1918
The Unexpected Victory

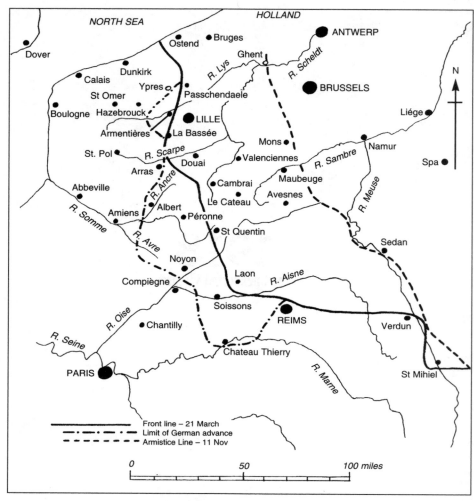

The Western Front, 1918

1918

The Unexpected Victory

J. H. JOHNSON

ARMS AND
ARMOUR

Arms and Armour Press
An Imprint of the Cassell Group
Wellington House, 125 Strand, London WC2R 0BB

Distributed in the USA by Sterling Publishing Co. Inc.,
387 Park Avenue South, New York, NY 10016-8810.

British Library Cataloguing-in-Publication Data:
a catalogue record for this book is available from the British Library

ISBN 1-85409-346-0

Designed and edited by DAG Publications Ltd.
Designed by David Gibbons; edited by John Gilbert;
printed and bound in Great Britain.

Contents

Acknowledgements

For permission to quote from The Private Papers of Douglas Haig 1914–1919 I am grateful to Earl Haig and Lord Blake, and similarly to Lord Hankey for his permission to quote from his grandfather's book The Supreme Command 1914–1918. I am also grateful to the Trustees of the Imperial War Museum for allowing access to their collection of private papers, in particular to the staff of the Department of Documents, and to each of the copyright holders for permission to quote from papers held by the Trustees and referred to in the Notes. I am also indebted to my friend Roger Webster who read through the whole of my draft and offered helpful suggestions; to John Weston for similar assistance; to Douglas Ellison, Ian Williams, Cliff Eydmann and Jack Brooks for companionship over the years on so many journeys to the old Western Front; to George Day for permission to quote from the unpublished diary of Captain R. F. Petschler, M.C., R.E; to the staff of my local library in Bexhill-on-Sea for assistance in locating books; and to Philip Haythornthwaite for the provision of photographs.

Author's Note

For an understanding of the various British formations mentioned in the text of this book, it may be helpful to give an indication of their approximate sizes. The infantry strength of an army – i.e., excluding cavalry, artillery, engineers and medical personnel – was dependent upon the number of divisions employed. A division would total between 11,500 and 12,000 men, and, depending on the circumstances, an army could consist of four or five army corps of some 36,000 each. From these examples the following simplified table can be constructed using rounded numbers:

Unit	Strength	Rank of Commander	Unit	Strength	Rank of Commander
Company	250	Captain	Division	12,000	Major-General
Battalion	1,000	Lieutenant-Colonel	Corps	36,000	Lieutenant-General
Brigade	4,000	Brigadier-General	Army	180,000	General

It must be stressed that the foregoing figures represent established rather than actual strength. The average strength of a battalion going into action would be unlikely to be more than 800 officers and men, and often less.

Introduction

1917 HAD BEEN a sombre year for the Allies; three British offensives on the Western Front had failed to achieve their objectives; the French offensive in Champagne had not only been halted but had brought in its wake mutinies in the French army; Italian forces had suffered a disastrous reverse at Caporetto, and Russia had signed an armistice with Germany in December. For the Franco-British armies these serious reverses had followed unavailing attempts in 1915 and 1916 to break through the enemy's front and resume open warfare.

Ever since the dramatic German advance through Belgium and northern France in August 1914 had been halted at the Battle of the Marne in September, albeit after a wide-ranging Allied retreat, Germany had decided to remain on the defensive on the Western Front[1] while turning to the east to knock out Russia. In consequence, the Allied armies on the Western Front had been presented with seemingly little option but to assault the enemy-held entrenched positions that stretched from the northern border of Switzerland to the North Sea. They saw no feasible way around this barrier, no real possibility of a flank to be turned, and the opportunities for a breakthrough limited to the strategic areas occupied by the Allied armies; the British Expeditionary Force with its back to the Channel ports, and the French army concentrated in defence of Paris. The impasse on the Western Front had prompted thoughts of a diversion elsewhere ever since 1915, but after the failure of the Dardanelles expedition in that year the problem had preoccupied political rather than military minds. Lloyd George, who became the British Prime Minister late in 1916 had been the principal proponent of the diversion of significant reinforcements to the Italian front in the belief that Austria would collapse. The prevailing military view, however, was that the Germans, with their strong interior lines of communication, would always have the logistical advantage in being able to move reinforcements quickly to threatened sectors.

Britain had been singularly ill-equipped for a Continental land war because, unlike other European countries where conscription in the armed forces was the norm, she had always maintained a voluntary system. Her regular army numbered some 247,000 of which nearly a half formed permanent garrisons overseas, for example in India and Egypt. In 1908 the formation of a Territorial Army

7

had been proposed as a second-line support to the regular army, and by 1914 its strength was nearing 300,000 but, at the time, the terms of enlistment were for home defence only. The understanding reached with France some years before the war was that a British Expeditionary Force (BEF) of 120,000 would be positioned on the left wing of the French army near to the border with Belgium. This, however, was merely a token contribution since the mobilised strength of the French Army was almost four million. The casualties suffered following the Battle of the Marne in September and the defence of Ypres in October meant that the British Regular Army had almost ceased to exist, and a call for volunteers resulted in over a million enlistments in the Regular Army and the Territorials by December, and a further million by the end of 1915. All these men, however, had to be accommodated, clothed, equipped and trained, and because of the shortage of instructors it was to be many months before they could be sent overseas. Conscription was introduced in 1916, adding more than two million enlistments by November 1918.

After the German decision to remain on the defensive in the west, the Allies on the Western Front were faced with conducting a form of siege warfare, a circumstance for which they were neither trained nor equipped. Their pre-war training had envisaged that a future war would be essentially mobile, and little regard had been paid to the provision of heavy artillery. In attempts to break the siege and resume open warfare, the Allies launched a number of set-piece offensives in the years 1915 to 1917; the French mounted six, two in Artois, two in Champagne, Somme and the Aisne, and a similar number was undertaken by the British: Neuve Chapelle, Loos, Somme, Arras, Third Ypres (Passchendaele) and Cambrai. All these offensives resulted in insignificant gains in terms of ground and incurred over a million and a half casualties in the process. By the end of 1917 the situation on the Western Front had reached stalemate.[2]

The successive failure over the three years poses the question – why did they fail, and was nothing learned? Both the French and British General Staffs were slow to come to terms with the problems of conducting siege warfare. Both armies launched attacks in 1915 against well-prepared enemy entrenchments, but they proved fruitless without the heavy artillery necessary to destroy them, and in 1916 the shortage of heavy artillery for the British contribution to the Somme battles was exacerbated by the unreliability of shells and fuses because of the hurried expansion of armament factories and lack of skilled inspection. Before the war the British War Office had thought that shrapnel rather than high explosive shell would predominate in a mobile war, but shrapnel, whilst effective against troops in the open, was useless against fortifications. In consequence, Britain's tiny munitions industry was not geared to produce heavy guns or ammunition, and it was not until 1917 that the British army began to be adequately supplied.

Experience of failure produces its own lessons, and these were dearly bought in terms of casualties between 1915 and 1917. Until the Battle of Cambrai in November 1917, there appeared to be no alternative to destroying the enemy's front line defences other than by the preliminary artillery bombardment (lasting on occasions for days). This would then be followed at zero hour by the infantry assault. Once the infantry had left the forward trenches, the bombardment would lift to successive lines of enemy defences on a pre-determined programme, but where the preliminary bombardment had been ineffective, as in the case of the opening day of the Battle of the Somme, the waves of infantry were faced with uncut wire entanglements and murderous machine-gun fire, and with little or no prospect of the bombardment being resumed to deal with the obstacle. Later in the battle the creeping barrage was introduced – a rolling curtain of fire behind which the infantry advanced at a distance of about a hundred yards, and designed to keep the enemy's heads down until the last moment. This was a considerable improvement on the rigidity of the programmed artillery lifts, but the enemy had learned lessons as well.

For most of 1915 and 1916, German defence policy on the Western Front had been one of linear defence with a strongly manned front line; should this be ruptured, then ground lost had to be recovered irrespective of cost. With casualties mounting and Allied preliminary bombardments becoming increasingly heavy, the Germans decided late in 1916 to adopt a policy of defence in depth. Instead of manning a definitive front line, there would be a series of zones; the front zone would be thinly held to avoid casualties in the preliminary bombardment, and at the rear of the zone there would be a scattering of strongpoints. In the second zone, or battle zone, reserves would be positioned ready to counter-attack; and in the third zone, or rearward zone, further counter-attack formations could be utilised if necessary. The theory was that an attacking force would eventually become so disorganised, if not exhausted, in having to surmount a series of obstacles that the impetus of the attack would be seriously impeded. In consequence, when further progress of an Allied offensive was slowed by this resistance, or brought to a halt by counter-attacks, there would have to be a pause to enable the artillery to be called up to bombard the fresh set of obstacles. The guns, however, would have to be brought forward to new positions over the devastation of the battlefield, thus inevitably incurring delay and giving time for the enemy to bring up reserves.

There were, however, varying degrees of effectiveness in the impact of preliminary bombardments on the enemy's defences. Despite a bombardment lasting seven days before the opening of the Somme offensive on 1 July 1916, it failed to destroy the enemy's deep dug-outs and led to an unparalleled disaster on the day of assault. Conversely, at Arras in April 1917, where the German army commander had delayed introducing the new defence policy, the preliminary bombardment was successful in destroying the enemy's front defences, and since it was directed purposefully over artillery positions, it rendered his counter-battery fire largely ineffective. It also seriously disrupted the enemy's lines of communication. This success prompted an even heavier preliminary bombardment in July 1917 before the opening of the Third Battle of Ypres (Passchendaele), but conditions were very different from those at Arras. Not only was the enemy's new defence policy in operation, but British artillery positions were everywhere overlooked by the German heavy guns positioned on the Flanders Ridges and out of sight on the reverse slopes. The British artillery suffered severely, and the impact of the bombardment ultimately reduced the battlefield to a swamp because of the high water table and fragile drainage system. Forward movement by the infantry was thus seriously impeded.

It was not until late in 1917 that the British found a way of dispensing with the preliminary bombardment, and by this means achieving surprise – that rarest and most valuable offensive weapon. The preparation for a large-scale offensive involved a lengthy period of gestation, and the assembly of the large force necessary had little chance of escaping enemy observation. This knowledge enabled the enemy to make his dispositions: the only doubts remaining to him were where the brunt of the attack would fall and, of course, the date. The delivery of the preliminary bombardment was final confirmation of enemy suspicions that an attack was imminent. In November 1917, and in conditions of great secrecy, several hundred tanks were brought up by rail and concealed in woods fronting the enemy positions before Cambrai. At dawn on 20 November, nearly 400 tanks punched a massive breach in the formidable Hindenburg Line. At exactly the same time, and aided by newly developed techniques in identifying the positions of enemy batteries without preliminary registration, a thousand guns opened fire on artillery positions and defences. Nevertheless, despite this initial success, the advantage gained could not be exploited because of the lack of reserves, and the battle ended in failure.

Exploitation of initial success was a problem that was never solved over the three years. Haig always envisaged that cavalry would be the principal arm of exploitation once a breach had been made in the enemy's front. In March 1916 he told his Army commanders that 'The action of mounted troops under existing trench warfare conditions follows on the actions of infantry and artillery...' and that once a breach had been made 'we must at once endeavour to exploit it without a moment's delay...' Apart from their usefulness in skirmishing and reconnaissance in the first weeks of the war and, later, in emergencies when they fought in a dismounted capacity, cavalry's role as an arm of exploitation never materialised because cratered ground, wire entanglements, machine guns and depth of defence all compounded to nullify their use. Tanks, first introduced in 1916 (but then few in number), with a top speed of four miles per hour, but drastically reduced to a crawl of barely one mile per hour over cratered ground, were too slow and unreliable to exploit the position once a breach had been made. Ultimately the task fell to the infantry, but unless the entire front was pierced (an unlikely scenario) the penetration would be narrow, and exploitation made precarious should a determined enemy cut off the head of the advance and enfilade the flanks.

Finally, it will be evident that the Franco-British armies were facing many intractable problems in their endeavours to resume open warfare over the years 1915 to 1917. The experience gained from conducting a series of abortive offensives was truly a 'learning curve' of grievous proportions, and the failure of the Battle of Cambrai brought the three years to an end, both politically and militarily, in an atmosphere of profound disillusionment. From the summer of 1917, the British Army, at a heavy cost, had alone shouldered the main burden of offensive operations on the Western Front, and although the mutinies in the French Army following the ill-fated Nivelle offensive in 1917 had been put down, the army remained an unknown quantity in terms of its ability to undertake offensive operations in 1918. But looming over all was the menace of the German Army in the west, now substantially strengthened by the armistice with Russia; and the portents for 1918 were grimly prophetic of the struggles yet to be endured. As the year dawned, however, few, if any, could foresee that by its end, Germany would be defeated. The purpose of this book is to explore how this came about.

Notes

1. The exception to the German defensive role on the Western Front was the offensive launched against the fortresses surrounding Verdun in February 1916. The objective was not a breakthrough but an attempt to destroy French morale. The Germans expected that the French would be compelled to throw in every man they had, and if they did so 'the forces of France will bleed to death'. The battle ended in December with both the French and the Germans suffering severe casualties.
2. J. H. Johnson, *Stalemate: The Great Trench Warfare Battles of 1915–1917*, Arms and Armour (London, 1995)

1

'Soldiers and Statesmen'[1]

T he last three months of 1917 had seen a period of unprecedented political activity. At the end of September Haig had been asked by Lloyd George for an appreciation of the impact on British forces of a Russian armistice. Haig had replied on 8 October that it was only on the Western Front that Germany could be defeated and all possible force should be concentrated there. Commitments in other theatres should be reduced to the minimum; no more line should be taken over from the French, and the 62 divisions on the Western Front should be brought up to establishment so that offensive operations could take place once drafts had been trained. He concluded: 'One more indispensable condition of success on the Western Front is that the War Cabinet should have a firm faith in its possibility and resolve finally and unreservedly to concentrate our resources on seeking it, and at once.'

In this recommendation he had been supported by the Chief of the Imperial General Staff (CIGS), General Sir William Robertson.

Following the precedent set by his predecessor, Asquith, in 1914, Lloyd George decided to seek alternative military advice and invited Field-Marshal Lord French (the Commander-in-Chief of the BEF until December 1915 when he was replaced by General Sir Douglas Haig), and Lieutenant-General Sir Henry Wilson (formerly commanding IV Corps and latterly Eastern Command in England) to attend a War Cabinet meeting on 11 October. At that meeting Lloyd George proposed four possible strategies; first, to adopt Haig's proposal of single-minded concentration on the Western Front: second, to recognise that the main emphasis should be on the Western Front but to continue operations in other theatres with present forces: third, to adopt a defensive strategy on all fronts, maintain the blockade of Germany and await the arrival of American forces in strength;[2] and fourth, to concentrate on another theatre in order to defeat one of Germany's allies, for example, Turkey. At a talk with Sir Maurice Hankey, the Secretary to the War Cabinet, on 15 October, Lloyd George told Hankey that:

> What he wished to avoid in 1918 was the terrific losses that were bound up with an attack of this nature [Haig's proposal]. He admitted that a continuance of Haig's attacks might conceivably result in bringing Germany to terms in 1919. But in that case it would be the United States of America who would

deal the blow and not we ourselves. If our Army was spent in a succession of shattering attacks during 1918, it would, indeed, be in exactly the condition that the French Army was in at that moment, with its numbers reduced and its morale weakened. He was particularly anxious to avoid a situation at the end of the war in which our Army would no longer be a first-class one. He wished it to be in every respect as good as the American army, and possibly a revised Russian Army, so that this country would be a great military power in the world... [He] contemplated an overwhelming military defeat, which would absolutely compel the enemy to submit. This could not possibly be achieved in 1918 by any method.[3]

French and Wilson submitted their memoranda to the War Cabinet on 28 October. French strayed far beyond his remit by severely criticising Haig and Robertson, but in concluding that the third strategy was the only course to adopt, he advocated the establishment of a Superior War Council to direct future operations. Wilson's view was that it was only on the Western Front that a decision could be reached, but thought that there should be 'intelligent, effective and powerful superior direction'. Their opinions were welcomed (and, indeed, anticipated) by Lloyd George, and it now seemed to him that his long-held wish for unified military command was within sight. Ever since the Somme battles in 1916, when he had been appalled at the fearful cost in casualties for so little gain, he had not only distrusted Haig but also Robertson, believing him to be Haig's mouthpiece rather than an impartial military adviser of the War Cabinet. Accordingly, Lloyd George wrote to the French Minister of War (Painlevé) at the end of October proposing 'a kind of Inter-Allied General Staff to work out the plans and watch continuously the course of events, for the Allies as a whole'. On 2 November Lloyd George reported to the War Cabinet that the French Government had agreed to the establishment of a Supreme Inter-Allied Council (subsequently changed to Supreme War Council) with a Permanent General Staff.

The need for 'superior direction' was given emphasis by the disaster at Caporetto on the Italian front when on 24 October an Austro-German offensive was launched on the Isonzo. The Italian Second Army was routed, losing nearly a half of its strength. Although eventually the front was stabilised, partly due to the onset of winter, the crisis caused the dispatch of eleven British and French divisions from the Western Front. This grave situation brought about the Allied Conference at Rapallo on 7 November at which the Supreme War Council was formally constituted. It was composed of 'the Prime Minister and a Member of the Government of each of the Great Powers...' together with three Permanent Military Representatives – Generals Weygand, Wilson and Cadorna respectively for France, Great Britain and Italy.

Haig had met Lloyd George in Paris when the latter was on his way to Rapallo and recorded in his diary:

The Prime Minister first made a few remarks regarding the necessity for forming an Inter-Allied Supreme War Council and Staff and asked for my views. I told him that the proposal had been considered for three years and each time had been rejected as unworkable. I gave several reasons why I thought it could not work, and that it should add to our difficulties having such a body. The P.M. then said that the two Governments had decided to form it; so I said, there is no need saying any more then! [4]

The Council met again on 1 December at Versailles and was joined by General Bliss as the Permanent Military Representative for the United States. The French Prime Minister (Clemenceau) opened the meeting saying that the Council's first task was 'to consider the nature of the military campaigns to be undertaken in 1918'. He then suggested that the Permanent Military Representatives should 'study the whole situation in detail and ... advise us as to the operations they recommend'. The subsequent discussion ranged over the current state of affairs on the Western Front and Italy, and in the other theatres (Salonika, Palestine and Mesopotamia), and also the shipping resources necessary to transport American forces to France. (By this time in early December there were 130,000 American troops in France, mostly undergoing training.)

Meanwhile, Haig's Passchendaele offensive had halted on the Passchendaele Ridge: his original objective of denying the ports of Ostend and Zeebrugge to the enemy was now far beyond attainment, and the Cambrai offensive which had opened so brilliantly on 20 November had ended in a withdrawal in the face of German counter-attacks. He was aware that further operations on the Western Front would have to await the recommendations of the Permanent Military Representatives which, in turn, would have to be considered by the Council. He saw that the inevitable delay would give little chance of being able to resume an offensive in the spring, particularly as the possibility of divisions being transferred from other theatres to the Western Front seemed remote. Moreover, he was aware that he might have to take over more line from the French, and he still awaited the response to the appeal for his divisions to be brought up to establishment. He was forced to come to the unpalatable conclusion that he would have to adopt a defensive role, and addressing his Army commanders on 3 November, he told them:

... the general situation on the Russian and Italian fronts, combined with the paucity of reinforcements which we are likely to receive, will in all probability necessitate our adopting a defensive attitude for the next few months. We must be prepared to meet a strong and sustained hostile offensive. It is therefore of first importance that Army commanders should give their immediate and personal attention to the organisation of the zones for defensive purposes and to the rest and training of their troops.

On 14 December the Supreme War Council decided that the British should take over twenty-five miles of the French front covering the sector opposite St Quentin southwards to Barisis, but the extension had already been discussed at a conference at Boulogne in September 1917 when Lloyd George and Robertson met Painlevé and Foch to discuss French pressure to take over a larger portion of the front. As the Passchendaele offensive was in progress it was decided that the question should be left to Haig and Pétain to agree between themselves. Haig was not happy when he was informed of the decision, but by the beginning of November agreement was reached, albeit that Pétain would have liked a further extension to the Aisne. Although the extension had been the result of French pressure, it is possible that Lloyd George would have been sympathetic to the proposal in the sense that it was an indirect way of constraining Haig from undertaking another Flanders offensive. The extension was completed by the end of January and entailed the creation of a newly constituted Fifth Army with General Sir Hubert Gough brought from the Ypres sector to take command.

Meanwhile, the armistice reached on the Eastern Front on 15 December, which was followed a week later by peace negotiations, meant that Germany could now start transferring divisions to the west. By the end of December at least ten divisions had been transferred, and there were now 161 divisions in France and Belgium. According to the Official History, 'a forecast was made that if German troops were brought from Italy as well as from Russia and Romania the enemy might have 185 divisions on the Western Front by the end of February, 195 by the end of March and 200 by the 1st May...' Compared with an Allied total of 170 (excluding American divisions) the outlook was ominous. At a meeting of the War Cabinet on 7 January Haig, according to his diary, said he thought the next four months would be critical, and it was possible 'that the enemy would attack both the French and ourselves'. In that event 'they would ask for support either in the shape of British Reserves, or by taking over some of their line in order to set free French troops'. In his opinion, 'the best defence would be to continue our offensive in Flanders...'[5] Two days later, at a luncheon with Lloyd George, Haig said that as Germany had only one million as reserves for 1918, he doubted 'whether they would risk them in an attempt to "breakthrough". If the Germans did attack it would be a gambler's throw.' Haig, who was notoriously inarticulate, had muddied the waters, and Robertson wrote to him after the meeting:

> For a long time past they [the War Cabinet] have been trying to persuade me to say that the Germans may not attack this year. Unfortunately you gave as your opinion this morning that they would not do so, and I noticed, as Lord Derby [Secretary of State for War] also did, that they jumped at the statement.[6]

Haig endeavoured to clear up the muddle when meeting Lloyd George two days later, but it was unfortunate that Haig persisted in sending conflicting signals, not only as to the likelihood of a German offensive in 1918, but also concerning the quality of the divisions to be transferred from the Eastern Front. In October, when the Passchendaele offensive was still in progress, he had told the War Cabinet that the best German divisions were already on the Western Front, and that those remaining in the east were of 'low fighting value, and only 32 divisions are estimated as fit to take part in severe fighting on the Western Front'.[7] These signals were no doubt taken into account by the Cabinet Committee set up in December to consider manpower demands. Its recommendation was that the Navy, the RAF, ship-building, munitions, food production etc. should have priority over the army on the Western Front, and concluded that there 'the Allies ought to be able to hold their own ... until the period when American strength begins to alter the balance of advantage in their favour'. Thus out of the 615,000 men wanted by Haig, the Committee allocated to the army 100,000 Category 'A' men, with 100,000 men in lower medical categories.

Underlying this decision were two factors: the first was the belief that the failure of Allied offensives on the Western Front between 1915 and 1917 to gain any significant ground had persuaded the War Cabinet that a German attack would also be likely to end in failure, and second, giving Haig all the reinforcements he had requested would mean another costly Passchendaele offensive in the spring.

Another Committee recommendation was that, following French (and German) practice, the twelve infantry battalions in a division should be reduced to nine and the surplus created used to form additional divisions, constituting 'a mobile army of manoeuvre'. The thinking behind the recommendation was that 'In order to secure the fullest advantage from the new weapons now available – machine-guns, trench mortars etc. – and the greatly increased artillery strength, it was clearly necessary to attach full complements of these to as many infantry formations as possible.'[8]. This change met fierce criticism from the Army Council, but the War Cabinet would not be moved, although the idea of creating additional divisions was dropped. The Official Historian thought the change 'was eminently desirable – but the time selected for it was open to objection'. Lloyd George, in his War Memoirs, derided this comment:

> It would be interesting to know what better time than January and February – a quiet time at the front – could have been chosen for an 'eminently desirable' change. The diary of the War shows that there was a complete cessation of all serious military operations on the Western Front from the end of December, 1917, to the middle of March 1918. It was the longest quiet spell we had known for years.[9]

Haig had hoped to complete the reduction by 15 February, but it was not finally completed until 4 March. As a result, 115 battalions were disbanded, 38 were amalgamated to form new units, and seven converted into pioneers (Dominion divisions were unaffected). Whether the change had any significantly adverse effect on events to come can only be conjectured, but its timing was undoubtedly unfortunate, and its execution caused a great deal of dislocation:

> Needless to say, this astonishing and demoralising exercise took time – time during which the roads of France were filled with British units seeking their new 'homes', and during which an esprit-de-corps built up in years of common experience was thrown away.[10]

On 21 January the Permanent Military Representatives at the Supreme War Council issued a Joint Note with their recommendations for 1918. The security of the Western Front was regarded as essential, and provided the British and French armies were maintained at their existing strengths, reinforced by American divisions at two a month, defences strengthened and armaments increased (guns, tanks, aircraft), they considered that the enemy 'would be unable to gain a definite military decision on the Western Front in 1918'. Equally, however, they saw no possibility of the Allies securing a military decision in the west in 1918, but a series of crushing blows against the Turkish army in Palestine might lead to Turkey's collapse, thereby having 'the most far-reaching results upon the general military situation...'. Two days later the Representatives issued another Joint Note recommending the creation of a General Reserve for the Western and Italian Fronts. Both recommendations were discussed at meetings of the Council at Versailles between 30 January and 1 February. There was no consensus, however, regarding the Representatives' Joint Note of 21 January: Lloyd George was eloquent in his support for the Turkish proposal, but he was not only opposed by Clemenceau who regarded the security of the Western Front as paramount, but also (to Lloyd George's annoyance) by Robertson. As the Official Historian commented: 'Matters therefore stood for all practical purposes exactly where they had been two months earlier...' There was, however, unanimous agreement to the proposal to create a General Reserve 'provided it could be formed in addition to the reserves at the immediate disposal of Commanders-in-Chief and Army commanders'.

The proposal to create a General Reserve was delegated to an Executive Committee (renamed Executive War Board) to develop, with Foch as President. Although, in essence, the proposal had much to recommend it, there were three major problems to be resolved before it could be realised: who would command it, how many divisions would be required, and from where would they come? Robertson's view on the question of command was that a Committee would be unable to assess the strategical situation for employment of the General Reserve without having to balance the demands of the Commanders-in-Chief, which could possibly be conflicting. Moreover, they would be in the position of receiving orders from two different sources – their respective Chiefs of Staff and the Committee which could lead to confusion. His suggestion to Lord Derby was that the Chief of the Imperial General Staff should be the representative on the Committee and 'permanently represented by a deputy to act for him in case of urgency'.

Although the proposal to launch a major offensive against the Turkish armies remained in being, the difficulty was that it could only be mounted with substantial reinforcement from other theatres. For all practical purposes this could only mean withdrawals from the Western Front, but here the maintenance of its security was considered paramount. Thus Lloyd George's cherished desire to 'knock away Germany's props' was unlikely to materialise, and in his frustration he determined to knock away Haig's props (indeed, he would have liked to remove Haig himself, but this would have brought about a Cabinet crisis.) Brigadier-General Charteris, Haig's Director of Intelligence, who had been criticised for supplying Haig with over-optimistic reports of the decline in German army morale, had already been moved in December, and Lieutenant-General Sir Lancelot Kiggell, Haig's Chief of Staff since December 1915 and highly regarded by him, was moved to Guernsey as Lieutenant Governor in January. Although these changes were grudgingly agreed to by Haig, he resisted an attempt to move General Gough (Fifth Army commander).

Lloyd George then decided that Robertson would have to go. His unwavering support for Haig and his belief that a military decision could only be gained on the Western Front persuaded Lloyd George that it affected the quality of the advice he gave to the War Cabinet as its principal military adviser. His opposition at the meeting of the Supreme War Council to the Turkish proposal now brought to a head Lloyd George's dissatisfaction that had been simmering throughout 1917. Although the removal of Kiggell and Charteris had been achieved without much difficulty, Robertson's removal was a different matter; he did not have the full support of the War Cabinet, and Lord Derby had earlier threatened to resign if Robertson and Haig were removed. At a meeting between Lloyd George, Lord Derby and Haig on 9 February, the former proposed what he thought would be a solution: Robertson to be the Permanent Military Representative at Versailles, and Wilson, the current Representative, made CIGS. This was acceptable to Lord Derby, and the decision was made that the Representative should be 'absolutely free and unfettered on the advice which he gives, but he is to report to the CIGS the nature of the advice given for information of the Cabinet, and the CIGS will advise Cabinet thereon'. In his autobiography[11] Robertson recorded '... my first impulse was to accept the post, but after careful reflection I resolved that I could be no party to a system which established a dual authority for the military direction of the war'. He saw Lloyd George on the 16 February who tried to persuade him to accept the post, but he refused. He was offered, and accepted, Eastern Command in England, and General Sir Henry Rawlinson (formerly the commander of the Fourth Army) became the British Military Representative in Versailles.

On 27 February the Executive War Board wrote to Haig regarding the formation of the General Reserve and he replied on 2 March to the effect that he had already made his dispositions to meet an imminent enemy offensive, and 'if I were to earmark six or seven divisions from these troops the whole of my plans and dispositions would have to be remodelled'. Pétain initially offered eight, but subsequently said he had none to spare. Nevertheless the War Board remained committed to the establishment of a General Reserve and decided that the British and French divisions in Italy should form the nucleus. A committee composed of General Officers was set up to consider the details, but the Italians were opposed to an immediate transfer.

It will be evident that the establishment of the Supreme War Council had not progressed very far in meeting Lloyd George's desire for a unified command. The Official Historian commented somewhat acidly:

> In 3½ months ... the Supreme War Council, with its ancillary organs, the Permanent Military Representatives, the Executive War Board, and Committee of General Officers, had done nothing tangible towards meeting the imminent German assault; and the Council was not to meet again until the 1st May.[12]

Within less than a month, however, a unified command was to come about on the Western Front, but in circumstances that no one had foreseen.

Notes

1. Title of book by Field Marshal Sir William Robertson (2 vols.), Cassell (London, 1926)
2. The United States of America had entered the war in February 1917 as a result of the German decision to wage unrestricted submarine warfare. In April 1917 the strength of the regular army was some 130,000, including reserves, and conscription was instituted in the following month.
3. Hankey, Lord, *The Supreme Command 1914–1918*, Vol. 2, Allen & Unwin (London, 1961)
4. Blake, Robert, (ed.), *The Private Papers of Douglas Haig 1914–1919*, Eyre & Spottiswoode (London, 1952)
5. *Ibid.*
6. Bonham-Carter, Victor, *Soldier True*, Frederick Muller (London, 1963)
7. Lloyd George, D., *War Memoirs*, Vol. II, Odhams (London, 1938)
8. *Ibid.*
9. *Ibid.*
10. Terraine, John, *Impacts of War 1914 and 1918*, Hutchinson (London, 1970)
11. Robertson, Field Marshal Sir William, *From Private to Field-Marshal*, Constable (London, 1921)
12. Edmonds, Brigadier-General Sir James, (comp.), *Official History of the War: Military Operations France and Belgium 1918*, Vol. I, Macmillan (London, 1935)

2

The Lull Before the Storm

Our general situation requires that we should strike at the earliest moment,
if possible at the end of February or beginning of March, before the Americans can
throw strong forces into the scale. We must beat the British. – General Erich
von Ludendorff, November 1917

The Western Front stretched for some 450 miles from Switzerland to the North Sea, but the sector of approximately 150 miles from St Mihiel to the Swiss northern border had not seen any significant action since 1914, although for most of the war the French had harboured fears of a German advance through Switzerland. From St Mihiel northwards the French held 150 miles, the British 125 miles, and the Belgian army twenty miles north of Ypres to the sea. Thus some 300 miles were under threat from a German attack, and although the Allies had little doubt that the Germans would mount an offensive in the west, there was no unanimity of view as to when and where it would fall. Notwithstanding the armistice with Russia in December, a final settlement had not yet been reached, and in February Germany resumed hostilities by an advance eastwards. This factor persuaded the Supreme War Council that a German offensive in the west would not take place until late in the spring, but the British were unconvinced. The growing strength of American forces in France was, they thought, likely to prompt an early German offensive, probably in March, and the balance of options open to the enemy pointed to an attack on the British front with the likely objective of the Channel ports. The French believed, however, that an early attack would fall in the Champagne sector: a belief, as will be seen later, that would ultimately have a profound effect on the future direction of the war.

Similar deliberations were exercising OHL (Oberste Heeresleitung) – the German Supreme Command. In November 1917, Ludendorff had convened a meeting to formulate plans for 1918 with the Chiefs of Staff of the Army Groups commanded by the Bavarian Crown Prince Rupprecht and the German Crown Prince. One proposal discussed was an attack in Flanders, but the need to wait for dry weather until April would entail an unacceptable delay. Another proposal was an offensive at Verdun; it would have a serious impact on French morale if successful, and at the same time frustrate a possible Franco-American offensive. This was advocated by

Colonel von der Schulenberg (Chief of Staff to the German Crown Prince) and supported by Lieutenant-Colonel Wetzell (Head of Operations, General Staff). The latter considered that in an attack on the British front 'we [would] have a strategically clumsy, tactically rigid, but tough enemy in front of us' whereas

> The French have shown us what they can do. They are just as skilful in the tactical use of their artillery as of their infantry. Their use of ground in the attack is just as good as in the defence. The French are better in the attack and more skilful in the defence, but are not such good stayers as the British.

Ludendorff, however, considered an attack on Verdun to be unacceptable because he thought it unlikely that the British would come to assist the French and he might be faced with a second Flanders battle. He stressed that his available forces were only sufficient for one offensive – a second diversionary offensive would not be possible. He suggested an offensive farther south in the St Quentin area which if 'after gaining the Somme line, Ham–Péronne, operations could be carried further in a north-westerly direction ... and lead to the rolling up of the British front'. Nothing, however, was decided, and during the next few weeks the various options already discussed were mulled over. There was a further meeting at the end of December, and although nothing was finally settled, preparations were to be made for attacks near Armentières (code- named 'George') and near Ypres ('George 2'), near Arras ('Mars'), and on either side of St Quentin ('Michael'). Other attacks were to be prepared: south of the Oise, east of Reims and on the old Champagne battle-field, but preparations for an attack at Verdun were abandoned.

On 21 January Ludendorff made up his mind: 'George' and 'Mars' were rejected because of inherent difficulties, weather dependence for the former, and the British possession of Vimy Ridge for the latter. His choice was 'Michael' (with the right wing extended to the River Scarpe), set to take place about 20 March. 'Mars', however, would follow several days after 'Michael', and the two 'Georges' were to be ready by early April. (It is significant, as the British Official History noted, that neither the Kaiser, nor the Crown Prince nor, indeed, Hindenburg, attended these momentous meetings.) For the Germans, the choice of 'Michael' was opportune: the extension of the British front down to Barisis meant that the junction of the Fifth Army with the French was just south of the Oise:

> It may now be accepted that the British have taken over the front of the French III Corps... The Eighteenth Army will therefore have only British opposite to it. This will make the situation more favourable for us. The offensive is principally intended to strike the British. They now stand opposite to us on the whole front of the Group of Armies which is to make the offensive. It need

not be anticipated that the French will run themselves off their legs and hurry at once to the help of their Entente comrades. They will first wait and see if their own front is not attacked also, and decide to support their Ally only when the situation has been cleared up. That will not be immediately, as demonstrations to deceive the French will be made by the German Crown Prince's Group.[1]

During January Haig had made his preparations for dealing with a German offensive in Flanders where he anticipated that the main blow would fall, but he made allowance for an attack farther south (although this was thought likely to have only limited objectives) by transferring three divisions to the Fifth Army in February, and an additional division in March. After these transfers, the disposition of the British Armies from right to left was: Fifth Army defending forty-two miles of front with twelve divisions (plus three cavalry divisions); Third Army, twenty-eight miles with fourteen divisions; First Army, thirty-three miles with fourteen divisions; Second Army, twenty-three miles with twelve divisions. In addition, there were eight divisions in the GHQ Reserve allocated equally behind each Army. The French army, totalling ninety-nine divisions (excluding cavalry), had sixty in the line and thirty-nine in reserve, but the majority of the latter divisions were in the Champagne sector.

It will be evident that the Fifth Army was severely stretched: each division (excluding cavalry) defending three and a half miles of front compared with, for example, just under two miles in the Second Army sector. This disparity reflected Haig's defence policy; he was determined to keep his left wing strong should the main German offensive be directed towards the Channel ports. Constrained by the sea on his left flank, which was within less than fifty miles to the Channel ports, he would have far less room to manoeuvre than if the blow should fall on his right wing held by the Fifth Army where there was ample room to conduct an elastic defence. Moreover, as a consequence of the extension of the British line to Barisis, where it joined the French, it could be expected that help would be forthcoming as a result of the agreement reached previously with Pétain for mutual assistance.

On 1 February Gough wrote to GHQ with the warning of increased enemy activity opposite the Fifth Army front. He cited the construction of additional crossings over the St Quentin–Cambrai canal, new airfields, and a large number of divisions in reserve, where good railway facilities existed to bring them forward rapidly. He reasoned that, as the Germans were looking for an early decision, operations on the Oise–Scarpe front were more likely than farther north owing to the condition of the ground. He considered that 'if the Germans attack the British Army, the Fifth Army is likely to be involved'. In events to come the fourth paragraph of his letter was prophetic:

The more recent German attacks (i.e. Verdun, February 1916, Riga, the attack on Italy) have been characterised by a short bombardment up to about 6 hours, and the most strenuous efforts to obtain surprise. These efforts I cannot be sure of defeating: consequently in his initial attack the enemy might find me disposed as at present with the equivalent of 8 divisions on a 40 mile front; this would go far towards ensuring him success, especially in view of the state of my defences.

Elsewhere in the letter he referred to the poor state of his defences and the need for additional labour.

His letter brought forth two replies from GHQ. The first, from Major-General Davidson (General Staff), dated 4 February, put forward for consideration whether 'the main resistance in the Fifth Army area should not be behind the line of the River Somme', but after failing to reach a conclusion 'considered that we should make our preparations to fight East of the Somme [although] we must however be prepared to be forced back to the line of the Somme'. The second, from Lieutenant-General Hon. Sir H. Lawrence (Chief of the General Staff), dated 9 February, stated that 'in the event of a serious attack being made on your Army on a wide front, your policy should be to secure and protect at all costs the important centre of Péronne and the River Somme to the south of that place...'. He considered that the ground protected by the Forward and Battle Zones was not important enough to justify 'the battle being fought out in the Battle Zone unless the general situation at the time makes such a course advisable. It may well be desirable to fall back to the rearward defences of Péronne and the Somme while linking up with the Third Army on the North, and preparing for counter-attack.' As events will prove, these less than precise instructions from GHQ prompts the belief, albeit reached in hindsight, that despite the effect on morale, a withdrawal behind the Somme would have been the better course, particularly because of the fragmentation of scarce labour resources on defences in two different areas.

On 16 February Haig met his Army Commanders at Doullens. Brigadier-General Cox (GHQ Intelligence) believed that the indications were that the enemy would attack the British, and Haig thought that the attack might fall on a wide front 'possibly from Lens to the Oise'. The possibility of the main German attack being directed towards the Channel ports had lessened because there were no indications of an imminent large-scale attack between the Scarpe and the La Bassée canal, but enemy activity in the St Quentin–Cambrai sector could mean preparations for either defence or offence. Haig noted in his diary that all his Army Commanders 'felt confident on being able to hold their front'.[2] (It is doubtful, however, whether this was a confidence entirely shared by Gough.) There was another Army Commanders' conference on 2 March when from Intelligence sources there now seemed to be a strong possibility that the 'enemy intends to attack on the Third and

Fifth Army fronts, with the object of cutting off the Cambrai salient [Flesquières] and drawing in our reserves'. Haig noted in his diary:

> I emphasised the necessity of being ready as soon as possible to meet a hostile offensive of prolonged duration. I also told Army Commanders that I was very pleased at all I had seen on the front of the three Armies I had recently visited. Plans were sound and thorough, and much work had already been done. I was only afraid that the enemy would find our front so very strong that he will hesitate to commit his Army to the attack with the almost certainty of losing very heavily.[3]

At this time German divisions on the Western Front had reached 181 with seventy in reserve, but a week later the total had risen to 185 with seventy-seven in reserve, of which forty-seven were thought to be opposite the British front. On 10 March the weekly Intelligence summary concluded 'it is probable that the main offensive will be between the rivers Scarpe and Omignon...', and the summary issued on 17 March gave no reason to change this view.

On 14 December 1917 GHQ had issued instructions for the organisation of defences. These were based on the system adopted by the Germans in 1917 involving the preparation of three zones of defence, the Forward, Battle and Rear. The Forward Zone was the existing front line, and where, in the words of the Official History, it should be 'sufficiently garrisoned and strengthened to guard against surprise and compel the enemy to employ strong forces for its capture'. Local reserves should mount counter-attacks if it should be penetrated. The Battle Zone was generally between one or two miles behind the Forward Zone, 2,000–3,000 yards in depth and containing two-thirds of the guns. It was where any over-running of the Forward Zone should be brought to a halt, using if necessary corps or Army reserves. The Rear Zone (known as the 'Green Line') was to be between four and eight miles from the Forward Zone and occupied in the event of failure in the Battle Zone to stem the enemy's attack. Owing to lack of labour, it was 'to be constructed as opportunity offered'.

There was, however, a serious flaw in the adoption of the German zonal system. The German Forward Zone was, in effect, an outpost zone, lightly held and designed merely to delay and fragment an attack, leaving the bulk of the divisions in the other defensive zones to counter-attack. In contrast to the German system, the Forward Zones in the Third and Fifth Army sectors were relatively heavily garrisoned, holding at least one-third of each Army's strength, and where their role was to 'do all in their power to maintain the ground against every attack'. This situation may have been forced on the Fifth Army because of the length of front defended, but this was not the case for the Third Army holding a much shorter frontage.

Adverse weather in January seriously affected work on the construction of defences. Those in the Forward Zones of both Armies were considered good; instead of a definitive front line, with its vulnerability to a sustained artillery bombardment, the trenches, although continuous, were garrisoned intermittently with outposts and strongpoints. This economised in men, but the system depended for its efficiency on being able to cover the intervening ground with cross-fire and thus required good visibility. Those in the Battle Zone were incomplete. The Fifth Army lacked dug-outs of any kind, and there were no dug-outs for machine guns in the Third Army area. There were marked differences between the two Armies in the construction of defences in the Rear Zone (Green Line): those in the Third Army consisted of two lines of trenches (albeit shallow-dug) and were fully wired, but in the Fifth Army sector recently taken over from the French 'there had been neither time nor labour to do very much except to mark out the front line, erect a little wire at tactical points, and show the best position for machine-guns by notice boards...'[4]

It was now increasingly evident that the German attack would be against the fronts defended by the Third and Fifth Armies, although it was still not certain whether it would be the main offensive. The terrain occupied by the two Armies forms the watershed between the basins of the Somme and Oise rivers. In 1918 it was open, unfenced and generally flat in the area occupied by the Fifth Army, except around St Quentin. Farther north in the sector held by the Third Army, the ground rises to form the chalk ridges (ranging from 300 to 500 feet above sea level) extending north-westwards almost to the Channel coast. Immediately behind both Armies was the area devastated by the Germans in the retreat to the Hindenburg Line in 1917, and in the rear of the Third Army lay the ruins of the old Somme battlefields. It was not, on the face of it, an ideal choice for an offensive, particularly as the right of the Fifth Army lay on the marshes of the Oise, considered by the Allies to be a formidable obstacle.

The Germans were aware that their preparations for Operation 'Michael' could not be wholly concealed from the British, but they endeavoured to mislead the Allies as to their true intentions. Their principal aim was to persuade the French that the main blow would fall on their front, and they hoped to achieve this by the spreading of rumours and false reports indicating that the attack would be in Champagne and north of Verdun, accompanied by smaller attacks on the Aisne and in Alsace-Lorraine. To emphasise the deception, a heavy artillery bombardment was opened in Champagne on 20 March, accompanied by attacks in some strength in the Verdun and Reims sectors. These deceptive techniques were eminently successful in persuading the French, but on 19 March information gained from prisoners and deserters pointed to either the 20th or 21st for the commencement of operations on the Third and Fifth Army fronts. Thus the British now possessed final confirmation that an attack was imminent, but whether it was the main attack or merely a diversion, and whether the French would also be attacked, remained in doubt.

Notes

1. Quoted in Edmonds, Brigadier-General Sir James, (comp.), *Official History of the War: Military Operations France and Belgium, 1918*, Vol. I, Macmillan (London, 1935)
2. Blake, Robert, (ed.), *The Private Papers of Douglas Haig 1914–1919*, Eyre & Spottiswoode, (London, 1952)
3. *Ibid.*
4. Edmonds, *op. cit.*

3

The Great Retreat: March 1918

The divisional commander stood by the roadside a few miles west of Roye,
and watched the remnants of his proud division march by. What brutes we all looked,
with dust and mud caked on our clothes, and horrible beards grown on our faces! None
of us had washed or shaved for four days. But as each section came up to where the
general was standing, every man held himself erect, and turned his head sharply
to the left, in the salute, as if unconscious of his appearance.[1]

The weather forecast for 20 March by the Meteorological Officer at GHQ was for
ground mist gradually developing by 5 p.m. and ground fog by 9 p.m. The fog
became dense after midnight, and for the infantry in their scattered outposts in
the Forward Zone the fog not only muffled sound, but gave an uneasy sense of iso-
lation. At 3.30 a.m. on the 21st the British artillery opened fire on likely troop assembly
points, but their sound was entirely eclipsed shortly after 4.30 a.m. when the heaviest
artillery bombardment of the war was delivered by some 6,000 guns on the fronts of
the Third and Fifth Armies and, in order to mislead, on part of the First Army's front.

So intense was the bombardment that the earth around us trembled. It was a dark
night, but the tongues of flame from the guns – 2,500 British guns replied to the
German bombardment – lit up the night sky to daylight brightness. Mixed up
with the high explosive shells crashing on our trenches, were the less noisy, but
deadly gas shells. Trenches collapsed, infantry in front line positions, groping
about in their gas masks, were stunned by the sudden terrific onslaught...
   Machine-gun posts were blown sky high – along with human limbs. Men
were coughing and vomiting from the effects of gas, and men were blinded.[2]

The bombardment was timed to last five hours, and designed, by its sheer weight
and ferocity, to stun the defenders, destroy communications and silence the
artillery. The first two hours was concentrated mainly on drenching the gun positions in the Battle Zone with gas; then, in the remaining three hours, a mixture of
high explosive and gas swept to and fro over the Forward and Battle Zones, focusing
primarily on the infantry in the front positions. The situation in the Forward and
Battle Zones, after the conclusion of the bombardment, was one of almost total
chaos. The destruction of underground cables caused a breakdown of communica-

tion between divisional and brigade headquarters, and also between front line positions and the artillery who, unable to see their aiming posts, could only respond by
firing on 'known' positions. The fog prevented visual communication by SOS
signals and also aircraft observation. A lieutenant in the Royal Garrison Artillery
recorded his impressions after emerging from his dug-out:

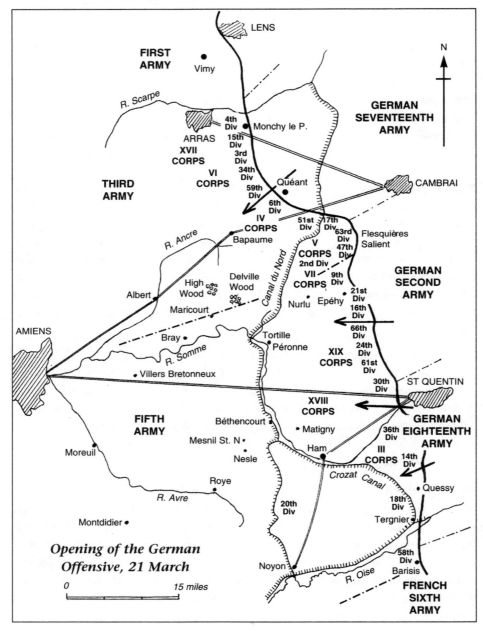

*Opening of the German
Offensive, 21 March*

It was still almost dark and there was a thick mist. I was not sure at first whether the mist was all due to gas, or whether there was a natural mist as well. I soon found that there was a very thick natural mist, which lasted to about midday. Shells were falling everywhere. It was perfect hell – no words can describe how utterly beastly it was, so I'm not afraid of exaggerating. I felt my way up the sunken road towards the guns – it was quite impossible to see the way. The eye-pieces of the respirator got fogged immediately and you could see nothing. I eventually found myself by the guns... The layers were experiencing the utmost difficulty in laying the guns as they could not see the aiming posts owing to the mist, and they had got their respirators off their faces in order to see better, retaining the nose-clip and mouthpiece. I sent a man out with an electric torch to hold over the picquet to lay on, but even this could be seen only with the utmost difficulty. So I went to the map room and took the magnetic bearing of the target they were firing on, and then, armed with a prismatic compass I laid the guns with this as accurately as I could... I should not like to vouch for the accuracy of the fire, but the great thing was to get some shells over, and they may have done as much good as if they had been exactly on the target each time.[3]

At zero hour, 9.40 a.m., the bombardment was replaced by a creeping barrage behind which specially trained Storm Troops equipped with flamethrowers and light machine guns advanced with instructions to by-pass centres of significant resistance:

... the Germans commenced to open rapid machine-gun fire, and we noticed several white lights being fired in our direction, and after a time from the direction of these lights the fire became most intense. I found out later that these lights were fired by small parties of the enemy who pushed forward and, on finding a weak spot in our line, fired a white light which was the signal for the Germans to concentrate against the weak places in the hope of breaking through and rolling up the flanks. This concentration was done by dribbling up small parties each with a light machine gun until an overwhelming volume of machine-gun fire was obtained under cover of which the enemy advanced.[4]

They found the front-line garrisons virtually annihilated. The survivors, blinded by the fog, and having to wear their gas masks for hours, were first aware that the assault had begun when, looming out of the fog, the leading waves engulfed them. Many outposts fought on, refusing to surrender, but were ultimately crushed by the following waves. Very few managed to find their way back into the Battle Zone.

The Fifth Army front was held from right to left by III Corps (Lieutenant-General Sir R. Butler), XVIII Corps (Lieutenant-General Sir I. Maxse), XIX Corps (Lieutenant-General H. E. Watts) and VII Corps (Lieutenant-General Sir W. Congreve), in all comprising twelve divisions, which were faced by forty-three German divisions of two German Armies (Eighteenth and Second) The Forward Zones of all corps were penetrated soon after 9.40 a.m. and many outposts overrun. Although there was desperate resistance in and around the Battle Zones, these were still held except in the III Corps sector where the main weight of the attack had fallen. By mid-morning Gough became aware of the extent of the weight of the attack on his front, and early in the afternoon his instructions to his corps commanders were to hold the enemy by fighting a delaying action and not to attempt a last-ditch defence of positions. By this means he hoped to maintain some sort of defence, perhaps for two or three days, until reinforcements could arrive, but these could only consist of two divisions from GHQ reserve. None was forthcoming from the French. General Humbert, commanding the embryo French 3rd Army on his right, came to see him at 1 p.m. but could offer no assistance, only sympathy, He promised, however, to report the position to Pétain, who although still fearing an attack in Champagne, ordered three divisions to be ready to move the next day to assist the Fifth Army.

Later that day Gough ordered III Corps to fall back behind the Crozat canal (linking the Somme and Oise canals), XVIII Corps to swing back its right to conform with the withdrawal of III Corps, XIX Corps to incline its left to link with VII Corps, and VII Corps to move similarly in order to maintain the connection with the right of the Third Army. According to the Official History, Gough's report to GHQ of these movements 'was misleading in so far as it showed the line to be continuous...' and that 'the Fifth Army stood in a better condition to continue the fight than actually was the case, and induced General Byng to delay the evacuation of the Flesquières salient'.[5] As will be seen later, this was to have serious consequences.

The movements of the four corps were carried out during the night without interference. The Crozat canal (some ten miles in length) was considered to be a formidable obstacle – thirty to forty feet in width and unfordable. All road bridges were demolished in the early hours of the morning together with two railway bridges. Unfortunately one railway bridge (the largest) was left, owing to the lack of sufficient explosives.

Thick fog also shrouded the Third Army front held from right to left by V Corps (Lieutenant-General Sir E. Fanshawe), IV Corps (Lieutenant-General Sir G. Harper), VI Corps Lieutenant-General Sir J. Haldane) and XVII Corps (Lieutenant-General Sir C. Fergusson), comprising fourteen divisions. The German attack by nineteen divisions of the Second Army was directed at the shoulders of the Flesquières salient held by V Corps rather than along the whole front: the salient had been spared the bombardment, but had been drenched with mustard gas. The German plan was to pinch out the salient by attacking IV and VI Corps: XVII Corps on the extreme left of the front was not attacked. Thus the weight of the attack, comprising eleven divisions, was to fall on the five divisions of IV and VI Corps. The Forward Zone of IV Corps was soon overrun and the garrisons either killed or captured. By 2 p.m. most of the Battle Zone between the 51st Division and the Bapaume–Cambrai road had been lost, and the 6th Division was engaged in a fierce struggle to defend the front of the Battle Zone. The situation was worse in the VI Corps sector where the Forward Zone held by the 59th Division had been overwhelmed, and the Germans were pressing against the rear defences of the Battle Zone. The assault against 34th Division was delayed until 11.30 a.m. with the object of driving a wedge between the 34th and 59th Divisions and then pushing north-westwards. By early evening only the left of the Forward Zone was held, but the arrival of the leading battalions of the 40th Division from GHQ reserve helped to contain the situation for the time being.

It was now evident that the position of V Corps in the Flesquières salient was becoming perilous. The German attacks on either side of the salient could, in the ultimate, result in V Corps being cut off, and in the early evening Byng ordered the withdrawal during the night from the apex of the salient to an intermediate position. This was a strong position with deep dug-outs forming part of the old Hindenburg Line that had been so successfully breached in November 1917 at the opening of the Battle of Cambrai.

The *Official History* in its view of the events of 21 March considered that:

The main reason for the failure of the defence as a whole ... is to be found in the fact that the British Army was extended over too great a length of front for its strength. Never before had the British line of 126 miles been held with so few men and so few guns to the mile; and the reserves were wholly insignificant... The losses of the previous year had not been made good, and the presence of too large a proportion of untrained and unseasoned officers and men further weakened the units – since no less than 19 out of the 21 divisions in the front line of the Third and Fifth Armies had been engaged in the Passchendaele battles in which they lost a large proportion of their best soldiers whose places had been filled, if filled at all, by raw drafts and transfers.[6]

It is undeniable that the Fifth Army front was over-extended (although less so than that of the Third Army), but there were other factors contributing to the success of the German attack. For most of the previous three years the British Army had fought offensive battles; it had not stood on the defensive since 1914. Thus there was virtually no experience of conducting an elastic defence nor, indeed, was there any time or labour to construct anything other than rudimentary defensive positions; and too much reliance was placed on natural obstacles such as rivers and canals, although, as earlier mentioned, it was believed that any loss of ground in the Fifth Army sector would not be so strategically damaging as it would be farther north.

The Forward Zone was not a continuous front line but an arrangement of mutually supportive outposts and strongpoints so sited that they could cover with fire the intervening ground. It would not appear, however, that any thought had been given to the incidence of fog. On the face of it, the dense fog experienced during the morning hours was a significant factor in nullifying the defence system and aiding the enemy's infiltration tactics. Ludendorff, however, thought otherwise: 'Fog impeded and retarded our movements, and prevented our superior training and leadership from reaping its full reward. This was the predominant opinion, but a few thought it an advantage.' It can only be conjectured as to what would have been the impact of the attack had visibility been good. It would seem certain that the enemy would have suffered greater casualties, not only from the surviving garrisons in the Forward Zone but from artillery in the Battle Zone. It is perhaps significant that when the fog cleared, particularly on the Third Army front, the momentum of the assault was slowed by machine-gun and small arms fire, and also from artillery firing over open sights. Nevertheless, there seems little possibility that the attack could have been held after a bombardment of a weight without parallel, and followed by an assault in such overwhelming strength.

Gough had visited his corps commanders in the afternoon of the 21st, warning them that the lack of reinforcements might force a general retirement. He amplified this on the morning of the 22nd with a written instruction:

To all corps, Fifth Army. In the event of a serious hostile attack corps will fight rear-guard actions back to forward line of Rear Zone [Green Line], and if necessary to rear line of Rear Zone. Most important that corps should keep close touch with each other and carry out retirement in complete co-operation with each other and corps belonging to Armies on flanks.

Fog again cloaked the battlefield on the morning of the 22nd, enabling the enemy to mass troops for the assault on the Crozat canal in the III Corps sector, and although several attempts made to cross the canal during the day were repulsed, a bridgehead was secured at the southern end of the canal at Tergnier and Quessy. The French 125th Division, however, arrived at noon with the promise of more to come.

If the position of III Corps was relatively stable, the very reverse applied to XVIII Corps, its neighbour. The withdrawal of III Corps to the Crozat canal had left the 36th Division on the extreme right of XVIII Corps holding a salient with its right flank along the Somme. This came under attack, and although a strongpoint in the division's battle zone held out for most of the day, the divisional commander, who, according to the *Official History*, was prepared 'to fight the battle out', was told after midday to withdraw to the Green Line. This instruction applied to all divisions in the corps, and by 5 p.m. virtually the whole corps was on the Green Line, but not to stay. The corps commander had decided that it was not suitable for defence as the trenches were mere scrapes in the ground, and the order was given for a night-time retirement to the left bank of the Somme.

This somewhat precipitate retirement of XVIII Corps appears to have been brought about by the interpretation of Gough's verbal instructions on the previous day when visiting his corps commanders, and his written instructions on the morning of the 22nd. In the words of the *Official History*, the Fifth Army diary, after giving the instructions, continued, 'accordingly orders were issued as follows: III Corps to stand fast, XVIII Corps to retire to the Somme and hold the Ham defences, XIX Corps to hold the Péronne bridgehead, VII Corps to hold forward portion of Rear Zone'.[7] These orders, however, were timed at 9.57 p.m. on the 22nd. It appears, however, that later in the morning of the 22nd, Fifth Army headquarters informed all corps by telephone of the imminent French reinforcement, and that Gough intended to stand on the line of the Somme. Thus it would appear that this telephone call transposed the qualification 'if necessary' into a definite order. Whatever the cause, the withdrawal of XVIII Corps in daylight, incurring heavy casualties in the process, was to have serious consequences. The withdrawal also had its effect on French civilians who were forced to leave their homes. Major R. S. Cockburn of the Reinforcing Battalion of the 20th Division (XVIII Corps) managed to obtain some food at a village inn and saw the people packing up their possessions:

> There was an old woman superintending the operation, who was all the time sobbing and crying. The family were packing all that they could take with them, evidently intending to abandon their home before the Germans should come: probably they had orders to leave the village. One Frenchman was talking in an angry tone, and cursing the war; he was the only one that spoke. As he collected his worldly goods and the bundles, he said he had been a prisoner of the Germans before, and was not intending to chance that happening again. 'Jamais, jamais,' he shouted, waving his arm and throwing open the door. 'Adieu', and then he went out with his bundles slung over his shoulder, and slammed the door behind him.
>
> Several poor people had already started to leave the village, and when my companion and I came out of the inn we saw them. They walked off pushing before them wheelbarrows loaded up with sacks. These old men, young girls and small children, form sad little bands, and I often wonder whether some of them got very far without falling down from exhaustion.[8]

XIX Corps was attacked all along its front, and the corps commander (Watts), following Gough's instructions, ordered his two divisions to withdraw to the Green Line if the Battle Zone could not be held. The VII Corps commander (Congreve) was advised by Gough on the telephone to delay the enemy as long as possible, but if forced to withdraw to stand on the Green Line. In the event, because of heavy enemy pressure, a withdrawal to the Green Line became necessary, although the remnants of XIX Corps' divisions took up positions behind the Green Line because the defences were wholly inadequate. Only VII Corps held a portion of the Green Line.

The acute problem faced by corps commanders was that although one division might successfully repel attacks and hold its position in the Forward or Battle Zone, its neighbours might be less fortunate: for example, the ground held might be less favourable for defence or enemy pressure heavier or, for one reason or another, a division might be less resolute under attack. Thus in the event of enemy penetration and the ever present concern about flank protection, a corps commander, because of the lack of reserves, and in the knowledge that he had been instructed not to fight a decisive battle, had little choice but to withdraw his divisions in line to the next defensive position.

If it had not been for the precarious situation of V Corps in the Flesquières salient, the Third Army would have been in a relatively better position than the Fifth Army. Nevertheless, the likelihood of further attacks on IV Corps on the northern flank of the salient and VII Corps on the southern would imperil V Corps. In the early afternoon Byng gave orders for its withdrawal to the front of the Battle Zone during the night, but in the evening he ordered a further withdrawal into the Battle Zone.

IV Corps was attacked at 7 a.m. but the enemy made little progress. The arrival of twenty-five tanks assisted in stemming a further advance although only nine ultimately survived. On the right of the sector, however, the enemy had penetrated over a mile north of the Bapaume–Cambrai road. On the corps left, the 3rd Division was still in its Forward Zone, but pressure on the 34th and 40th Divisions (the latter from GHQ Reserve replacing the 59th Division) forced a swing back of the corps right. XVII Corps, on the northern boundary of the Army, had not been attacked, but the swinging back of VI Corps had exposed its southern flank, and withdrawal would mean the loss of Monchy le Preux. A hill-top village with excellent observation, it had been a prime objective during the Battle of Arras in 1917, and its abandonment would be a bitter blow. Nevertheless, the withdrawal of VI Corps had left the village and its defenders in a vulnerable position, and at 8.30 p.m. Byng ordered XVII Corps to swing back its right and evacuate Monchy if necessary. Soon after midnight V Corps was ordered to withdraw as soon as possible to the Green Line, and IV Corps to conform. Accordingly, Monchy was evacuated in the early hours of the morning.

It could be argued that Byng's reluctance to release his hold on the Flesquières salient was an error. In December 1917 Haig issued instructions that the 'salient was only to be held as a false front', and that 'the troops occupying it, if seriously attacked, were to fall back on the Battle Zone'.[9] This instruction was repeated on 10 March. The *Official History* was forthright in its criticism:

> The retention of the Flesquières salient by the Third Army was a mistake; it
> led to the useless sacrifice of a great proportion of the infantry of 2nd Division

and part of that of the 63rd (Royal Naval) Division, when the enemy shelled the salient with mustard gas [over 7,000 gas casualties] – the loss, one may say, of a division. This later caused serious difficulties, from the consequent lack of reserves, at the junction of the Fifth and Third Armies.[10]

Apart from the gas bombardment, the salient had not suffered infantry assault, and although in a sense it had not been 'seriously attacked' the heavy pressure directed on the shoulders of the salient should have alerted Byng much earlier to the even worse possibility of V Corps being cut off.[11]

Fog was dense on the morning of the third day of the German offensive, but more so in the Fifth Army sector than farther north. Only two corps of the Fifth Army remained on their Green Line. XVIII and XIX Corps were now positioned in a deep re-entrant. Crozat canal was still held by III Corps, and Gough hoped that the French would soon be able to take over the corps sector, thereby releasing two divisions, albeit much reduced in strength, into reserve: the 58th Division south of the Oise was already under French command. During the morning, however, the Germans, despite determined resistance, succeeded in crossing the canal at several points. 'A certain bewilderment was caused to the defenders at first as the Germans appear to have gained their first footing west of the canal disguised in British uniforms from the fallen men of the 2/2nd Londons.'[12] By 2 p.m. the defenders had been driven back two miles. Another serious development was the news that the enemy had crossed the Somme at Ham, threatening III Corps communications. The important bridge-head at Ham had been defended by the 89th Brigade (30th Division), although the engineers had had little time to construct anything but rudimentary defences to cover the town, and there were only three weak battalions to hold the line. Bridges over the Somme in the 30th Division's sector had already been destroyed, but the bridge on the Ham–Noyon road was to be left to the last as the main escape route for the garrison. A subaltern of the 201st Field Company had been ordered to destroy the bridge in the event of the enemy being in possession of the bridgehead. On arrival at the bridge in the afternoon of the 22nd he found that it had been already prepared for demolition. During the day traffic streamed ceaselessly over the bridge, but in the early hours of the 23rd it had dwindled, and his diary records:

> The stragglers got fewer and in smaller parties, and I continually asked N.C.Os or officers if there were more to follow, and the answer was, 'No, not many.' The machine-gun fire was now very intense and occasional bullets passed over the bridge. In the distance I saw an officer leading about a platoon of men, and when he approached he said he was the last of the infantry... [He later] came running back and said his commanding officer ordered the bridge to be blown up. I did not do it immediately and waited for at least a quarter of an

hour. Then I heard a tremendous burst of cheering, it was the Huns entering the town. Bullets were now flattening themselves on the walls and road near me. Presently through the mist I thought I saw a movement, and then it was unmistakeable; a small party of Huns were rushing for the bridge. I waited until they first set foot on the bridge and then pressed down the handle of the exploder for all I was worth. Up went the bridge with a terrific crash and it was quite some minutes before the pieces stopped falling, and then, strange to say, the cheering which had been very loud up to then, suddenly stopped and there was dead silence for a few minutes but only for a time, and then a tremendous burst of machine-gun fire was directed along the street.[13]

According to the *Official History*, 'The explosion had cut the girders in the centre, but their shore ends stayed on the abutments and the hanging ends fell on the lock walls, so that the gap was small.'

Two French divisions arrived during the afternoon, and a mixed formation of British and French troops struggled to stem the enemy advance. With one minor exception, the arrival of the French meant that they had now taken over the III Corps front, and although this was a welcome development, Gough had not been aware until early in the morning that XVIII Corps was now behind the Somme, and he ordered XIX Corps to conform. Report of this retirement reached VII Corps before dawn, placing them in an immediate difficulty because they would have to follow suit, and contact had not been established with the 47th Division on the extreme right of the Third Army. The retirement of VII Corps began at 6 a.m. but by the afternoon enemy pressure had become so heavy that the intended line of defence could not be held, necessitating another withdrawal. During the evening a division arrived from Second Army, but VII Corps, while retaining touch with XIX Corps, had lost contact with V Corps of the Third Army.

Gough had had no personal contact with Haig since 21 March, which might be thought surprising bearing in mind the overwhelming nature of the German assault and the desperate position of his Army. In fact GHQ had played little part in dictating events, merely to insist that the Third and Fifth Armies should remain in contact. Haig, however, came to see Gough in the afternoon of the 23rd, and noted in his diary:

I was surprised to learn that his troops are now behind the Somme and the R. Tortville. Men very tired after two days' fighting and long march back. On the first day they had to wear gas masks all day which is very fatiguing, but I cannot make out why the Fifth Army has gone so far back without making some kind of a stand.[14]

After meeting Gough, Haig, now conscious of the impending crisis, returned to his advanced headquarters where he met Pétain, and his diary records:

General Pétain arrived at 4 p.m. He has arranged to put two Armies under General Fayolle on my right to operate in the Somme Valley and keep our two Armies in touch with one another. P. seems most anxious to do all he can to support me and agrees that the only principle which should guide us in our movements is to keep the two Armies in touch. In reply to my request to concentrate a large French force (20 divisions) about Amiens, P. said he was most anxious to do all he can to support me, but he expected that the enemy is about to attack him in Champagne. Still, he will do his utmost to keep the two Armies in touch. If this is lost and the enemy comes in between us, then probably the British will be rounded up and driven into the sea! This must be prevented even at the cost of drawing back the North Flank on the sea coast.[15]

Pétain suggested, and Haig agreed, that Fayolle should command all troops between the Oise and Péronne, and in consequence the French left boundary would extend along the line of the Somme from opposite Péronne to Amiens. Thus, with the exception of VII Corps north of the Somme, the remnants of the Fifth Army would be commanded by Fayolle.

The need for reinforcements was now critical, and after Haig had consulted the commanders of First Army (General Sir H. Horne) and Second Army (General Sir H. Plumer), a total of five divisions (including three Australian and one New Zealand), with an additional division if the Belgians co-operated in extending their right flank, was formed under the command of Lieutenant-General Morland.

Meanwhile, in the early hours of the 23rd, orders reached the divisions of V Corps in the Flesquières salient to withdraw to the Green Line commencing at 10 a.m. Apart from an abortive attempt to turn the flank of the 47th Division on the boundary with the Fifth Army, where a gap now existed because of the retirement of the 9th Division, the withdrawal was achieved without too much difficulty, By the evening, however, the enemy had succeeded in penetrating the gap, although further progress was halted by the arrival of reserves. By the end of the day all corps of the Third Army were on the Green Line except for some two miles on the right:

No words ... could convey any picture of the confusion of the night of 23rd/24th March: troops wandering about to find their brigades and battalions, in an area without landmarks, devastated a year before by the enemy; dumps burning and exploding; gaps in the line; the Germans attacking almost behind the V Corps front; the atmosphere charged with uncertainty, and full of the wildest reports and rumours.[16]

From the German viewpoint, progress so far had not been unalloyed. Despite the sweeping success of the Eighteenth Army, and to a slightly lesser extent, the left of the Second Army in their operations against the Fifth Army, the progress of the

Seventeenth Army and the right of the Second Army on the frontage extending from the Flesquières salient to just beyond Arras had not been nearly so satisfactory. Ludendorff was now in a dilemma: the problem he had to solve was, 'Should the victorious course of the Eighteenth Army be arrested and a decision forced on the right wing of the attack by increased pressure, in spite of the enemy's strong resistance? Or did the tactical situation demand a change of the original plan?'[17] On the 23rd he made up his mind:

> The object now is to separate the French and the British by a rapid advance on both sides of the Somme. The Seventeenth and Sixth Armies and later the Fourth Army will conduct the attack against the British north of the Somme, in order to drive them into the sea... The Seventeenth Army will take St Pol as the main direction and will push with its left wing via Doullens in the direction of Abbeville. South of the Somme the operations will be conducted offensively against the French by a wheel to the line Amiens–Montdidier–Noyon and then an advance south-westward...[18]

In effect this amounted to a change of plan in that the French and the British were to be attacked simultaneously. 'This meant shifting the whole attack to the left.' The position of the Fifth Army on 24 March was now becoming desperate:

> The divisions ... were now fighting and moving in small bodies, often composed of men in different units, frequently with parties of Germans mixed up with them, so that it was impossible for corps or divisional staffs to ascertain the position of the front line. After three days of battle, with each night spent upon the march or occupied in the sorting out and reorganisation of units, the troops ... were tired almost to the limit of endurance.[19]

III Corps was now under French command, and at 6.30 a.m., confronted by a renewed enemy attack, was forced to fall back. Two divisions (20th and 30th) of XVIII Corps still held the line of the Somme with two French divisions behind them, and with a further two some six miles in the rear. The enemy, however, had crossed the Somme at several places, thrusting through the 30th and 36th Divisions and compelling the former division to fall back.

> As dusk approached, the enemy attacked the troops on our left, before Mesnil-St-Nicaise. There was much rifle fire, but we ourselves could see nothing of the Germans as they were advancing over sunken ground beyond the ridge. Suddenly we saw all the troops on our left retiring hastily and in disorder. Some were running as fast as they could. It was disgusting to watch, and as this withdrawal meant that we were left in the air, so to speak, you may imagine our alarm and anger. I consulted with the battalion commander, and

we agreed that there was at present no reason for our men to leave our trenches; though our position would be a ridiculous one should the Germans capture Mesnil-St-Nicaise. These men continued to retreat, in spite of loud protests made by others on their right, who remained in their trenches. Very soon it became clear that the Germans were attacking in force, for we saw their white lights rising in great numbers; while after a time we heard shouts, whistles, cheers, and trumpets being blown in Mesnil, and saw our troops running out of the village as if hotly pursued... Rightly or wrongly, we thought it was no use staying where we were, for the enemy were right behind us; and we went back slowly ourselves. How many times did the same thing happen, through the retreat of one sector causing the positions of the sectors on its flanks to become untenable? Alas! our New Army had been trained to attack, but had never been taught how to rereat![20]

The river crossing near Béthencourt forced the 20th Division to retire and by nightfall both the 20th and 30th Divisions had taken up a position behind the Canal du Nord and in touch with two French divisions. XIX Corps succeeded in holding on to the Somme position except on the right where Béthencourt was lost, but VII Corps was holding a somewhat disjointed forward position which was soon penetrated by the enemy, causing a retirement. On the left flank of the VII Corps front, the commander (Brigadier-General F. S. Dawson) of the South African Brigade (9th Division) had been told that its position must be held 'at all costs'. But by 4 p.m., after maintaining a dogged defence and suffering grievous casualties, the brigade was virtually surrounded and its commander captured. A German officer wrote in his diary:

There was a corner of a little wood where the English [sic] put up a desperate resistance, apparently with a few machine guns, and finally with only one. When the defence was broken down, out from the lines of our advancing infantry, which I was following, appeared an English General, accompanied by a single officer. He was an extraordinary sight. About thirty-five years old, excellently – one can almost say wonderfully – dressed and equipped... Brushed and shaved, with his short khaki overcoat on his arm, in breeches of the best cut and magnificent high laced boots, such as only the English bootmakers make to order, he came to meet me easily and without the slightest embarrassment... I said 'Good morning', and he came to a stop with his companion. By way of being polite, I said with intention: 'You have given us a lot of trouble; you stuck it for a long time.' To which he replied: 'Trouble! Why we have been running for five days and five nights!' [sic] It appeared that when he could no longer get his brigade to stand he had taken charge of a machine gun himself... All his officers except the one with him had been killed or wounded, and his brigade hopelessly cut up. I asked for his name, to remind me of our meeting, and he gave it. He was General Dawson, an Equerry of the King.[21]

By nightfall only the right of the corps held the line of the Somme. Shortly before midnight GHQ ordered the divisions of VII Corps north of the Somme to join the Third Army, and those to the south to join XIX Corps.

At 3 a.m. on the 25th, following the agreement reached between Haig and Pétain on the 23rd, the command of the Fifth Army passed to Fayolle and, as a result, Gough would receive his orders from GAR (Group d'Armées de Reserve) and not from GHQ.

German pressure on the Third Army was mainly concentrated on cutting off V Corps in the Flesquières salient. Byng ordered the two divisions in the salient (2nd and 63rd) to retire to the rear of the Green Line (termed the Red Line) which was accomplished by the afternoon. But enemy pressure on VII Corps (Fifth Army) on the right of the Third Army, causing its retirement, had opened up a gap of over four miles between the two Armies. Shortly before 4 p.m. Byng decided to swing back the right of his Army in an endeavour to join with the left of the Fifth Army. By nightfall this still had not been achieved and, furthermore, contact had been lost with IV Corps on the left. In the morning IV Corps had still been on the Green Line, but the corps commander, on learning of Byng's instructions to swing back the Army's right, ordered a retirement to a new line. The position of the remaining corps, VI and XVII, was relatively stable and they remained in their positions on the rear of the Battle Zone.

Events were now rapidly approaching a crisis. Late that evening Haig was told that Fayolle could not expect to receive any reinforcements for four days, and at 11 p.m. Pétain arrived at Haig's advanced headquarters. According to Haig's diary, Pétain seemed 'almost unbalanced and most anxious':

> I explained my plans ... and asked him to concentrate as large a force as possible about Amiens astride the Somme to co-operate on my right. He said he expected every moment to be attacked in Champagne and he did not believe the main German blow had yet been delivered.
>
> He said he would give Fayolle all his available troops. He also told me that he had seen the latter today at Montdidier where the French reserves are now collecting and had directed him (Fayolle) in the event of the German advance being pressed still further, to fall back south westwards towards Beauvais in order to cover Paris. It was at once clear to me that the effect of this order must be to separate the French from the British right flank and so allow the enemy to penetrate between the two Armies. I at once asked Pétain if he meant to abandon my right flank. He nodded assent and added, 'it is the only thing possible, if the

enemy compelled the Allies to fall back still further'. From my talk with Pétain I gathered that he had recently attended a Cabinet Meeting in Paris and that his orders from his Government are to 'cover Paris at all costs'. On the other hand, to keep in touch with the British Army is no longer the basic principle of French strategy. In my opinion, our Army's existence in France depends on keeping the French and British Armies united. So I hurried back to my Headquarters at Beaurepaire Château to report the serious change in French strategy to the C.I.G.S. and Secretary of State for War, and ask them to come to France.[22]

Haig's next diary entry was for the 25th, presumably not long after midnight:

Lawrence at once left me to telegraph to Wilson (C.I.G.S. London) requesting him and Lord Milner [War Cabinet member] to come to France at once in order to arrange that General Foch or some other determined General who would fight, should be given supreme control of the operations in France...[23]

For the first time since the opening of the offensive there was only a ground mist, rather than fog, on the morning of the 25th, which, however, soon disappeared. The three corps, III, XVIII and XIX of Fifth Army were now part of the French 3rd Army commanded by General Humbert. The day did not begin well: on the III Corps front the enemy continued his advance, bringing about an early retirement of French divisions to south of the Oise. By the end of the day the French had relieved III Corps except for the 58th Division south of the Oise, but as the French divisions had been fighting without ammunition supply or artillery, they retained the corps field artillery.

Today saw a fierce battle in progress in front of Maricourt. A great effort was being made to hold the Hun up. We were firing all day, and from the battery position you could hear the rattle of machine guns.

The road past our battery afforded some evidence of the fighting that was in progress in front of us. Wounded men continued to pass all day – the slightly wounded glad of the opportunity to get out of the firing line, helping the badly wounded; men wounded in the legs supporting themselves by the shoulders of men wounded in the arms; here and there, but at rare intervals, a Hun prisoner under the escort of a perfectly good Tommy.

We spoke to some of them, to learn how the battle went, but none had anything very cheering to relate. The general impression seemed to be that we were up against a hopeless task – that there would be no stopping them here – more reinforcements were needed... There were on the other hand, some reinforcements brought up. Small detachments of dusty, tired looking men, in charge of a young officer, passed the battery from time to time, making for the fighting line. Our men were given a bit of a cheer as they passed... It always seemed to cheer them a bit to find a battery in action, and it certainly cheered us to see reinforcements brought up.[24]

XVIII Corps was positioned on the Canal du Nord, and two British divisions (30th and 20th) held the centre and left, with a French division on the right. There was a gap, however, on the left, with the right of XIX Corps, which was soon penetrated by the enemy. In an attempt to close the gap, a counter-attack by the French 22nd Division was arranged in cooperation with the right of XIX Corps, but this did not materialise. Indeed, according to the *Official History*, 'the 22nd Division began ... to go not forward, but southward, marching away from the gap'. The French division on the right soon came under a heavy attack and, because of III Corps' retirement, was forced to fall back. With their flanks 'in the air', the two British divisions were forced to conform to the retirement. Since the general direction was south-westwards towards Roye, the gap already existing with XIX Corps would become even wider; so the corps commander ordered the 20th Division, retiring with the French 22nd Division, to change direction after arriving at Roye and move northwards to fill the gap.

All preparations had been made by XIX Corps to join with the French in a counter-attack, and although the 24th Division attempted to advance, they were anticipated by the enemy and it came to nothing. Elsewhere enemy pressure was unremitting, causing small-scale retirements to avoid flanks being turned. As a consequence, however, of the French retirement south-westwards, together with that of the VII Corps north of the Somme, orders were issued at 6 p.m. for withdrawal of the corps.

The situation was equally bleak on the Third Army's front. While VI and XVII Corps on the left flank were virtually on their original positions, the right of V Corps had retired some seventeen miles and taken up positions in trenches in the High Wood area, some existing from the Somme battles in 1916.

High Wood! The words [brought] poignant memories to many in the 47th Division. An ironic joke of Fate, surely, to send us back through High Wood. Our troops passed the cross erected there to those brave fellows of the 47th who succeeded in 1916 where others had failed, and many vowed we would have no peace until High Wood had been wrested again from the Germans.

The desolation of the Somme country was in keeping with our feelings. Feet were sore with marching over rough country; mouths parched; bodies tired with a heavy, numbing fatigue; these things produced a desolate feeling akin to the quiet sorrow of the surrounding country.[25]

On the afternoon of the 25th GHQ instructed the Third Army to fall back to the line of the Ancre (a tributary of the Somme). The withdrawal began at 9.30 p.m. and was carried out with little enemy interference, although because it had to cross the ruins of the old Somme battlefields, movement was mainly restricted to roads already congested with all forms of traffic.

Days and nights came and went without marked difference, on and on all the time until at last we linked up with the retreating infantry and during the whole of this dreadful march we were shelled, shelled, shelled, and if there can be monotony in the expectation of death – then the very din of battle became monotonous. Eventually, it seemed untold ages, we reached the open country of the Somme, and those on foot made across the fields in the direction of Delville Wood, while the transport kept to the road. The day was fine and warm and the majority of us shed our greatcoats and any such clothing we felt we could do without to give us greater freedom of movement... Everybody was on the move and all in the same direction – away from the line with the enemy pressing behind... Crowds of troops were either wounded or captured but still that extraordinary British spirit which knows not defeat kept up our hearts and what is more to the point kept us on our feet. We regained the road somewhere near Delville Wood and the remnant of the company halted. Some of the company who had seen previous fighting called it Delville Wood but to look at it, there were only a few dead stumps that remained. By a remarkable stroke of luck, the quartermaster also chose this spot wherein to pull in his train, and in a very short time had brewed up some tea ... and the sight of a cooker in full blast helped considerably at the moment. We were just about to draw our ration of the precious liquid when along galloped a staff officer in the kind of rage into which only a brass hat can work himself, his face was purple and his eyes literally bulged, he harangued us thus: 'What the hell are you men doing? Can't you see the enemy advancing?'... so we sorrowfully poured our tea into the ditch and bolted![26]

Notes

1. Cockburn, Major R. S., Papers of, held in the Department of Documents, Imperial War Museum, London.
2. Crutchley, C. E., (ed.), *Machine Gunner 1914–1918* , Bailey Bros & Swinfen (Folkestone, 1975)
3. Allfree, Lieutenant E. C., Papers of, held in the Department of Documents, Imperial War Museum, London
4. Petschler, Captain R. F., Private diary
5. Edmonds, Brigadier-General Sir James, (comp.), *Official History of the War: Military Operations France and Belgium 1918*, Vol. I, Macmillan (London, 1935)
6. *Ibid.*
7. *Ibid.*
8. Cockburn, *op. cit.*
9. Edmonds, *op. cit.*

10. *Ibid.*
11. After the war, Byng claimed that an early retirement from the salient would have had a detrimental effect on morale.
12. Grimwade, F. C., *War History of the 4th Battalion, The London Regiment (Royal Fusiliers)*, Regimental Headquarters, (London, 1922)
13. Petschler, *op. cit.*
14. Blake, Robert, (ed.), *The Private Papers of Douglas Haig 1914-1919*, Eyre & Spottiswoode (London, 1952)
15. *Ibid.*
16. Edmonds, *op. cit.*
17. *Ibid.*, quoted
18. *Ibid.*
19. *Ibid.*
20. Cockburn, *op. cit.*
21. Binding, R. G., *A Fatalist at War*, Allen & Unwin (London, 1929)
22. Blake, *op. cit.*
23. *Ibid.*
24. Allfree, *op. cit.*
25. Maude, A. H., (ed.), *The 47th (London) Division 1914–1919*, Amalgamated Press (London, 1922)
26. Polley, D. J., 189th Machine Gun Company, 63rd (Royal Naval) Division, Papers of, held in the Department of Documents, Imperial War Museum, London.

4

Unified Command

Following a War Cabinet meeting on 23 March, Lloyd George asked Lord Milner (a member of the War Cabinet) to cross to France the following day to consult the French Government and French and British military authorities on the crisis. Thus unbeknown to Haig, Milner was already in France at the time of his telegraph. After visiting GHQ at Montreuil (Haig was at his advanced headquarters) he went on to Versailles, arriving there in the early hours of the 25th. Later that day he saw General Rawlinson, the British Permanent Military Representative, and was then asked to meet Clemenceau in Paris. According to Milner, Clemenceau showed 'no despondency or confusion' but was clearly concerned about the possible loss of contact between the French and British Armies. Afterwards it was arranged that Milner should meet President Poincaré, Clemenceau, Loucheur (War Minister) and Foch at Compiègne.

The meeting took place at Pétain's headquarters at which Pétain expressed himself as 'very pessimistic about the Fifth Army which, he said, had ceased to exist. He was bringing up all the divisions he could spare in support. Six divisions were already engaged and he was bringing up nine more. That was all he could spare at the moment.'[1] Foch disagreed, and thought the danger was such that all risks should be taken. Poincaré and Clemenceau were in agreement with Foch and asked Milner what the British would do to establish co-operation between the two Armies. Milner could not respond without consulting Wilson (who had arrived in France) and Haig, and suggested a meeting the next day when both would be present. It was subsequently arranged that the meeting would take place at Doullens where Haig had already arranged to meet his Army commanders.

It seems inevitable that any event of great historical importance should afterwards be subjected to various interpretations, and the fateful meeting at Doullens is no exception. According to Lloyd George's *War Memoirs* (published some fifteen years after the event), he and Milner had decided that 'there was only one effective thing to do and that was to put Foch in control of both armies'. Wilson had arrived at Montreuil at 11.30 a.m. on the 25th, and his diary records:

> Interview at once with Haig and Lawrence. After much talk I told Haig that in my opinion we must get greater unity of action, and I suggested that Foch should co-ordinate the action of both C.in C.s. In the end Douglas agreed...[2]

The implication is that initially Haig had had objections, but this appears to conflict with the substance of his telegram sent to London in the early hours of the morning with the plea 'that General Foch or some other determined general who would fight should be given supreme control...'

Wilson travelled with Milner to Doullens on the 26th when 'they fully agreed to making Foch the co-ordinating authority. Milner was in a difficult position, seeing that he was furnished with no authority from the War Cabinet to commit that body...'[3] According to Lloyd George's *War Memoirs*, he certainly had his authority, unless it was a case of a belated claim for the credit.

Shortly before the Conference commenced, Milner 'then talked to Haig alone about Foch and was delighted to find that, far from resenting the thought of Foch's interference, he welcomed the idea of working with him'.[4] The Conference then assembled: President Poincaré in the chair, Clemenceau, Foch, Pétain, Haig, Wilson and Milner. Haig spoke first. He outlined the events of the last five days and stressed that there was no question of falling back on the Channel ports, that he was determined to hold on north of the Somme, and he was bringing up every division he could spare. It was then Pétain's turn. He described the efforts made since 22 March: twenty-four divisions were on their way, with more to follow; Amiens must be defended at all costs. Foch then said: 'We must fight in front of Amiens, we must fight where we are now. As we have not been able to stop the Germans on the Somme, we must not now retire a single inch.' According to the *Official History*: 'On this outburst Field-Marshal Haig was heard to say, "If General Foch will consent to give me his advice, I will gladly follow it." '[5]

Milner then asked to see Clemenceau alone:

> I told him ... that Foch appeared to be the man with the greatest grasp of the situation. Could he not be placed by both Governments in a position of general control, as Foch himself had suggested to Wilson? Clemenceau agreed but said he must speak to Pétain. When he took Pétain aside I did the same with Haig. When I explained to Haig what was contemplated he seemed not only willing but really pleased.[6]

Clemenceau, after seeing Pétain, proposed the following:

> General Foch is charged by the British and French Governments with the co-ordination of the action of the British and French Armies in front of Amiens. He will arrange to this effect with the two Generals-in-Chief, who are invited to furnish him with the necessary information.

According to the Official Historian, Haig 'pointed out the difficulty of such a task unless General Foch had full authority over all operations "on the Western Front". To this General Pétain at once agreed...' and the proposal was amended accordingly.[7]

Meanwhile German pressure continued on the front of the Fifth Army now held almost equally by the French and British (eighteen and nineteen miles respectively). The former III Corps area was held by the French (although they had arrived with little ammunition or artillery) with a scattering of British units. The French soon experienced the enemy infiltration tactics that had beset the British, causing withdrawal when flanks were turned. Ultimately they were forced to retire some five miles, losing Roye in the process and widening the gap with the right of XIX Corps.

XIX Corps was in a pronounced salient and thus dangerously exposed: there was a gap on its right with the French of three miles, and on its left, the Third Army was set back four miles in the corps' rear. The enemy opened a strong attack at 6.30 a.m., forcing the retirement of the 39th and 66th Divisions, and at 9.30 a.m. the corps was ordered to retire to a new line five miles to the rear. At the end of the day the French and British held a line from south-east of Noyon to the Somme west of Bray, but the retirement of VII Corps meant that there was no contact with the Third Army.

The Third Army front was relatively stable, although Byng still feared further pressure on his right flank. At 2.20 a.m. he issued a warning order for a further retirement, although emphasising that 'no retirement is to take place unless the tactical situation imperatively demands it'. This order had been telephoned in advance to corps commanders, and it would appear that the VII Corps commander (Congreve) assumed 'that all that was expected of VII Corps was a series of rearguard actions to cover the retirement of Third Army...'[8] Shortly after 1 p.m. an attack on a brigade of the 35th Division was repulsed, but at 2.30 p.m. the divisional commander issued orders for a retirement to the Ancre. Following a message from Third Army headquarters, however, received at corps headquarters, that 'no voluntary retirement from our present line is intended. Every effort must be made to maintain our present line', Congreve endeavoured to halt the division's retirement; but it was too late, and as a result a gap of five miles opened between the two Armies.

After six days the German offensive was beginning to slow down. The dense fog of the previous mornings had now virtually disappeared, thereby assisting the defenders in the choice of targets. The rapidity of the advance had on a number of occasions outdistanced the artillery and supplies, and it had now reached the devastation of the old Somme battlefields where only the roads were passable. One factor contributing to the slowing down of the advance was an epidemic of looting:

Today [28th March] the advance of our infantry suddenly stopped near Albert. Nobody could understand why. Our airmen had reported no enemy between Albert and Amiens... I jumped into a car with orders to find out what was causing the stoppage in front. Our division was right in front of the advance, and could not possibly be tired out. When I asked the Brigade Commander on the far side of Meaux why there was no movement forward he shrugged his shoulders and said he did not know either... I turned round at once and took a sharp turn with the car into Albert. As soon as I got near the town I began to see curious sights... There were men driving cows before them on a line; others who carried a hen under one arm and a box of notepaper under the other. Men carrying a bottle of wine under their arm and another one open in their hand.

When I got into the town the streets were running with wine. Out of a cellar came a lieutenant of the Second Marine Division, helpless and in despair. I asked him, 'What is going to happen?' It was essential for them to get forward immediately... He replied, solemnly and emphatically, 'I cannot get my men out of this cellar without bloodshed.'[9]

Similar scenes took place elsewhere when the Germans came across the vast quantity of stores left behind in the retreat.

The failure of the 17th Army to make any significant progress immediately south of Arras was a disappointment to Ludendorff, but on the other hand he was tempted to capitalise on the success of the Eighteenth Army against the French south of the Somme. Accordingly he directed the Eighteenth and Second Armies to push south-westwards to the Avre river, and Amiens to be captured by the latter Army's centre. They would be joined in this advance by the Seventh Army while the Seventeenth Army was to push westwards in conjunction with the Sixth and Fourth Armies. 'Translated into simple language, the orders meant the Seventh, Eighteenth and Second Armies were to form a great barrier to keep off the French, whilst the Seventeenth and Sixth defeated the British, and the Fourth Army, the Belgians.'[10]

* * *

The events of each of the six days culminating on 26 March have been described in some detail because they not only brought about the virtual destruction of the Fifth Army, but also produced the second great crisis of the war. Moreover, they appeared to demonstrate that the key to a successful breakthrough on the Western Front had at last been found. Any analysis of why this should have been so is complicated by the various underlying, and often conflicting, strands of political and military decisions made before the offensive. The *Official History* blamed the War Cabinet (and, by implication, Lloyd George) for the success achieved by the German offensive because it denied Haig the reinforcements he needed to bring his Armies up to strength; but he required these for mounting a Flanders offensive in the spring rather than for resisting a German offensive. David Woodward, in *Lloyd George and the Generals*,[11] argued that no blame should be attached to Lloyd George. On the contrary, at a Manpower Committee on 15 December he was on record as pressing for men to be sent from the Home Forces to France. The objections, however, came from the War Office representatives, partly on the grounds that Haig had stated that he could hold on for eighteen days in the event of a German offensive, giving ample time for reserves to be transported to France.

A material factor in the success of the German breakthrough was that its main weight fell on the extension of the British line to Barisis. The line had been taken over in January from the French, and although the front line position was in good condition, 'it was of the old type, not developed in depth into a Forward Zone. Behind this there was no more than a belt of wire ... so that the Battle Zone and Rear Zone had to be constructed.'[12] The fact that the Fifth Army was overstretched in holding the line has been mentioned earlier, but Haig placed too much reliance on the policy of mutual assistance previously agreed with Pétain: it does not appear to have occurred to either commander that the strategic object of the offensive would be to separate the British from the French. On 10 March the routine GHQ Intelligence summary warned that an attack would be made in the Arras–St Quentin sector, but it was not known whether this was the main attack or merely a diversion. Haig expected that although some ground might be lost, he was confident that the attack would ultimately be held, with the prospect of the enemy suffering severe casualties; indeed, a mirror image of his own experiences in past British offensives. He still believed that the strategic direction of the main offensive would be against the Channel ports, whereas Pétain, because of the success of enemy deception techniques, was convinced that it would be in Champagne. It is a matter for conjecture whether Haig would have offered material assistance to Pétain in that eventuality.

Lawrence's letter of 9 February had instructed Gough that the enemy should not be held in the Battle Zone 'unless the general situation at the time makes such a course desirable'. The emphasis was on making a stand behind the Somme, and it was this instruction that Gough had in mind on the second day of the offensive when it was clear that he could not expect reinforcements, or assistance from the French, in time to save his Army if it stood its ground. There appeared to be no alternative to a fighting retreat by day and an orderly retirement by night: 'orderly' in the sense that it was vital that corps should not lose touch with each other. This, however, was not to be; fog, the breakdown of communications, the insecurity brought about by enemy infiltration, and the closeness and weight of the enemy pursuit all compounded to produce an atmosphere of crisis. In some cases it was only after the event that corps commanders were aware of the retirement of their neighbours, and a number of withdrawals were made in daylight without the provision of an adequate protective screen, causing, on occasions, heavy casualties. Moreover, the Fifth Army's retirement was not to a series of well-prepared defensive positions but sometimes to little more than scrapes in the ground, sometimes wired, sometimes not. The planned ultimate point of retirement, the Somme, did not prove to be a very formidable obstacle. Owing to a dry winter, the river was at a low level, allowing the enemy to cross by causeways. The arrangements for destruction of bridges were not always effective; the abutments often remained, as did vestiges of the bridges themselves, affording passages for small parties.

It is clear that the Fifth Army had the task of defending the indefensible. GHQ had instructed that the ground protected by these zones was not important enough to justify fighting for it, raising the question why the decision was not made to withdraw from it. It could not have been foreseen in November, when agreement was reached on the extension of the British front, that it would be the focal point of the enemy offensive, but on 1 February Gough warned GHQ that enemy activity pointed to an attack on his Army. Even then it could not be certain that it would be the enemy's main blow. GHQ, in its memorandum of 4 February, put forward for consideration the advisability of a withdrawal behind the Somme, but failed to come to a conclusion. One of the disadvantages cited was 'the moral effect', and it is probable that this was the deciding factor. The Germans had faced a similar problem almost exactly a year earlier because of British pressure on the Ancre. The withdrawal had straightened out a dangerous salient and shortened their front by twenty-five miles. 'The decision to retreat was not reached without a painful struggle [wrote Ludendorff]. It implied a confession of weakness bound to raise the morale of the enemy and lower our own. But it was necessary for military reasons – we had no choice.'

The German withdrawal, however, had been to the strong defences of the Hindenburg Line, whereas a British withdrawal would have been to the so-called 'Emergency Line' – a line that existed only on paper. The line (between two and three miles behind the Green Line) extended from the Oise along the western bank of the Somme through Péronne, passed east of Bapaume and finally joined the Arras defences. Withdrawal to this line would have shortened the British front by some fifteen miles, and if labour resources had been concentrated on strengthening the natural obstacle of the Somme instead of being fragmented in two alternative areas, it is possible, in hindsight, that the German offensive might have been blunted.

Foch, in his new command role, ordered that there should be no further retirement: present positions held should be maintained, Amiens must be covered, there should be no separation of the French and British Armies and the Fifth Army front should be reinforced. Indeed reinforcements were on the way: the 5th British Division from Italy, four ANZAC (Australian and New Zealand Army Corps) divisions from the Second Army, and, ordered by Pétain, five more divisions to be sent to south of the Somme. In addition, over the following four days nearly 40,000 troops crossed to France from the United Kingdom, and in the first week of April almost 74,000.

Despite the firm direction of Foch and the arrival of reinforcements, the situation on the Western Front remained critical, particularly south of the Somme where on the 27th the Germans launched a heavy attack on the French defences from Noyon to the River Avre. The French V Corps (including the British 2nd Cavalry Division) in the Noyon area held their ground throughout the day, but despite Foch's insistence that there should be no further retirement, the French VI and II Cavalry Corps holding a position south-west of Roye were forced to withdraw, allowing the Germans to capture Montdidier, thereby creating a re-entrant some ten miles in

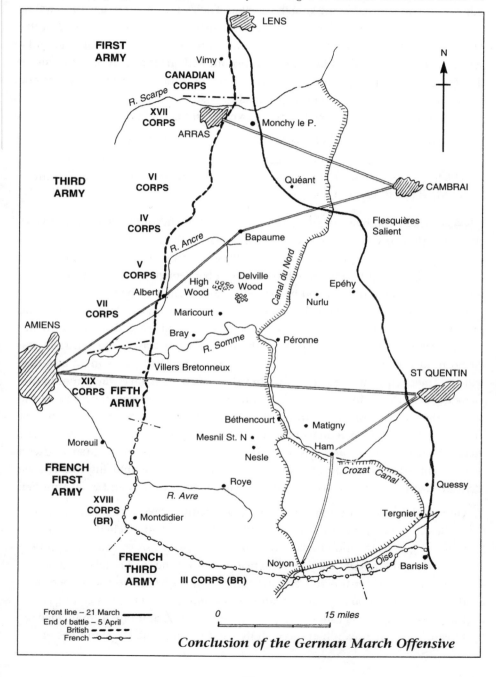

Conclusion of the German March Offensive

width and depth. This retirement carried with it the British XVIII Corps which then formed a defensive flank. Farther north the gap along the Somme caused by the retirement of VII Corps (Third Army) on the previous day was exploited by a determined German thrust, forcing Gough to obtain Foch's agreement to a withdrawal of XIX Corps. This withdrawal, however, had established contact with the right of the Third Army. North of the Somme the Germans made only small gains notwithstanding the attacks having been pressed forward with great resolution. This failure had been an acute disappointment to the Germans, and Crown Prince Rupprecht regarded it as 'the turning point in the great offensive'.

It was on this day that Gough was removed from his command:

> The Chief of the Imperial General Staff, with the approval of the Government, had chosen to regard General Gough as responsible for the British retirement which in their eyes was a grave disaster, and ordered his removal from command of the Fifth Army.[13]

His place was taken by General Sir H. Rawlinson (British Military Representative at the Supreme War Council), formerly commander of the Fourth Army. Gough had been unpopular in London ever since the Passchendaele battle in 1917, but Haig had resisted an attempt to replace him in December. Gough had been given a virtually impossible task, but he, and his Army, were ultimately to be vindicated.

German pressure was maintained south of the Somme on the 28th, although the French mounted a successful counter-attack on their right wing, driving the enemy back towards Montdidier. Nevertheless the critical point was in the centre of the Allied front held by the battered divisions of XIX and XVIII Corps in an awkward salient. The enemy attacked at 10 a.m. but the French soon gave way, exposing the flank of XVIII Corps and forcing a withdrawal. As mentioned earlier, because of the gap on the left wing of XIX Corps, Foch had agreed to a retirement, but late receipt of the consent forced a retirement in daylight closely pursued by the enemy. The main German effort, however, was north of the Somme (Operation 'Mars'). After a fierce bombardment, the advance of the Seventeenth Army, employing twenty-nine divisions with sixteen in reserve, was brought to a halt by artillery and small arms fire:

> One of the most thrilling sights in these exciting days was watching our artillery. Often they did not retire until the infantry had reached them, and then the gun teams and limbers would thunder down the road at a mad gallop to get the guns, and would very soon tear past us on the road to take up a new position. No sooner was this accomplished then off would go the limbers at the same mad gallop to the rear to bring up ammunition. Often in getting out the guns the gunners came to hand to hand fighting, and one little incident I heard was that a team had successfully crept through the German lines one

night, limbered up some guns which had been captured and galloped back with them.[14]

Only on the right of the attack in the Arras sector was some ground gained, but by the afternoon the attack was called off. This was yet another severe disappointment for Ludendorff who ordered that the 'Mars' attack should not be renewed. Instead he decided to attack the British front on the River Lys early in April in the direction of Hazebrouck, but pressure would still be maintained south of the Somme with the objective of capturing Amiens.

For the next three days the Germans made only limited progress south of the Somme, and none at all north of the river. As a result, Ludendorff decided to postpone operations until 4 April. Between 1 and 3 April there was a lull in enemy activity, but it was evident to the Allies that this was only a presage of a renewed offensive. There was no certainty as to where this would take place, although Haig was convinced that it would fall on the British front. It seemed clear, however, that an attack against the French (other than south of the Somme) was unlikely, pointing therefore to a renewal of operations between the Oise and the sea.

There was an Inter-Allied Conference at Beauvais on 3 April at which Foch's authority was enlarged. The agreement reached on 26 March had charged him with the 'co-ordination of the action of the British and French Armies', but it was agreed at the Conference that he would be entrusted with 'the strategic direction of military operations' covering British, French and American Armies. Each commander-in-chief would retain tactical control of his Army, with the right of appeal to his Government if it was considered that his Army was endangered by any order received from Foch. Following the Conference, Foch issued a General Directive in which he considered that an offensive north of the Somme to be most likely. He therefore called for a counter-offensive south of the river by the French, with the British attacking astride the Somme. The objective was to free Amiens from enemy pressure.

On 4 and 5 April the Germans made one more effort to reach Amiens. The attack was made on a fifteen-mile front between Montdidier and the Somme. The French were driven back some two miles, but attacks against the British front met strong resistance; the infantry, advancing virtually shoulder to shoulder, suffered severe casualties, particularly from artillery fire. Ludendorff considered: 'It was an established fact that the enemy's resistance was beyond our strength. [OHL] was forced to take the extremely difficult decision to abandon the attack on Amiens for good.'[15]

Notes

1. Milner diary
2. Callwell, Major-General Sir C. E., *Field-Marshal Sir Henry Wilson*, Cassell (London, 1927)
3. *Ibid.*

4.   Milner, *op. cit.*
5.   Edmonds, Brigadier-General Sir James, (comp.), *Official History of the War: Military Operations: France and Belgium, 1918*, Vol. I, Macmillan (London, 1935)
6.   Milner, *op. cit.*
7.   Denis Winter, in *Haig's Command*, Viking (London, 1991) claimed that Haig's intervention was a fiction introduced by the Official Historian. He also implied that Haig opposed Foch's appointment.
8.   Edmonds, *op. cit.*
9.   Binding, R. G., *A Fatalist at War*, Allen & Unwin (London, 1929)
10. Edmonds, *op. cit.*, Vol. II, Macmillan (London, 1937)
11. Woodward, David, *Lloyd George and the Generals*, (University of Delaware, 1983)
12. Edmonds, *op. cit.*, Vol. I
13. Edmonds, *op. cit.*, Vol. II
14. Petschler, R. F., Private diary
15. Ludendorff, General, *Concise Ludendorff Memoirs*, Hutchinson (London, 1933)

5

'Backs to the Wall': The Battle of the Lys, April 1918

Early in April a German soldier in the 371st Infantry Regiment wrote in his diary:

> Near Lille we were resting up from our enterprises, also to be re-equipped for the great push to come, which was supposed to take us to the English Channel. Many familiar faces had gone to be replaced by new faces, to become soon familiar and then suddenly to vanish. The army had struck lately quite successfully against the French and the British. Our superiors and newspapers assured us that big events were approaching. As far as we were told there were only 30,000 Americans [in reality over 400,000], most of them inexperienced soldiers. There were more Americans to come, but then we had hundreds of submarines that controlled the seas. Now that the whole Eastern army had been transferred to the west, a million strong, it seemed to us imminent that the next offensive would bring victory and peace.[1]

Haig's conviction that the next German offensive would strike against the British front was strengthened by Intelligence received pointing to an attempt to pinch out Vimy Ridge, coupled with an attack in the Neuve Chapelle area. Haig met Foch at Abbeville on 7 April to discuss means of reinforcing his Armies in the north. Foch, however, considered the safety of Amiens to be paramount and to this end he planned a joint offensive by the French First and British Fourth Armies to regain the line previously held between the Avre and the Somme. He refused to provide Haig with any reinforcements either by way of relieving British divisions south of the Somme, or by mounting a large-scale counter-offensive on the Montdidier front. Haig was told on the 8th by the First Army commander (General Sir Henry Horne) that all the signs pointed to a renewed enemy offensive the next day. Haig thereupon immediately appealed to Foch to relieve six divisions in the Ypres sector, but Foch refused.

The River Lys lies in the Flanders plain rising near Aire-sur-la-Lys, and passes through Estaires, Armentières and Comines on its journey to join the Schelde. 'The surface is everywhere clayey. The water-table, or level of subsurface water, is always fairly high, and any depression or excavation quickly fills with water.'[2] It was for this reason that Ludendorff had decided against launching a Flanders offensive before the middle of April, but the exceptionally dry spring of 1918 now persuaded him that an offensive was possible. The original German plans formulated at the end of 1917 were for Operation 'Mars' to take place after 'Michael', followed in turn by the two 'George' operations – 'George 1' near Armentières, and 'George 2' near Ypres. The frontage for the original 'George' attack was to have extended from the La Bassée canal to near Ypres, but this had now been modified to an attack (code-

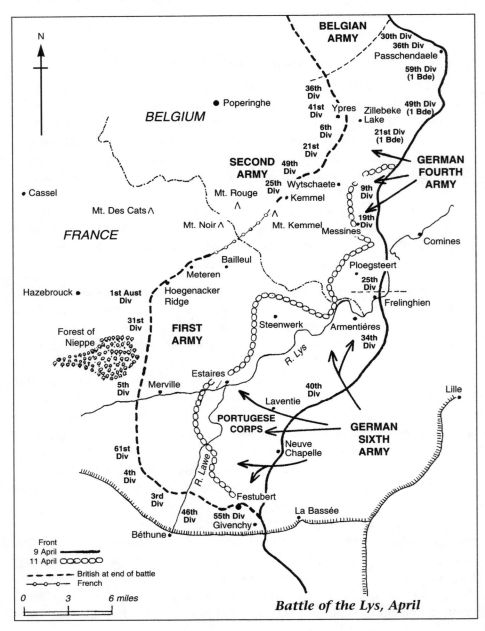

Battle of the Lys, April

named 'Georgette') extending over twelve miles from the La Bassée canal to just short of Armentières with, if all went well, complementary attacks north of Ypres. The sector from the canal to Armentières was held by the left wing of the British First Army comprising four divisions, one of which was Portuguese and overdue for relief.[3] The defences had been organised into zones: the front of the Battle Zone was termed the 'Corps Line', and the Green Line was the 'Army Line'. The ground between the front line and the Corps Line

> ... was already well organised and bristled with switch lines, defended locali-ties, machine-gun posts (some of concrete), belts of wire and wired hedges; gun positions had been wired prepared for all-round rifle and Lewis-gun defence, so that they could be held independently if the enemy should break through.[4]

At 4.15 a.m. on the 9th a heavy bombardment of high explosive and gas shells was opened on the back areas between the La Bassée canal and Frelinghien (three miles north-east of Armentières) lasting for four and a half hours. The main weight of the bombardment fell on the sector between Givenchy and Laventie held by the Portuguese division and the 55th Division. As on 21 March, there was thick fog hampering response by the British artillery, but communications, with some excep-tions, were virtually intact because of deep-buried cables.

The assault was delivered at 8.45 a.m. by eight divisions with six in support; all the divisions were fresh. No less than four divisions struck the three Portuguese brigades in the front line, with disastrous results. Large numbers of Portuguese were seen retiring even before the attack was launched, and by 10 a.m. it had become a rout. By 11 a.m. 'virtually the whole of the division, including its artillery, had left the battlefield'. The 55th Division on the right of the Portuguese stood firm (and was to remain so for the rest of the battle), but on the left, the Portuguese retire-ment had forced the 40th Division to withdraw. The effect of these withdrawals was to create a re-entrant ten miles wide and nearly six miles deep.

The news reached Haig shortly after midday at a meeting with Foch. Haig proposed shortening his front in order to create a reserve to protect the Channel ports, and once again suggested that the frontage held by six divisions in the Ypres area should be taken over by the French. Haig wrote in his diary:

> Foch declined to take over any part of the British Line, but is determined to place a Reserve of four French divisions with their heads on the Somme imme-diately west of Amiens. In case of necessity he proposes to march these N.E. to take a share in what he calls the 'bataille d'Arras'...
>
> I found Foch most selfish and obstinate. I wonder if he is afraid to trust French Divisions in the battle front.[5]

Although the German attack in the morning had gone well, largely because of the Portuguese retirement, it was not a repetition of the success gained on 21 March. Ludendorff wrote:

> In the afternoon the attack seemed to progress more slowly. The ground was soft in places and this made it very difficult to bridge the enemy's trench-system. It took a long time to get up guns and ammunition. In the evening we were advancing towards Armentières, had reached the Lys and were approaching the Lawe. In the direction of Béthune we made little progress. On the left at Givenchy and Festubert, we were held up. The result was not satisfactory.[6]

One contributory reason, on occasions, for the slowing down of the German advance was the discovery of the vast amount of stores left behind in the British withdrawal, and the stocks of food remaining in village shops after their owners had fled. A German soldier entering the town of Steenwerk described the scene:

> On the other side of the street was a large market and grocery store. Other soldiers had entered there already. The place was filled with ham, sausages, cans of delicacies and white bread. Duty was forgotten. More soldiers piled in bringing with them bottles of wine and beer. Outside in the street whistles shrilled. The officers were trying to assemble their men again, but nobody paid any heed. Different regiments were arriving by now, but they too followed our example and pretty soon the whole town was filled with men, who probably for the first time in long years, lost the respect before Prussian discipline. They broke into houses, demolishing the interiors. They discovered a brewery and started rolling barrels of beer into the street, breaking them open with bayonets and spades, to drink to their heart's content. Here and there arguments ensued, to be followed by fist fights, and if the British could have returned now, they would have captured some of the very best German divisions without difficulty.[7]

Fog again enveloped the battlefield on the 10th. The Germans attacked on both sides of Armentières in the direction of Hazebrouck. By noon the villages of Ploeg-steert and Messines had been captured, although the latter was recaptured in the afternoon. Armentières, however, was outflanked, and GHQ ordered it to be evacuated. The situation was now alarming. Haig ordered two cavalry divisions from south of the Somme to move northwards, but he had no other reserves to call upon. Withdrawal from the Passchendaele salient would shorten his line, but Foch had stressed the importance of holding the present front; he feared that a withdrawal would be interpreted as a sign of weakness and thus invite attack.

In thick fog on the next day (11th) the Germans renewed their offensive at 4.30 a.m. The heaviest assault was in the centre of the great re-entrant formed after the

Portuguese retirement two days earlier. The three divisions holding the centre were forced to give ground, further deepening the re-entrant and giving rise to the possibility that additional pressure would drive a wedge between the First and Second Armies. Haig wrote to Foch asking him to place at least four four French divisions between St Omer and Dunkirk. Foch's reply was that the British must 'hold on where they stood', and emphasised the importance (as if Haig needed reminding) of stopping the German advance on Hazebrouck. He promised, however, to send a cavalry corps to support the Second Army. It was on this day that Haig issued Special Order of the Day. He expressed the admiration he felt 'for the splendid resistance offered by all ranks of our Army under the most trying circumstances'. The concluding paragraph read:

> There is no other course open to us but to fight it out. Every position must be held to the last man: there must be no retirement. With our backs to the wall and believing in the justice of our cause each one of us must fight on to the end. The safety of our homes and the Freedom of mankind alike depend upon the conduct of each one of us at this critical moment.

Ludendorff now believed that not only Hazebrouck was within his grasp but also the Channel ports. The loss of Hazebrouck with its important railway junction would sever the Second Army's line of communication running behind the Flemish hills of Mt Kemmel, Mt Rouge, Mt Noir and Mt des Cats which, although only 300–350 feet high, dominate the Flanders plain. Only the forest of Nieppe lay between the enemy and Hazebrouck.

> One last obstacle lay before him, the forest of Nieppe, where in the earlier days of the war soldiers employed in wood-cutting had seen startled wild boars rushing through the undergrowth. Its fringe was lined, or rather dotted, with exhausted men; divisions and even brigades were mixed up with one another, No reinforcements could arrive at Hazebrouck until the evening, or reach the scene of action until late on the 13th. Those engaged had either just emerged from the ordeal of the last battle or were lads of eighteen, who had been sent out of England in defiance of pledges under the stress of imminent peril.[8]

The German gains on the 12th were limited to enlargement of the deep re-entrant, now over eleven miles wide. At the conclusion of the day's fighting, which had seen desperate resistance by tired troops, Hazebrouck was less than six miles away. There was a shortage of officers, and divisional staffs could not exercise much control because the front was constantly shifting: it was, as the Official Historian wrote, 'a brigadiers' and soldiers' battle'. An example of this was on the 13th when two companies of a machine-gun battalion were dispatched 'in a lorry, forcibly appropriated', to stem the German advance on Meteren. 'After occupying a line about a mile south of the village, the machine-gunners were able to keep off the Germans and rally the returning troops.'[9] This bare narrative conceals the reality, graphically described by the battalion commander, Lieutenant-Colonel G. S. Hutchison:

> In Meteren there stood an A.S.C. [Army Service Corps] motor-lorry column. I requested the use of a lorry, but the officer in charge refused it. I hit him on the head with the butt of my revolver, and instructed the driver, a bright young fellow who rendered yeoman assistance to the Division during the ensuing days, to drive off.
>
> We halted at the farm-house, where I had installed my headquarters, and within a few minutes half a company of machine-gunners, guns, and ammunition complete, had been packed into the lorry, while I myself, with my Adjutant, sat beside the driver at the wheel, revolvers in hand. We drove straight towards the Ridge on which stood the Hoegenacker Mill, which became the fulcrum of the fighting.
>
> On the way we surprised the advance guard of the enemy in a ditch. From our seat beside the driver my Adjutant and I loosed off our revolvers and killed the gun crew, German storm troops, and captured their machine-gun...
>
> Masses of British Infantry [in] grave disorder and often led on by their own officers, were retiring on to Meteren. At the revolver-point I halted one Battalion led in retreat by its Commanding Officer, ordering the men to turn about and occupy the Hoegenacker Ridge. Three times I gave my order and put it also into writing. The men refused to move. Finally I gave the officer, whose men said they would accept no order except through one of their own officers, two minutes in which to decide, with the alternative of being shot out of hand. At the end of those two minutes I struck him; and the Regimental Sergeant-Major exclaimed, 'That's what I've been waiting for all day, sir.'[10]

Although it could not be foreseen by the Allies or the Germans, the high point of the offensive on the Lys had been reached on the 12th, and on the 14th Foch told a surprised Haig that 'la bataille d'Hazebrouck est finie'. Between the 14th and the 18th, notwithstanding intermittent attacks, some of them heavy, the Germans gained little ground of any significance. In the afternoon of the 14th, the German Sixth Army reported to Ludendorff 'that its offensive had, to all appearance, fizzled out and that the troops were completely exhausted: each day the divisions were ordered to attack but did not do so'.[11] Between the 19th and the 24th there was something of a lull in enemy operations in Flanders with only persistent gas shelling and minor actions taking place. On the 20th 'OHL decided to stop the offensive in Flanders, but, as the two wings of the attack were hanging back, that the operations against Festubert-Givenchy by the Sixth Army, and against Kemmel by the Fourth Army should be continued so as to have more elbow room'.[12]

During this period there had been little enemy activity south of the Somme, although Villers Bretonneux was shelled with gas on the 17th. A German prisoner taken by the French on the previous day revealed that an attack on the town was planned for the 17th, and air observation disclosed an increase in the movement of enemy batteries. No attack took place on the 17th, however, but gas shelling continued. The German objective was not the capture of Amiens but in the nature of a diversion to hold Allied forces on the Villers Bretonneux front and occupy the plateau on which the town stands in order to shell railway communications at Amiens.

On the morning of the 24th, a bombardment on the same lines as that delivered on 21 March, but lasting just over two hours, fell on a four-mile frontage west and south-west of Villers Bretonneux. In thick fog, with visibility reduced to no more than forty yards, the assault began at 6 a.m., and a vanguard of thirteen enemy tanks[13] followed by infantry crossed No Man's Land virtually unseen. The defence was broken where tanks appeared, but held elsewhere. Nevertheless, where enemy penetration had succeeded, the flanks were forced to withdraw in order to conform, and Villers Bretonneux was lost. There were twenty British tanks in the area – thirteen Mark IVs and seven Whippets[14], and the appearance of enemy tanks was to result in a landmark in the history of armoured warfare. Three British tanks, one 'male' armed with two 6-pounder guns, the others 'female' armed only with machine guns, appeared at 9.30 a.m. An enemy tank promptly knocked out the two 'females', and disabled one of the 'male's' guns, but the crew brought the other gun into action and disabled one of the enemy tanks, its crew abandoning the machine. Two more enemy tanks appeared on the scene; one was fired on and backed away, the other turned and followed its companion. Farther south the Whippets charged and scattered enemy infantry, causing hundreds of casualties. At 10 p.m. a counter-attack was mounted and, in fitful moonlight, two Australian and one British brigade recovered most of the lost ground and Villers Bretonneux was recaptured.

Not only was Villers Bretonneux retaken but the new line established beyond where the old one had run and a lot of prisoners and guns were captured. It was much the most wonderful performance of which I had direct knowledge during my service. Remembering that the pick of the Australians were killed in Gallipoli, I have often wondered whatever they can have been like. I have no patience with the journalistic tendency to see anything even slightly exotic as necessarily better than the home-grown article, and a good experience of English County battalions has left me with a high opinion of them. Nevertheless, it is my considered opinion that the Australians, even in 1918, were better in battle than any other troops on either side. They were not popular. They had a contempt for Britishers to begin with – that is some Australians voiced such a contempt: I myself heard the expression, 'not bad for a Britisher' used by one about a successful feat of British arms; they were untidy, undisciplined, 'cocky', not 'nice' enough for the taste of Thomas Atkins; but it seems to me indisputable that a greater number of them were personally indomitable, in the true sense of the word, than any other race.[15]

On the 25th began what was to be the last major effort by the Germans on the Flanders front. A total of eleven divisions attacked the front between Bailleul and Ypres with the twin objective of taking Poperinghe and isolating the British in Ypres. The ten-mile frontage attacked was held by three French and three British divisions. Following a bombardment at 2 a.m., the assault was launched in thick fog at 6 a.m. Mt Kemmel was soon overrun, 'the French resistance collapsed like a pack of cards', and, north of the French, the British 9th Division held on for a time but was ultimately forced to retire because its right flank had been exposed by the French withdrawal. Although the loss of Mt Kemmel was a serious blow, the Germans failed to exploit it. A counter-attack, by a French and a British division, was arranged by the commander of the Second Army (General Sir Herbert Plumer) to take place at 5 p.m. with the objective of retaking Mt Kemmel, but the French division was not ready, and the counter-attack was postponed until 3 a.m. on the 26th. In the event it proved abortive: because of ground conditions, the British 25th Division was unable to keep up with the barrage, and the French division, starting half an hour later, was stopped after meeting strong resistance. The 25th Division was forced to withdraw, but the counter-attack had the effect of disrupting an assault by three German divisions on the Kemmel sector. Farther north, the enemy made some limited gains, albeit at heavy cost, in the Second Army's outpost line and, as a precautionary measure, Plumer ordered the withdrawal of the main British line nearer to Ypres.

There was a pause in German operations on the 27th and 28th, but on the 29th, after a two-hour gas bombardment, followed by forty minutes of high explosive, an attack by eleven divisions was launched at 5 a.m. on the French and British positions from Meteren to Zillebeke lake (an outpost position) and on the Belgian position north of Ypres. The weight of the assault on the Franco-British positions caused the French to give some ground, but this was regained by a counter-attack. The assault on the Belgian position near Langemarck was a failure. The German view was:

The whole 'Georgette' operation was finished; the Fourth and Sixth Armies had exhausted their powers of attack.

The storming of Kemmel was a great feat, but, on the whole, the objective set had not been attained. The attack had not penetrated to the decisive heights of Cassel and Mont des Cats, the possession of which would have compelled the evacuation of the Ypres salient and the Yser position. No great strategic movement had become possible; the Channel ports had not been reached. Our troops in the conquered trenches were in a very unfavourable situation, as they were strongly enfiladed by the enemy... The second great offensive had not brought about the hoped-for decision. [16]

Ludendorff decided on the evening of the 27th not to persevere with the Lys operation. He knew that Foch had been transferring reserves to the Amiens area and he intended to create a diversion by attacking the French front on the Chemin des Dames; plans for this attack had been in preparation since the middle of April. Nevertheless, Ludendorff still considered the British front in Flanders to be the prime objective, and preparations were to be made for an attack, code-named 'New George', in June.

Notes

1. Meisel, F., Papers of, held in the Department of Documents, Imperial War Museum, London
2. Edmonds, Brigadier-General Sir James, (comp.), *Official History of the War: Military Operations France and Belgium 1918*, Vol. II, Macmillan (London, 1937)
3. Portugal, traditionally Britain's oldest ally, had joined the war officially in 1916 on the side of the Allies, and by the middle of 1917 there was a Portuguese Expeditionary Force of some 40,000 on the Western Front. Their morale, however, was poor. The officers were allowed home leave, but not the men. Moreover, many were in sympathy with the revolution that had broken out in Portugal in December 1917.
4. Edmonds, *op. cit.*
5. Blake, Robert, (ed.), *The Private Papers of Douglas Haig 1914–1919*, Eyre & Spottiswoode (London, 1952)
6. Ludendorff, General, *Concise Ludendorff Memoirs*, Hutchinson (London, 1933)
7. Meisel, F., *op. cit.*
8. Cruttwell, C. R. M. F., *A History of the Great War 1914–1918*, Clarendon Press (Oxford, 1934)
9. Edmonds, *op. cit.*
10. Hutchison, Lieutenant-Colonel G. S., *Warrior*, Hutchinson (London, 1932)
11. Edmonds, *op. cit.*
12. *Ibid.*
13. The Germans were slow in building tanks: only thirteen (A7Vs) were available at Villers Bretonneux, and, indeed, only fifteen were ever built. They were huge machines weighing 33 tons, had a crew of eighteen and were armed with a 57mm. gun and six machine guns. They were unwieldy machines and difficult to manoeuvre over broken ground.
14. The Whippet was a light tank armed with three machine-guns and with a maximum speed of 8 mph
15. Ledward, Lieutenant P. A. (23rd Brigade, 8th Division), Papers of, held in the Department of Documents, Imperial War Museum, London
16. Quoted in Edmonds, *op. cit.*

6

High Tide: The German Diversionary Offensives: May–July 1918

THE BATTLE OF THE AISNE: MAY 1918

There was a pause in German operations following the failure of the Lys offensive and this, to the more sanguine observer, might have indicated exhaustion or a decline in morale or, indeed, both. Intercepted German wireless messages pointed to a suspension of operations in Flanders, but the ingenuity of German methods of deception did not allow of any relaxation by the Allies. Haig remained convinced that the next blow would fall in Flanders, and with the weakened and tired forces at his disposal, he was not only fearful of his ability to contain it, he was also worried about being separated from the French, believing that 'it meant absolute disaster, as both army and ports would be lost'.[1] Supporting Haig's contention were the indications of German strength: south of the Oise to the Swiss border there were estimated to be 60 divisions, whilst between the Oise and the sea there were no fewer than 204, compared with 64 and 106 Allied divisions respectively. British casualties in the March and April battles had amounted to over a quarter of a million, but reinforcements received only totalled 133,000 – mostly boys of eighteen and a half and those recovered from wounds.

Foch's main concern was the creation of a substantial General Reserve to be placed not only in support behind the Franco-British front in the north, but to be used, when the time was right, to mount a counter-offensive. He was sure that there were plenty of men in khaki available in the United Kingdom for this purpose and he put pressure on Wilson to increase the flow of reinforcements. As a result Wilson agreed to provide 70,000 men additional to the 20,000 reinforcements per month that had been agreed would be sent to France during the three weeks commencing 20 May. Nevertheless, these extra drafts would not succeed in bringing the British divisions up to establishment, and the remedy appeared to lie in increasing the transportation of American forces to France. The total strength of the American Expeditionary Force in France at the beginning of May was 430,000, but this had increased to 650,000 by the end of the month. Those already in France had been undergoing training in quiet French sectors, but under an arrangement reached between Lord Milner and General Pershing (Commander of the American Expeditionary Force) in April, it had been agreed that six of the eight divisions arriving in May would be trained by the British Army. This was discussed at a meeting of the Supreme War Council on 1 May, and Haig's diary noted:

... a great deal of time was wasted discussing the agreement made by Lord Milner and General Pershing regarding bringing 120,000 American Infantry to France in May to join the British Army. I thought Pershing was very obstinate, and stupid. He did not seem to realise the urgency of the situation.

Finally, the arrangement for May is to hold good and Pershing is to decide in a fortnight whether the same arrangement will continue for June. He hankers after a 'great self-contained American Army' but seeing that he has neither Commanders of Divisions, of Corps, nor of Armies, nor Staffs for same, it is ridiculous to think such an Army could function unaided in less than two years' time.[2]

According to Haig's diary entry for 19 April, he had received a letter from Foch stating 'that he was anxious to maintain 15 French Divisions in Reserve behind the British Army. To enable him to obtain these Divisions it would be necessary to put tired British Divisions in the positions now held by the French Divisions which he wants.'[3] After a discussion with Lord Milner, who had arrived in France, Haig agreed, somewhat reluctantly, to send four divisions. At the end of April, however, Foch suggested that this number should be increased to between ten and fifteen divisions, but Haig, while accepting the need for a General Reserve, would not agree to the increase because of the prevailing uncertainty regarding enemy intentions.

Throughout most of May, French and British Intelligence sources failed to glean any reliable information as to where and when the next German offensive would open, but as early as 25 April the Americans had forecast that the sector between Reims and Montdidier (which included the Chemin des Dames ridge and the River Matz) seemed a likely objective. It would not appear, however, that this remarkably accurate prediction by the fledgling Intelligence branch of the American Expeditionary Force had much impact; the British, based on observed enemy preparations, believed in an attack on the Somme–Arras front, but Foch's opinion was that it would fall in Flanders. To offset this, Foch suggested a counter-offensive on the Festubert–Robecq front by the Canadian Corps which, coincidentally, Haig already had in mind. On 26 May, however, British Intelligence reported the move of four enemy divisions, with heavy artillery, in the direction of Laon – nine miles north of the Chemin des Dames sector.

The impending German attack in the Chemin des Dames sector was 'a matter of an attack to draw off the enemy reserves. The old main object, defeat of the British, still remained unaltered. The great offensive against the British was to follow the diversion attack against the Chemin des Dames as soon as possible.'[4] Ludendorff, however, remained concerned about the state of morale in the German Army:

Officers of all ranks complained of the tired and discontented spirit which was being brought into the Army from home. The leave men had been exposed to

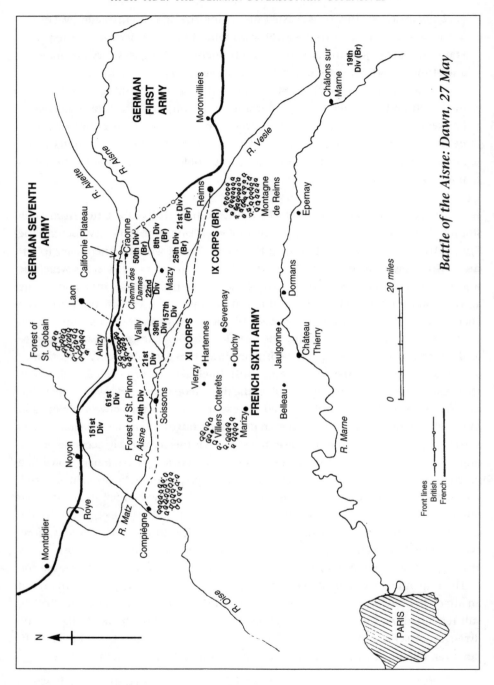

Battle of the Aisne: Dawn, 27 May

the influence of agitators, and the new drafts had a bad influence on discipline. All this was lowering the fighting value of the Army. Among a number of drafts very serious irregularities had occurred, particularly among those from Bavaria and the East.[5]

The original objective was the line of the Aisne, to be reached after crossing the River Ailette and the Chemin des Dames ridge. This would entail a relatively modest advance (by 1918 standards) of less than ten miles, but during May, the objective was extended to the River Vesle, virtually doubling the length of the advance. The attack was to be delivered by forty-one divisions: of which thirty divisions and 1,150 batteries were already in position on 27 May. This great assembly had been undetected by the French largely because the infantry had been hidden in woods around Laon and within only a day's march of the battlefront.

As a result of Foch's request to exchange tired British divisions for fresh French divisions, Haig released five: four divisions (8th, 21st, 25th and 50th) under IX Corps were attached to the French 6th Army commanded by General Duchêne on the Aisne front west of Reims, and the remaining division (19th) to the French 4th Army near Châlons sur Marne. The British had been assured by the French that the front was 'suitable and quiet', and although this view had been accepted with some misgivings, all five divisions had suffered severely during the March and April battles, and it was essential that they should be allowed to recuperate and build up their strength for future operations. They had received reinforcements (mostly inexperienced young recruits) but not enough to bring them up to establishment, and there was little possibility yet of replacing losses of experienced officers and NCOs. 'The company officers were completely untrained, almost without exception. The simplest orders were misunderstood, whilst the frontage allotted to the division [50th], some 11,000 yards, reduced the force available to a minimum.'[6] All the divisions were in position by 19 May.

To the battered, battle-weary troops, whose only knowledge of France was based on experience of the northern front, the Champagne country in the full glory of spring was a revelation. Gone was the depressing monotony of Flanders, drab and weeping, with its mud and its mist, its pollards and its pavé: gone the battle-wrecked landscapes of Picardy and the Somme, with their shattered villages and blasted woods. Here all was peace. The countryside basked contentedly in the blazing sunshine. Trim villages nestled in quiet hollows beside lazy streams, and tired eyes were refreshed by the sight of rolling hills clad with great woods.[7]

The Chemin des Dames ridge extends for some twenty-four miles from Craonne in the west to midway along the Soissons-Laon road. It is a bare hog's back with a flat top mostly between 350–400 yards wide, steep on the northern side, and although less so on the southern side, it is cleft by numerous small valleys where 'ascent is a matter of climbing on hands and knees'. At the foot of the northern slope is the Ailette, a canalised river some 60 feet wide. The ridge had been no stranger to conflict: in September 1914 the summit had been reached by a Franco-British force, but lost by the French in 1915 and ultimately recovered in October 1917. The ridge was held on the right by the British 8th, 21st and 50th Divisions, and the French 45th Division. The 50th Division was holding the Californie plateau, the highest point and a prime enemy objective. In the centre and left were three French divisions (22nd, 21st and 61st), and behind the Aisne were four French divisions and the British 25th. Further back there were three more French divisions and the British 19th. Against this total of sixteen Allied divisions situated 'in a position from which it was difficult either to make a counter-stroke or retire' were arrayed forty-one German divisions and over a thousand heavy batteries.

The ridge itself was undoubtedly a strong position: the French thought it impregnable. Although Pétain had feared an attack there in March, the fact that this had been directed against the British front only tended to confirm French views of its strength. The defences were arranged in Forward, Battle and Rear (Green Line) zones: termed First, Intermediate and Second positions by the French. The British were unhappy with the state of repair of defences in the Forward Zone, but the French thought them 'complete and perfectly kept up' probably on the grounds that they were adequate for a quiet front. They were soon to be proved entirely inadequate.

In his dispositions, Duchêne had committed a cardinal error. Pétain's instructions that the Forward Zone should be lightly held in order to disrupt the enemy advance, and that the Battle Zone was where the enemy should be halted, had been ignored. Duchêne decided to place his main force in the Forward Zone, and in this he had received the assent of Pétain who had decided 'to let his subordinates prepare in their own way a battle of which they would have the immediate charge'. This surprising, albeit reluctant, approval to a policy that ran counter to his own defensive doctrine was probably influenced by political pressure. Cruttwell, in his *History of the Great War*, believed that 'the Chemin des Dames had, next to Verdun, the greatest moral importance for French opinion. It was therefore worthwhile making unusual sacrifices to hold it.'[8]

The first signs of enemy preparations were noticed by the British IX Corps; aircraft had observed dust clouds on the roads south of Laon, and at night there had been heard the unmistakable sounds of troops on the move. The IX Corps commander interpreted these developments as a portent of enemy concentration, and although the French were informed, they still remained unconvinced that an attack was imminent. Prisoners taken by the French XI Corps at noon on the 26th, however, revealed that an attack would be launched on the next day, or the day after, and that the bombardment would commence soon after midnight. This at last persuaded the French to take precautions, and although all troops had been placed on the alert by the early evening there was no time to take anything more than rudimentary counter-preparations.

The information extracted from the two prisoners proved to be correct. At 1 a.m. on the 27th a storm of high explosive and gas shells descended on twenty-four miles of the front held by the four French and British divisions, with the greatest density on the French 22nd Division and British 50th Division holding the centre. A German account reads:

Contrary to previous procedure, in which the fire-preparation of an attack had begun with the comprehensive engagement of the enemy's artillery, this time from 1 a.m. for the first ten minutes, all guns and trench mortars, using gas ammunition, simultaneously devoted themselves at the highest rate of fire to all targets within reach. This was designed to create at the very start irremediable confusion and moral effect among the enemy. After this, the mass of the batteries turned their fire for 65 minutes, with gas and high explosive mixed, on the Allied artillery...'

The bombardment, considered even heavier than that delivered on 21 March, lasted for almost 2½ hours, and in that time the infantry in the Forward Zone were overwhelmed. All communications had been cut, and the artillery, if not destroyed, rendered almost powerless to respond. At 4 a.m. the German infantry began their advance behind a creeping barrage, their path over the ridge virtually unopposed. The heaviest thrust was in the centre against the French 22nd Division, a division that had already suffered severely in the March battles. Outnumbered five to one, it was swept from the ridge and forced back across the Aisne, where although the demolition charges had been laid to destroy the bridges, there had been no time to fire them.

The engineer parties detailed were caught at work by the enemy. Nowhere did they receive the order to fire the charges in sufficient time, and all initiative on their part was forbidden by the defence plan. Moreover, the first enemy parties arrived mixed up with the last of the retreating French troops. It was in these circumstances that the bridges between Vailly and Maizy fell intact into the hands of the Germans.[9]

The retirement of the 22nd Division placed the 150th Brigade of the British 50th Division on the Californie plateau in a difficult position. The Brigade Commander (Brigadier-General H. C. Rees) wrote in his diary:

My telephone connection with the 4th East Yorks was destroyed almost at once, also all lines to artillery... Luckily the buried line to Colonel Thomson's headquarters on the plateau and to our most valuable observation post remained intact... I talked to Col. Thomson and he told me that the shell fire was terrible but that he was still through to one of his company commanders on the forward edge of the plateau.[10]

Attacked on both flanks, the brigade was forced to withdraw although an attempt was made to counter-attack, but this failed with heavy losses. In his last message to General Rees, Thomson said:

> 'I'll say good-bye, General. I'm afraid I shall not see you again.' I said, 'Try to escape, the British army can't afford to lose you.' I subsequently heard that after fighting to the last he ran for it and was killed... He was one of the finest characters I've met...

By 8 a.m. the brigade, as a fighting unit, had ceased to exist, and its neighbouring brigade (151st) suffered so severely that it was 'no longer an organised formation'. The remaining brigade (149th) put up a desperate fight, but confronted by tanks, the survivors were forced to retreat over the Aisne. The 50th Division, including its artillery, had been all but destroyed. General Rees decided to escape himself: 'I felt I must stop to see whether there were any stragglers. In almost all battles there are stragglers, but this time I saw none... The battle was now across the Aisne and on the open ground between us and the Aisne, was a German field battery in action.' Rees reached the Aisne at 11 p.m. but was eventually captured. On his way into captivity, he and two British officers, accompanied by a German staff officer, were driven by car to Craonne where the three were ordered to get out. Rees's diary continues:

> I was furious as I imagined we were being taken to see some corps commander and thought it was deliberately humiliating. I made a remark to Laverack to this effect. The German staff officer with us overheard it and said, 'When you reach the top, you will see His Imperial Majesty the Kaiser, who wishes to speak with you.' When we approached, the Kaiser was apparently having lunch, but stepped forward on to a bank and told me to come and speak to him. He asked me numerous questions with regard to my personal history, and having discovered that I was a Welshman, then said, 'Then you are a kinsman of Lloyd George.' He asked no questions which I could not answer without giving away information and made no indirect attempts to secure information of this character either. Presently he said, 'Your country and mine ought not to be fighting against each other, we ought to be fighting together against the third. I had no idea that you would fight me. I was very friendly with your royal family with whom I am related. That, of course, has now all changed and this war drags on with its terrible misery and bloodshed for which I am not responsible.' He added some further comments on the intense hatred of Germany shown by the French, and then asked, 'Does England wish

for peace?' Everyone wishes for peace I replied. He then after a pause said, 'My troops made a successful attack yesterday. I saw some of your men, who had been taken prisoner, they looked as if they had been through a bad hour. Many of them were very young.' I then said that I hoped my troops had fought well against him. He said, 'The English always fight well', and bowed to intimate that the interview was at an end. I withdrew.[11]

The two remaining front line divisions in the British IX Corps (8th and 21st) had suffered grievous casualties in the bombardment. Their defences in the Forward and Battle Zones were overwhelmed, and the survivors forced to fight a rearguard action back to the Aisne. A battalion of the Devonshire Regiment that had been in reserve sheltering in a hillside tunnel escaped the worst of the bombardment and succeeded in holding up the advance for several hours. For this action the French subsequently awarded them the Croix de Guerre.

It was a similar story in the west. The French 21st Division, on the left of the 22nd Division, was attacked frontally and on its right flank by three divisions and driven south-eastwards towards the Battle Zone where a stand was made. Nevertheless its commander informed his corps commander that it was 'a delusion to think of defending the First Position [Battle Zone]; that his regiments were at the end of their powers; and that the Second Position [Green Line] should be occupied'. The division on the left of the French XI Corps held a position north-west of the ridge. Attacked by three divisions, it was forced to withdraw, although three battalions held out in the Forêt de Pinon for some hours and considerably impeded the German advance.

The situation at nightfall was that the Allied divisions in the centre and left of the front had been driven back over the Aisne, but in the centre the German battering-ram had swept over the Second Position (Green Line) and in a number of cases the advance had reached the Vesle.

In the course of a summer day the enemy had crossed two, and in places, three rivers; he had driven a salient twenty-five miles wide at the base and extending nearly twelve miles into the Allied line; he had destroyed four of the divisions originally in the line, and nearly destroyed two more, besides two others sent up from the reserve.[12]

Notwithstanding their success, the Germans had worries. Their advance had been the longest made in a single day ever made on the Western Front since the onset of trench warfare, but the salient thereby created was too narrow:

In spite of all, however, the situation of the Seventh Army was not completely satisfactory. Nearly all the great German attacks on the Western Front had come to a standstill because the outer edges of the attack – caught by flanking fire and

71

fallen upon by hostile reserves – could not keep up with the central thrust... So the Seventh Army commander had to consider whether anything could be done to help forward the wings of the Army which were hanging back.[13]

As will be seen later, the failure to broaden the wings of the advance was ultimately to cause the failure of the offensive.

For the Allies, however, worse was to come on the 28th. Duchêne had five fresh French divisions at his disposal plus the remnants of the divisions shattered on the first day. But, once again, he was further to demonstrate his unfitness to command: Pétain's instructions for the employment of reserves were that counter-attacks should not only be made in the 'zone of penetration' but also on the flanks. In a rapid advance the head is strong and the flanks vulnerable, as the Germans themselves realised. Nevertheless Duchêne's decision was to meet the advance head-on.

The German advance continued on the 28th with the greatest progress in the centre and left. There was street fighting in Soissons, and although the French tried to maintain a bridgehead, they were ultimately driven out of the town and across the Aisne without, unfortunately, destroying the bridges. A reinforcement division arrived to support the two French divisions in the centre, but this was to no avail as eventually all were driven back. On the right the British IX Corps withdrew behind the Vesle, but succeeded in mounting a local counter-attack.

Only four divisions had so far been sent by Pétain to assist the 6th Army, but the growing crisis prompted the dispatch of another four from north of the Oise; however, they would take time to arrive, and thus could do nothing immediately to stem the German advance. Just before midnight on the 28th Pétain issued a Directive stressing that it was the duty of all 'to maintain their positions without troubling about the thrust of the enemy's advanced units'. His plan was to use the reinforcements to attack the wings of the salient.

The next day saw further progress by the enemy in the centre, forcing the French back over seven miles. On the evening of that day Pétain planned converging attacks by eight divisions on the wings of the salient to take place on the 31st. Meanwhile assistance was forthcoming from the American 3rd Division still undergoing training south of Chaumont:

> The sight of these magnificent youths from over the seas, of these clean-shaven lads in their twenties, brimming over with vigour and health under their new equipment, produced a prodigious effect. What a striking contrast they made with our own regiments, clad in garments soiled and worn out by so many years of war, the men of which, haggard, their hollow eyes lit up by sombre fires, were no more than bundles of nerves held together by a will-power of heroism and sacrifice. All felt that they were to be witnesses of the magical operation of a

transfusion of blood. Life was arriving in floods to reanimate the mangled body of France bleeding to death from four years of innumerable wounds.[14]

Pétain, however, needed still more divisions and wanted Foch to release the French Tenth Army (four divisions) from the General Reserve, plus nine divisions in Flanders. Foch, ever mindful of the threat of a German attack in Flanders, refused but asked the Belgians to extend their right flank down to Ypres, thereby relieving a British division. To this the Belgians agreed.

The Germans made the second greatest advance of the offensive on the 31st. Once again it was in the centre, and during the morning their advance parties had reached the hills above Château Thierry, and by the evening they held ten miles of the Marne's north bank. They had made little progress, however, in broadening the wings of the salient: attempts to debouch from Soissons on the left and capture Reims on the right were checked. Even so, the crisis was rapidly deepening for the Allies. Their resistance was weakening, and it seemed that there was little to stop the Germans if they decided to cross the Marne and head towards Paris, only forty miles away. Reinforcements, however, were on the way: Foch yielded to Pétain by giving him the Tenth Army, and Pétain gave Duchêne two American divisions (73rd and 2nd). Nevertheless politicians in Paris 'were demanding the head not only of General Duchêne, but also, above all, that of General Pétain'.[15]

It would appear that Ludendorff's objective of diverting Allied reserves from the north was being achieved, but the extent of the German advance was now creating its own problems. It had gone too far too fast, and the lack of progress on the flanks was now causing great concern. To overcome this OHL decided to broaden the front of the attack by extending it west towards Noyon and capturing Reims in the east. Once this was achieved the offensive could be stopped, a defensive line secured and the emphasis shifted to Flanders. Foch and Haig had always believed this to be Ludendorff's intention, but the French High Command was convinced that Paris was the objective.

On the last day of May there were signs that the situation was becoming stabilised. The French counter-attacks planned to take place on the wings of the salient were scaled down to an attack in the west only. This, while gaining some ground, proved abortive because of enemy counter-attacks, but it had the effect of hampering German efforts to broaden the wings of the salient. Although there were indications that the Germans were tiring, Pétain was still intent on extracting divisions from the north. In a letter to Foch he emphasised that only fourteen fresh divisions would be available in the next ten days 'to feed the battle', and it was imperative that he had a mobile reserve to meet contingencies:

The only means I can see of providing this is to send American reserves from the British zone to relieve French divisions in the trenches in the Vosges and

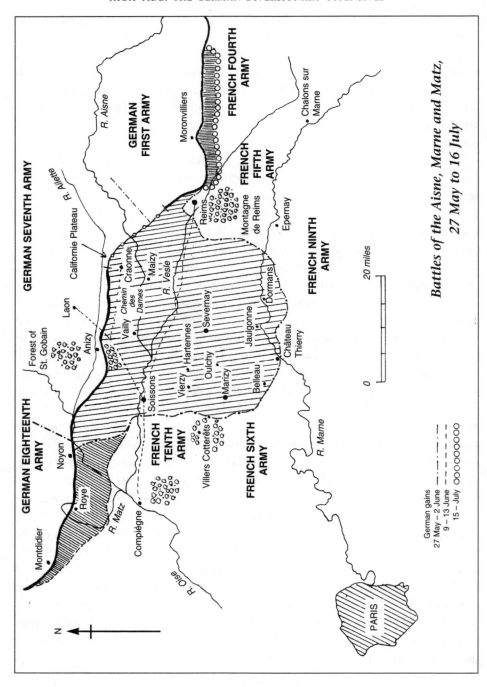

Battles of the Aisne, Marne and Matz, 27 May to 16 July

Lorraine. Also British reserves should be sent to the Oise, and, if necessary, to the Marne.

Foch's response was non-committal: he stressed the need for a foot-by-foot defence to prevent a German march on Paris, but was silent on the request to transfer British reserve divisions.

The Supreme War Council met on 1 and 2 June where the atmosphere at times was somewhat acerbic. At the preliminary meeting between Lloyd George, Lord Milner, Wilson and Haig, the latter opposed any suggestion that American troops training with the British Army should be sent to relieve French divisions:

> In discussing this problem, I pointed out that the most important fact was whether the French Army was fighting or not. From what I heard from Foch and Weygand, I inferred that French reserves once in the battle did not last out but 'melted away': this was due to coddling them last summer, and to want of discipline and to the lack of reliable officers and N.C.Os.[16]

At the afternoon's meeting with Clemenceau and Foch, the transfer of American divisions was not discussed as Foch believed it could be settled between Haig and himself, but he commented critically on the scale of reinforcements from the United Kingdom, claiming that 'nothing had been done'. According to Haig's diary, 'Lloyd George denied this strongly, and insisted that the British Government had made great attempts to get men before the battle of March 21 began. And so these people went on wrangling and wasting time.'[17]

Apart from some local operations, the battle had run its course and by 6 June had come to an end. The British contingent stayed on for some weeks (the French were reluctant to let them go), but by the 30th the last of the five British divisions had returned to the British sector. Their casualties had amounted to almost 29,000 out of an Allied total of 163,000 of which 60,000 were prisoners. German casualties were about equal, if an estimate for lightly wounded is added.

On 3 June Haig agreed to release five American divisions training in the British sector to relieve French divisions, and on 4 June Foch telegraphed Haig with the request that he move three divisions from his General Reserve to astride the Somme west of Amiens where 'they can act either to the profit of the British or to the profit of the French Army'. Although Haig agreed to this request he was alarmed at the implication in the telegram that if the Germans marched towards Paris it might 'call the Allied forces to the great battle'. He immediately entered a formal protest against the removal of any portion of the British Army 'until it is beyond doubt that most of the reserves available for Crown Prince Rupprecht's Group of Armies have been absorbed in the battle'.[18] Meanwhile Pétain, convinced that Paris was the next German objective, pressed Foch to extract more British divisions even to the extent of a radical scaling down of the British front from the Somme to Dunkirk. The divisions thus freed would be included in two Allied masses which would 'feed the front to cover Paris as economically as possible, and counter-attack the flanks of the enemy advance'. Foch, apart from informing Pétain that three British divisions would be moved to the Somme, ignored the proposal.

The strength of the British Army in France in early June was fifty-six divisions (of which eight were cadre divisions) plus the five divisions still in the Chemin des Dames area. These, together with six French divisions supporting the Second Army, faced at least 100 German divisions in Flanders. The threat of any cut-back in British divisions was of great concern to Haig, and following his report to the War Office of Foch's demands, Lloyd George asked Lord Milner and Wilson to meet Clemenceau and Foch. The meeting took place in Paris on 7 June: Lord Milner and Wilson were accompanied by Haig and Lawrence. Wilson's diary records:

> Milner opened [the] discussion by saying that the Government had been made rather anxious by the constant withdrawals of troops from Haig's command, while Rupprecht's divisions remained intact, and now Haig had been asked to move down 3 divisions to astride the Somme. The Field-Marshal, while not thinking that a disastrous point had been reached, did nevertheless consider that if further reductions were made he would formally have to appeal to his Government, unless Rupprecht's strength was sensibly reduced.[19]

Foch, sensing a possible crisis in Franco-British relations, explained that 'he was only asking Haig to make plans for moving his divisions away... [and] he was sure that Haig would only protest in future if he [Foch] committed 'des imprudences', and that in that case he [Foch] would agree with the Field-Marshal'. So a crisis was averted, and Wilson's diary concluded, 'This meeting has done a vast deal of good and has been well worth the trouble.'[20]

The German offensive on the Chemin des Dames, whilst exceeding all expectations in terms of ground gained, had created a salient, or pocket, too deep and too narrow. After the failure of his attempt in March to separate the French from the British, Ludendorff's plan had been twofold: to divert Allied reserves from north of the Somme, and then to create a strong defensive line along his great southern flank. But the depth of the pocket, with its extremity resting on the Marne, was a serious flaw in his design since the wings would always be vulnerable. Ludendorff then decided that to complete the Chemin des Dames offensive the western flank of the pocket would have to be widened. Accordingly, in an operation code-named 'Gneisenau', eighteen divisions of von Hutier's Eighteenth Army would attack on a frontage of some twenty-four miles between Noyon and Montdidier on 9 June. No ultimate objective had been planned, but it was hoped to establish a line Montdidier–Compiègne

THE BATTLE OF THE MATZ: 9–14 JUNE 1918

The Matz is a tributary of the Oise that joins it some six miles north of Compiègne and flows north-westwards, and then due north, to Roye. In effect it divided the battlefield, heavily wooded in the east, cultivated and undulating in the centre, but open in the west; the river itself is little more than a stream and only a few feet deep. The position was held by the French 3rd Army comprising four divisions with three due to arrive. The defences were in three positions – front, intermediate and second – but as they had only been constructed since March they were somewhat rudimentary. Pétain instructed that the first position should be lightly held to escape the worst of the enemy's preliminary bombardment, and that the attack should be held in a line of resistance some 3,000–4,000 yards in the rear of the first position. Unfortunately, because of shortage of time and 'the repugnance of certain commanders to modify the mistaken practice hitherto followed', almost half of the defending infantry were positioned little more than 2,000 yards from the front line.

Ever since the end of May the French had suspected that the Germans were preparing an attack on the Noyon–Montdidier front, but they could not be sure whether this was yet another exercise in deception. Information taken from prisoners on 7 and 8 June revealed, however, that an attack was imminent, and final confirmation was received when a deserter gave details of the date and the hour. At midnight on the 8th an intense bombardment began on the entire front from Noyon to Montdidier. It lasted for nearly three and a half hours, and at dawn fifteen German divisions attacked, gaining an immediate success in the centre where they battered their way through the line of resistance and the second position. By the evening they had advanced nearly six miles. On the next day the Germans pushed forward a further two miles in the centre, but on the right a retreating division forced the withdrawal of the entire right wing to avoid being cut off. The Germans made no further move on the 11th, but just previously the French had decided to mount a counter-attack on this day on the western wing of the salient. To achieve this, Foch placed five divisions together with 144 tanks under the command of a General Mangin (who had been without a command since the ill-fated Nivelle offensive in 1917). The final paragraph of Foch's orders read:

> Tomorrow's operations should be the end of the defensive battle which we have been fighting for more than two months. It should mark the definite check of the Germans and the renewal of the offensive on our part. It must succeed. Let everyone understand this.

Mangin's force, attacking in misty conditions at 11.30 a.m., surprised the enemy, and although it made some progress it was stopped by mid-afternoon by artillery fire. It was continued at 3.30 a.m. on the following day, achieving only partial success on the extreme right. On the same day the Germans mounted an attack

(Operation 'Hammerschlag') on the western side of the Aisne battlefield to assist the 'Gneisenau' offensive, but this was brought to a halt by artillery fire. On the evening of the 12th the OHL ordered both operations to be stopped. From then until the 18 June there were only attacks of a local nature. On the Matz front the French advanced their line in the west by two miles. and on the 18th the Germans attacked at Reims on a front of ten miles with three divisions. Although encircled on three sides, the defence, holding the massif of the Montagne de Reims, held firm.

Although the Matz offensive had failed, 'the German High Command, in spite of the enormous expenditure of divisions [since 27 May] still kept in hand considerable forces. The near future, therefore, remained full of anxieties.'[21] On 13 June Foch wrote to Pétain and Haig. He calculated the distribution of enemy reserves between the Somme and the sea to be thirty-five to forty divisions, and ten to twelve divisions between the Somme and the Swiss frontier. As the bulk of the reserves were 'behind the Armies opposed to the British Armies' he thought that it was there that the next attempt would be made. Nevertheless, because of their communication facilities it would 'permit them to transport their mass of manoeuvre rapidly to any point on the whole Franco-British front'. Thus the 'Allied reserves must take part in the battle wherever it is fought'. He therefore asked both commanders to draw up plans for the transport of reserves to whichever front was seriously threatened.

Pétain remained certain that the Germans intended to march on Paris, and he continued his demands for the handing over of British reserves on the grounds that as 'the British Armies had already had two months' respite to reconstitute themselves and absorb their reinforcements ... they are therefore in a position to look after themselves and give the French Armies time to reorganise in their turn so as to be ready to resist a new shock in the direction of Paris which cannot fail to materialise'. This approach, however, was brushed aside by Foch.

Meanwhile no clue could be gleaned of future German intentions, and bad weather in the last fortnight of June prevented air reconnaissance of enemy preparations. Rumours surfaced of an attack against Verdun, but the British thought the next attack would be on the Lys salient. On 28 June, however, French Intelligence believed that the next attack would be 'a continuation of attacks in the direction of Paris along the valleys of the Oise and the Marne...' and fixed a date of 15 July. On the same day, based on information from prisoners, the French Fourth Army reported the collection of bridging material for a Marne crossing between Epernay and Château Thierry, and that the attack would take place in July. Although not conclusive confirmation that the next blow would fall on the Marne, it was enough to persuade Pétain to begin to move reserves to strengthen the front. In all, the twenty-six divisions in the line and in reserve were increased by nine, although as a precautionary measure, Foch ordered three French divisions to be assembled in the Amiens area and on hand to assist the British in the event of a Flanders attack.

Haig was still convinced that this would be the decisive German effort (which indeed was Ludendorff's intention), and that an attack on the Marne would be yet another diversion to draw reserves away from his front. Foch, however, was soon to undergo a sea-change. Pétain persuaded him that the enemy was 'about to engage the greater part of his shock troops' in the Marne offensive, and Foch summoned Lawrence (Haig was on leave) to a conference on 12 July and warned him of the possibility of British reserves being called upon. He wanted two British divisions moved to south of the Somme, and the British Army to be prepared to launch an offensive on the Festubert front to free the coal-mining area around Béthune.

Lawrence agreed to move the 12th and 18th Divisions, but on the next day Foch's demands escalated. He telegraphed GHQ requesting that four divisions be sent to the French 4th Army, and this was followed almost immediately by another telegram asking for a corps headquarters to be sent in addition, and for a further four divisions also to be prepared to follow. In sum, this amounted to a request for ten divisions. Accordingly, Lawrence arranged to move the 51st and 62nd Divisions, but this was countermanded by Haig on his return from leave. He immediately informed Wilson of Foch's requests and demanded an interview with Foch to learn the reasons why the original arrangement, which envisaged the use of British reserves only when the enemy marched on Paris, had been changed. Haig received scant comfort from Wilson who telephoned him with the War Cabinet's response, to the effect that if he considered that the British Army was endangered, or if Foch was not acting solely on military considerations, they relied on the exercise of his judgment. Haig noted somewhat acidly in his diary that it was 'a case of heads you win and tails I lose. If things go well, the Government take credit to themselves and the Generalissimo [Foch]; if badly, the Field-Marshal will be blamed!'[22] At the meeting with Foch on the 15th, Haig explained that because of evidence of enemy preparations pointing to an attack on the British front in the near future he was reluctant to move any reserves.

> Foch agreed with me but said his first object was to hold up the present attack at all costs as soon as possible. He only wanted my Divisions as a reserve in case of necessity, and they would be in a position ready to return to me at once in case the British front was threatened. Under these circumstances I agreed to send the next two Divisions as arranged.[23]

THE SECOND BATTLE OF THE MARNE: 15 JULY–6 AUGUST 1918

The first battle of the Marne had taken place in September 1914 when it seemed that there was little to stop the German First Army advancing on Paris: indeed, its nearest troops were within twenty-three miles of the capital. The French Army and the tiny BEF had been in virtually constant retreat since the outbreak of war in August, but on 5 September they turned and struck back, forcing the enemy across the river. It was the turning point in the war which then, for three long years, lapsed into the sterility of trench warfare. As will be seen, the second battle was to prove to be another turning point.

In contrast to the battle of the Aisne in May, the French were prepared. From the Argonne to Château Thierry were positioned thirty-three divisions including two American and one Italian, and poised for the counter-offensive were twenty-four divisions including four American and three cavalry divisions. In reserve were thirteen divisions, and it was planned to add three more, including two British divisions. To assemble this considerable force had meant drawing on other French fronts to the extent that the cupboard of reserves was almost bare. Excluding Allied reserves, the French Fourth Army of fourteen divisions was confronted by twenty-five German divisions, and the French Fifth and Sixth Armies of twelve divisions by eighteen German divisions. Although heavily outnumbered in artillery, the French were well equipped with aircraft, including nine RAF squadrons. (The Royal Flying Corps had become the Royal Air Force on 1 April 1918.)

Prisoners taken on 14 July by the 4th Army revealed that the bombardment would commence at 12.10 a.m. on the 15th. Shortly before midnight the French opened counter-preparation artillery fire on the troops assembling for the assault, causing, according to German accounts, considerable disruption. The German bombardment commenced shortly after midnight, lasting for nearly three and three-quarter hours, and at dawn the German infantry advanced. East of Reims the enemy succeeded in reaching the Intermediate Position, but there he was stopped: an action in which the American 42nd (Rainbow) Division played a notable part. West of Reims the attack achieved some success by crossing the Marne between Dormans and Jaulgonne, 'capturing a bridgehead on either side of Dormans 3 miles deep and 7 to 9 miles wide', and by so doing threatened to delay Pétain's plans for the counter-offensive on the 18th. The Germans made no progress east of Reims on the following day, and although they achieved small gains west of the city, a French counter-attack regained the Intermediate Position, and the American 3rd Division drove the enemy back across the Marne near Jaulgonne.

Two of the four British divisions (51st and 62nd) requested by Foch had already moved into the area, and the other two (15th and 34th) were en route. On the 17th, however, GHQ, increasingly alarmed at new evidence of enemy preparations on the British front, was on the point of requesting their return when a letter arrived from Foch seeking to know which parts of the British front were threatened by an early attack, but stressing that reserves could 'only be found by withdrawing them from fronts which are not threatened for the benefit of that which is in danger'. This effectively discounted the possibility of the early return of the four divisions, particularly when Foch, in a further letter to Haig, considered that there would be no large attack against the British front 'for the moment', and that if even if there were, their return would take over a week.

The bridgehead gained by the Germans over the Marne on the opening day of their offensive was now turning out to be a serious liability. The French had concentrated on attacking the Marne bridges by bombing and artillery fire, causing severe casualties, and in the evening of the 17th OHL agreed to the withdrawal of the troops in the bridgehead, but deferred issuing the final order. Although it was not evident to the Allies, or indeed to the Germans, the high tide of the offensive had been reached: the ebb was soon to follow, but the tide would not turn again.

The time had now arrived for the French counter-offensive. Poised for the attack were the Tenth and Sixth Armies comprising twenty-four divisions, including four American and two British divisions. The French plan was to thrust against the western flank of the German salient between Soissons and Château Thierry where penetration would cut the road between Soissons and Reims and disrupt enemy communications. Equally important to the Germans was the railway junction at Soissons which, if captured or rendered unusable, would sever vital communications between the north and the salient. The ever-cautious Pétain, however, wanted to delay the counter-offensive because of his concern that the German advance over the Marne might threaten the Montagne de Reims; he ordered that preparations for the western flank attack should be postponed and the 2nd American division, already en route from the Sixth to the Tenth Army, returned. Foch, on learning of this, immediately counter-manded the order. He was determined that nothing should delay the counter-offensive, and he made this abundantly clear in a message to Pétain:

> Please understand that, until you inform me of some fresh crisis there can be no question of slowing down in any way, still less of stopping, Mangin's preparations. In case of urgent and absolute need, you may take from him the troops absolutely indispensable, letting me know at once.

After an uncomfortable night of heavy rain, thunderstorms and high winds the French artillery opened up at dawn on 18 July along the entire salient, and at 4.35 a.m. Mangin's Tenth Army, dispensing with a preliminary bombardment, advanced from the cover of the forest of Villers-Cotterêts behind a creeping barrage and preceded by an armada of light Renault tanks. The Germans were taken completely by surprise; before noon the left wing of the attack was overlooking Soissons, and on the right the Americans advancing on either side of the Moroccan division had captured Vierzy, six miles from its jumping-off point. South of the Tenth Army, the 6th Army met with similar success, forcing the enemy to retreat to a line between Marizy and Belleau and threatening the important communication centre at Oulchy. From a tactical aspect the attack was not particularly damaging – the Germans were adept at swiftly organising defensive measures – but it was enough for the German Crown Prince to order the evacuation of the Marne bridgehead. The strategic implications, however, were very much greater. Ludendorff had been attending a conference in Tournai to discuss the projected Flanders attack (code-named 'Hagen') timed for the beginning of August, when the news of the Mangin attack reached him. He returned to his headquarters at Avesnes 'naturally in a state of the greatest nervous tension'.[24] Indeed, he was in the grip of acute indecision: to commit reserves, already on their way to Flanders, to the defence of the Marne salient would mean that his cherished 'Hagen' operation would either have to be postponed or, at worst, abandoned. If the latter, the German armies would have to revert to a defensive role, with the implication that Germany had lost all hope of victory.

The Tenth and Sixth Armies resumed their attacks on the 19th, but the pace of the advance was being slowed as the Germans tenaciously defended their threatened flanks. The troops in the Marne bridgehead were evacuated on the night of the 19th/20th, destroying the bridges as they crossed the river and preparing defensive positions on the northern bank. On the 19th the two British divisions (51st and 62nd) on the eastern side of the salient south-west of Reims were ordered to relieve the Italian corps which had suffered heavy casualties, losing almost 40 per cent of its fighting strength and most of its artillery. The two divisions in company with two French divisions attacked across the Adre valley on the 20th, but the creeping barrage fell too far ahead of the infantry. Many enemy outposts armed with machine guns remained unaffected by the barrage, and in the difficult conditions of fighting in wooded country with inadequate maps, none of the divisions could make much progress.

It was now evident that the best policy was to capitalise on the success achieved on the western flank of the salient. Accordingly Pétain ordered reserves to move to strengthen the Tenth and Sixth Armies, and Foch agreed to allow two British divisions (15th and 34th) and two American divisions (32nd and 42nd) to be employed. The Germans were now aware that the salient was becoming increasingly vulnerable, and Allied air reconnaissance had revealed substantial troop movements northwards. The French plan was 'not merely a matter of driving the enemy from the Château Thierry pocket, but also of cutting off his retreat to the north and capturing the bulk of his forces'. On the 20th Ludendorff came to the conclusion that 'Hagen' would yet again have to be postponed: Crown Prince Rupprecht in Flanders had informed him that 'the decision of the War could certainly not be expected from a weakened, narrowed and considerably less well mounted attack, particularly against a foe who knew German intentions...' Ludendorff replied that 'in view of the possibility of a offensive British action, the Hagen operation will probably never come to execution'.

There was little French progress over the next few days, although Château Thierry was reoccupied on the 21st. The Germans, however, now realised that the salient could no longer be held, and on the 27th the German Crown Prince telegraphed OHL:

If the battle is to be fought out in the area south of the Aisne and Vesle, the dispatch of fresh forces of all arms, including the general artillery reserve, is necessary... It can be expected with all certainty that the enemy will continue the battle. In these circumstances the Group of Armies does not believe that it is expedient to fight the struggle south of the Vesle.[25]

Ludendorff was reluctant to agree to the withdrawal, but on the 30th OHL issued orders for it to commence on the night of 1/2 August. In the early hours of 1 August, however, two corps of Mangin's Tenth Army (including the British 15th and 34th Divisions) struck a heavy blow at the German defences between Severnay and Hartennes, and by the evening French cavalry had reached the outskirts of Soissons, which was abandoned by the Germans on the next day. It was now the turn of the Fifth and Sixth Armies to exploit the Tenth Army's success, and by 3 August the Germans had retreated across the Vesle. On 5 August the battle came to an end, although Pétain issued instructions to the effect that it was still the intention of the three Armies to push the enemy north of the Vesle and the Aisne 'but without exposing themselves to useless losses or to failure with a river behind them'. Allied casualties had amounted to 117,000, of which total the French had suffered 95,000. German casualties have been estimated at 168,000, of which nearly 30,000 were prisoners.

Crown Prince Rupprecht had said of Ludendorff that he was a good tactician but not a great strategist. The truth of this remark is exemplified by the first of the diversionary offensives, the Chemin des Dames, where the original intention had been to construct a defensive line on the Aisne. The dramatic success of the breakthrough tempted Ludendorff to push on to the Marne – two rivers too far, and the deep pocket so formed, with the vulnerability of its flanks, brought about the abortive Matz attack. The Marne offensive, the largest of the diversions, was the final attempt to draw away Allied reserves from the north, and, indeed, was the last German offensive of the war. This time the French were prepared, and their counter-offensive on 18 July came as an unpleasant surprise to Ludendorff. Although initially the ground gained was not great, and contained by a stubborn defence, there was the realisation that not only had the Marne offensive failed, but that the Allies were strong enough to return to the offensive. Hindenburg's memoirs were explicit:

We could have no illusion about the far-reaching effects of this battle and our retreat... From the purely military point of view it was of the greatest and most fateful importance that we had lost the initiative to the enemy... How many hopes, cherished during the last few months, had probably collapsed at one blow! How many calculations had been scattered to the winds.[26]

Ludendorff summoned General von Lossberg (Fourth Army Chief of Staff) to OHL. Lossberg, an expert on defence, told Ludendorff that the Ninth and Seventh Armies were exhausted, and advocated a withdrawal of all the German armies to the Hindenburg Line. Ludendorff could not accept this drastic proposal, entailing as it would giving up all the gains achieved since March, because of its impact 'on the enemy, on our army and on the homeland'. There is no doubt that Ludendorff was showing signs of mental imbalance, a disability that would increasingly effect his future decisions. Hindenburg was nominally the supreme commander of the German Army, but he had been little more than a figurehead: it was Ludendorff who had borne the main burden of the conduct of operations on the Western Front over the last two years, and the strain was now becoming obvious. Although he knew that withdrawal behind the Vesle was inevitable, his vacillation in issuing the order meant that he expended reserves he could ill afford in the abortive defence of the salient. Seemingly oblivious to reality, he issued an appreciation of the situation to all his army commanders on the Western Front on 2 August: 'The situation requires, first, that we stand on the defensive, and, secondly, resume the offensive as soon as possible.'

Notes

1. Callwell, Major-General Sir C. E., *Field-Marshal Sir Henry Wilson*, Cassell (London, 1927)
2. Blake, Robert, (ed.), *The Private Papers of Douglas Haig, 1914–1919*, Eyre & Spottiswoode (London, 1952)
3. *Ibid.*
4. Edmonds, Brigadier-General Sir J., (comp.), *The Official History of the War: Military Operations France and Belgium*, Vol. III, Macmillan (London, 1939)
5. Ludendorff, General, *Concise Ludendorff Memoirs*, Hutchinson (London, 1933)
6. Rees, Brigadier-General H. C., Papers of, held in Department of Documents, Imperial War Museum, London
7. Quoted in Boraston, J. H. and Bax, C. E. O., *The Eighth Division in War*, Medici Society (London, 1926)
8. Cruttwell, C. R. M. F., *A History of the Great War 1914–1918*, Clarendon Press (Oxford, 1934)
9. Edmonds, *op. cit.*
10. Rees, *op. cit.*
11. *Ibid.*
12. Edmonds, *op. cit.*
13. Quoted from a German Monograph in Edmonds, *op. cit.*
14. Pierrefeu, J. de, *French Headquarters*, Bles (London, 1924)
15. Quoted in Edmonds, *op. cit.*
16. Blake, *op. cit.*
17. *Ibid.*
18. Edmonds, *op. cit.*
19. Callwell, *op. cit.*
20. *Ibid.*
21. Quoted from *French Official Account* in Edmonds, *op. cit.*
22. Blake, *op. cit.*
23. *Ibid.*
24. Ludendorff, General, *My War Memoirs*, Hutchinson (London, 1919)
25. Edmonds, *op. cit.*
26. Hindenburg, Field-Marshal Paul von, *Out of My Life*, Cassell (London, 1920)

7

Preparations for the British Counter-Offensive

O perations on the Western Front between May and July had been domi-nated by the German offensives on the Aisne, the Matz and the Marne, and this had allowed a period of relative quiet on the British front. The arrival of reinforcements had enabled Haig to build up the fighting strength of his divisions, and by the end of June he decided to undertake some operations of a limited nature. On 28 June two divisions (the 5th, which had returned from Italy, and the 31st) attacked the German position east of Nieppe forest in the Lys salient. Advancing behind a creeping barrage, they took the Germans by surprise and secured all their objectives. Nearly 450 infantry were captured together with a quan-tity of trench mortars and machine-guns.

The most significant operation, however, was by the Australian Corps on 4 July with the objective of Vaire and Hamel woods, and the village of Hamel, on the ridge between Villers Bretonneux and the Somme. Both woods and the village were strongly fortified, but the trenches were in a poor state and inadequately wired. The capture of the ridge would not only have several tactical benefits, but also enable the state of German defences and morale to be probed. Only a small force of infantry (ten battalions) would be involved, together with sixty tanks. The Australians had had an unhappy experience with tanks in their first attack on Bulle-court during the Arras offensive in April 1917 and refused to work with them when the attack was renewed. Before the attack on 4 July, however, General Rawlinson (Fourth Army Commander) overcame their objections by setting up practice sessions with tanks to show 'what they could do, and how to use them'. After the battle he wrote: 'Now the Australians can't say enough in praise of tanks.' The inclu-sion in the infantry of four companies of the American 33rd Division, and the choice of the date, were no coincidence. In a letter from Rawlinson to Colonel Wigram (a private secretary to the King) he wrote:

I selected the date of Independence Day, as it was the first occasion on which American troops had taken part in an actual attack alongside our own fellows; and I was not a little put out when, at the very last moment, I got a direct order from Pershing that no American troops were to be employed. It was then too late to withdraw them, so I am afraid I had to disobey the order.[1]

Meticulous preparations were made for the attack, and were a model of their kind. Surprise was the key element:

> In the early stages of preparation as little as possible was committed to paper, plans and details being arranged verbally at conferences held at Australian Corps headquarters, the final conference not taking place until three days before the attack... The additional troops required were told that they were to be employed to reinforce the line against an expected attack.[2]

There was to be no preliminary bombardment, the tanks would precede the infantry, and aircraft would co-operate by crossing over the enemy lines and bombing troop assemblies, guns and transport. It was hoped to conceal the advancing infantry by smoke shell and a screen of smoke fired by trench mortars; and, further to confuse the enemy, the artillery of III Corps would fire a creeping barrage, mixed with smoke shell, although its infantry would be not be taking part in the attack. Zero hour was fixed for 3.10 a.m. and during the night the tanks were brought up to within two miles of the front line, the noise of their arrival drowned by aircraft flying up and down the entire Fourth Army front. The barrage opened at zero hour, simultaneously with counter-battery fire, and the infantry moved off in waves. On the right, the 6th Brigade met some opposition in and around Vaire and Hamel woods, but this was overcome with the assistance of tanks. The 11th Brigade captured Hamel village, surprising the enemy in their dug-outs, and the 15th Brigade, north of the Somme, although meeting resistance from machine-gunners, gained their final objective by 5 a.m. Total Australian casualties were nearly 900, American 134, and five tanks were put out of action. Almost 1,500 prisoners were taken, together with a significant quantity of field guns, machine-guns and trench mortars. Thus the operation was a complete success and, although limited in scope, would serve as a valuable dress-rehearsal for a future offensive.

Foch had issued a General Directive on 20 May in which he had forecast that although the enemy had halted after the Chemin des Dames offensive, it was probable that he would resume operations. Nevertheless, 'whether he resumed the attack or not, the Allied Armies must be ready to pass to the offensive'. He considered that between the Oise and the North Sea important results could be obtained from (a) 'freeing of the railway Paris–Amiens, and the Amiens area...' and (b) freeing of the mines in the Lys region. If there should be a resumption of enemy attacks, circumstances might dictate an offensive on a smaller scale such as (b) above. He directed that preparations should be made for both offensives without delay.

On 12 July Foch suggested to Lawrence (Haig was in England) that the British should undertake an offensive on the Festubert–Robecq front (the Lys operation referred to in his Directive of 20 May), but Haig, on his return, wrote to Foch on 17

July saying that he could see no object 'in pushing forward over the flat and wet country between Robecq and Festubert. He proposed an alternative:

> The operation which to my mind is of the greatest importance, and which I suggest to you should be carried out as early as possible, is to advance the Allied front east and south-east of Amiens so as to disengage that town and the railway line. This can be best carried out by a combined French and British operation, the French attacking south of Moreuil and the British north of the river Luce.[3]

Foch replied to Haig's letter of 17 July, and whilst still maintaining that preparations for the Lys operation should be continued, he responded favourably to Haig's proposed operation:

> The combined operation of the British Fourth Army and the French First Army intended to free Amiens and the railway seems to me also one of the most profitable to execute at the moment by reason of the prospects which it offers... General Debeney, on his part, has been studying an offensive with the same objectives, but his proposals differ a little from yours.

Rawlinson submitted his plan to GHQ on 17 July. It would take the form of a three-stage advance by the Canadian, Australian and III Corps; the Canadian Corps had not been involved in any of the 1918 battles, but III Corps had suffered heavily in the days following the 21 March offensive. His objective was a line about three miles beyond the front at Villers Bretonneux, fanning out to the north across the Somme near Morlancourt, and south-westwards in the direction of Moreuil. The ground was suitable for tanks and cavalry, the German defences were poor, the morale of the defenders low, and few divisions were in reserve. Rawlinson, however, mindful of his experiences in co-operating with the French on the Somme in 1916, wanted to make the attack a wholly British operation, and for this purpose suggested taking over four miles of the French front. Except for this latter proposal, Haig approved Rawlinson's overall plan.

There was an Allied Commander-in-Chiefs' conference on the 24th, but before the formal proceedings took place Haig outlined Rawlinson's plan, which Foch approved with the modification that the French First Army should operate on the right of the Fourth Army. He directed that Rawlinson and Debeney (First Army commander) should meet and coordinate their plans. At the conference which followed there was a discussion on a memorandum prepared by Foch. In this he expressed his intention of passing over from defence to the offensive, and proposed the following operations:

> (a) freeing important railway lines such as Paris–Amiens, which would be by means of a combined operation between the British Fourth and French First

Armies, and the line Avricourt–Paris in the Commercy area by reduction of the St. Mihiel salient. This to be undertaken by the American Army.

(b) Driving the enemy from the northern coal mining areas, and finally from the neighbourhood of Calais and Dunkirk.

Three days later there was another conference with Foch attended by Haig, Lawrence, Rawlinson and Debeney at which the latter suggested a limited operation south of the River Luce. Foch, however, would not agree and directed that Rawlinson's operation should take place. Any hope that Rawlinson had of conducting the operation by the Fourth Army alone was dashed by Haig agreeing that the French First Army should take part, on the grounds that four French divisions would be available as reserves to exploit success. The date of the offensive was fixed for 10 August, and on 28 July Haig was asked to take command of the French First Army for the operation. In his letter of acceptance he indicated that the date of the operation could be advanced by two days if XXII Corps, whose four divisions had fought in the Marne battle, could be returned to him; this was immediately arranged.

The War Cabinet in London was unaware of the impending operation:

> The plan of attack was kept a profound secret. The first hint of a coming attack reached the Committee of Prime Ministers on August 1st, when Borden [Canadian Prime Minister] told them that on the previous evening he had learned in the greatest secrecy that the Canadian Corps was being moved from the Arras region to another part of the line with a view to a coming offensive. Even Henry Wilson [CIGS] did not admit to knowing anything of what was intended. The Prime Ministers were rather perturbed at this intelligence... It then transpired that this was limited to a series of attacks intended to rectify the line, which Henry Wilson had already advocated and which Foch had decided to undertake; no further objection was raised.[4]

There was an extraordinary air of secrecy surrounding the preparations for the attack, which would prove that the British had become as adept as the Germans in the techniques of deception:

> Surprise was the essence of Allied success. To ensure as much initial secrecy as possible and limit knowledge of the contemplated operation to as few persons as possible, the preliminary arrangements were settled in the Fourth Army by conferences of the principal officers concerned, held at different places with small numbers at first, increased only as time advanced. Sir Douglas Haig, on his part, sent a personal letter to General Debeney to explain that he refrained from meeting him in order not to awake suspicion. Both in the Fourth Army

and the French First Army the troops in the line were not to be acquainted with the intended operation until 24 to 36 hours before zero hour.[5]

Nevertheless, the assembly of so much material in the rear areas – guns, tanks, ammunition – could not be hidden from the troops, and a small notice headed 'KEEP YOUR MOUTH SHUT' was issued to all ranks. The first two paragraphs read:

> The success of any operation we carry out depends chiefly on surprise. DO NOT TALK. – When you know that your unit is making preparations for an attack, don't talk about them to men in other units, or to strangers, and keep your mouth shut, especially in public places.
>
> Do not be inquisitive about what other units are doing; if you see or hear anything, keep it to yourself.

Civilians had been evacuated from Amiens in March, and a 'Forbidden Zone' set up in the Fourth Army area 'in which only a few inhabitants, who were in possession of passes, were allowed to remain under the supervision of the Assistant Provost Marshal...' Every effort was made to give the impression of normality: to disguise the arrival of fresh batteries being brought into position, artillery fire was continued at its usual frequency and concentration, but under cover of this, registration of targets was carried out. All troop movements took place at night, but the move of the Canadian Corps from the First Army presented a problem, not so much in the logistics involved, but in the concealment of its relocation. The corps had not taken part in the March and April battles, and German Intelligence would be quick to interpret that a move south could herald its employment in an offensive. To mislead the enemy two Canadian battalions plus a wireless section were moved opposite Kemmel Hill in the Second Army sector. Wireless stations in both the First and Second Army sectors burst into activity with messages, and

> false moves were carried out, and noise and dust created in order to convey the impression that a concentration of tanks was taking place near St Pol... Road surfaces in the Fourth Army sector were strewn with straw, and wheels bound with ropes to deaden sound. The Canadian Corps arrived in the Fourth Army area between the end of July and 4 August, and on that day OHL informed the Second Army that 'apparently two Canadian divisions had been relieved from their hitherto front position after a short tour; particular attention should be given to ascertain their whereabouts...The front of the British Third and Fourth Armies requires particular attention.'[6]

On the night of 6/7 August the tanks were moved up to within three miles of the front. There were 342 Mark V tanks, 72 Whippets and 120 supply tanks[7] and, as before the Hamel attack, their engine noise was drowned by aircraft. The claim by some German troops that they had heard the sound of tanks was attributed to 'phantoms of the imagination or nervousness' by their higher staffs.

Arrayed for the battle in the Fourth Army sector were the Canadian Corps of four divisions (plus the British 32nd Division), five Australian, four British, one American and three cavalry divisions, and in the French First Army sector nine divisions plus a cavalry corps. Reinforcements to the existing artillery of the Fourth Army had brought the total to 1,386 field guns and howitzers, and 684 heavy guns. The French were equipped with 780 field and 826 heavy guns. Facing this onslaught were ten divisions of the German Second Army in the front line and four in reserve, and of these the army commander (General von der Marwitz) had informed OHL that only two divisions were 'fully battle fit'.

There was a significant difference between the forthcoming offensive by the Allies and those they had undertaken in previous years. The onset of open warfare in March 1918 had meant that they no longer had to fight their way through the three-zone system adopted by the Germans in 1917. The German defences were those reached at 'the high-water mark of the March offensive' and intended as jumping-off points for a further offensive rather than as a barrier to repel Allied offensives. Thus the German Second Army defences were not constructed on the three-zonal system: in effect they consisted of little more than a Forward Zone, sometimes consisting of a single trench, inadequately wired and with no deep dug-outs:

> The real strength of the defence, it was to be found, lay in the scattered machine guns, which were distributed in great depth, hidden in shell-holes and behind every piece of cover, but sometimes only concealed by the high corn.[8]

The greater part of the ground over which the battle would take place was south of the Somme. Between the River Avre and the Somme is the great Santerre plateau ideal for the use of tanks; there were a few woods, none of them of any size, mostly clustered around the villages. Running through the plateau, and parallel to the advance, is the River Luce, although little more than a stream. Intersecting the area are the two ruler-straight Roman roads running from Amiens due east to St Quentin, and south-east to Roye, the latter road forming the boundary between the Fourth Army and the French First Army. North of the Somme in the III Corps sector, however, the ground presented some difficulties:

> Its south bank, though undulating, has no specially marked hill features, but on the north the adjoining land rises to a considerable height on the spur which traverses the narrow wedge between the Somme and the Ancre. This plateau is furrowed by a number of deep gullies running northward from the

river, and the sharp hills between these gullies, falling in places by abrupt chalk cliffs to the Somme, form very commanding features from which it would be possible for a determined enemy to play havoc with any attempt to advance south of the river, for they completely dominate the south bank. The most marked of these spurs is the long saddle immediately east of the village of Chipilly. This feature is almost girdled by the Somme ... and projects almost a mile south of the general line of the river. It thus forms a barrier across ground for which the Australians would be responsible. The capture of the Chipilly Ridge was the task allotted to the 58th Division...[9]

There was a meeting on 3 August between Foch and Haig at which the plans for the Amiens offensive were discussed. It would appear that Foch was in an ebullient mood: he was happy to learn that the offensive was imminent, and at the end of the meeting gave his opinion that the Germans were breaking up. This may have underlined his wish that the advance should not be limited to the line Hangest–Méricourt. He wanted it to press on, and an objective 'some place south of Chaulnes' named. Haig explained that once the Hangest–Méricourt line had been secured it would be consolidated for defence, and the advance on Roye–Chaulnes would be continued with the ultimate objective of Ham, fifteen miles beyond Chaulnes. Thus Haig was extending Rawlinson's original objectives, symptomatic of his long-held 'bite and hold' policy, by no less than twenty miles. Rawlinson was informed of this change at a conference with Haig on the 5th when Debeney and Lieutenant-General Kavanagh (Cavalry Corps commander) were also present. Haig emphasised that the cavalry must keep in touch with the battle and 'be prepared to pass through anywhere between the River Somme and the Roye–Amiens road'. The 3rd Cavalry Division had been allocated to the Canadian Corps, and a cavalry brigade to the Australian Corps. Each corps would be provided with Whippet tanks to operate with the cavalry. Debeney explained the rôle of his First Army, which would be 'engaged successively from west to east against the junction of the German Second and Eighteenth Armies' with the main attack on the 9th from south of Montdidier. These plans, however, were changed by General Fayolle (commanding the French reserve armies) who directed that the principal rôle of the First Army was to cover the right flank of the Fourth Army by 'advancing between the Avre and the Amiens–Roye road'; the secondary rôle was the advance between Montdidier and Rollot.

On 6 August the day of attack was fixed for the 8th, and the zero hour left to Rawlinson and Debeney to agree between themselves. Accordingly the hour for the Fourth Army was 4.20 a.m., but forty-five minutes later for the French who were attacking without tanks and would need the extra time to deliver the preliminary bombardment. On the 6th, however, the Fourth Army received something of a shock when a German division attacked on a 4,000-yard front in the III Corps sector south of Morlancourt – a position held by the 58th and 18th Divisions. The objective was to recapture ground lost when the 5th Australian Division, as a farewell gesture, mounted a minor operation on 29 July shortly before they left the area. Unfortunately the German attack came at a time when the 18th Division, which had occupied the ground captured by the Australians, was about to be relieved. On the next day the 18th Division counter-attacked and regained some of the ground lost. *The War History of the 4th Battalion, The London Regiment*[9] records the dislocation caused by the attack:

> Another conference followed on the morning of the 6th, after which company commanders went forward to reconnoitre the point of assembly. On arrival at 54th Brigade headquarters [18th Division] it was found, however, that the enemy had just delivered a sharp attack and possessed himself of the very trenches from which we were to 'jump- off'...: rather disconcerting and possibly very serious for the whole attack, for the Hun had reached some of the dumps and gun positions prepared for the 8th, and it might be that they would guess our intentions. To guard against any possibility of failure on this score the barrage lines were completely rearranged. Prisoners subsequently captured stated that the British intention to attack had not been discovered, but the extraordinary defence which the Bosche made on the 8th, combined with the fact that his field guns were withdrawn east of Gressaire Wood throws some doubt on this. At all events the company commanders were forced to withdraw without seeing anything of their assembly position or of the ground over which they were to advance, and reported accordingly.[10]

On 4 August Ludendorff issued an Order of the Day:

> I am under the impression that, in many quarters, the possibility of an enemy offensive is viewed with a certain degree of apprehension. There is nothing to justify this apprehension, provided our troops are vigilant and do their duty.
>
> In all the open warfare conditions in the course of their great offensive battle between the Marne and the Vesle, the French were only able to maintain one initial tactical success due to surprise, namely that of July 18th, and this success ought to have been denied them...
>
> The French and the British infantry generally fought with caution; the Americans attacked more boldly but with less skill. It is to the tanks that the enemy owes his success of the first day... Henceforward, we can await every hostile attack with the greater confidence ... we should wish for nothing better than to see the enemy launch an offensive, which can but hasten the disintegration of his forces...[11]

It is ironic that Ludendorff's wish for an enemy offensive precisely echoed that of Haig's before the 21 March offensive.

Notes

1. Maurice, Major-General Sir F., *The Life of General Lord Rawlinson*, Cassell (London, 1928)
2. Edmonds, Brigadier-General Sir James, (comp.), *Official History of the War: Military Operations France and Belgium,* Vol. III, Macmillan (London, 1939)
3. *Ibid.*
4. Hankey, Lord, *The Supreme Command 1914–1918*, George Allen & Unwin (London, 1961)
5. Edmonds, *op. cit.*
6. *Ibid.*
7. The Mark V tank first appeared in March 1918. It was an improvement on the earlier Mark IV and could cover 25 miles on a single fill of aviation spirit, and had a top speed of 5 mph. (on uncratered ground). It suffered, however, from inadequate ventilation, and the conditions for the crew, particularly on a hot summer's day, with the heat so generated mixed with exhaust gases and cordite fumes was, at times, beyond endurance. The Whippet was a light tank armed with three Hotchkiss machine-guns. It had a top speed of 8 mph and was designed to work with cavalry in exploitation.
8. Edmonds, *op. cit.*
9. Grimwade, F. C., *The War History of the 4th Battalion The London Regiment (Royal Fusiliers) 1914–1919*, Regimental Headquarters (London, 1922)
10. *Ibid.*
11. Quoted in Edmonds, *op. cit.*, Vol. IV

August 1918

*As the sun set on the 8th August on the battlefield the greatest defeat which
the German Army had suffered since the beginning of the war was an accomplished
fact. The position divisions between the Avre and the Somme, which had been struck by
the enemy attack were nearly completely annihilated. The troops in the front line north
of the Somme had also suffered seriously as also the reserve divisions thrown into the
battle in the course of the day.* — German Official Monograph

During the night of 7/8 August the infantry moved up into their attacking positions. The night was fine, but some two hours after dawn ground mist began to form and gradually thickened reducing visibility to less than ten yards as the zero hour approached. Shortly before 4.20 a.m. the tanks advanced from their assembly positions ready to precede the infantry attack. The fog proved to be a hindrance as tanks and infantry moved off, and they could do little more than follow the line of the barrage. Nevertheless, it had the benefit, as on 21 March, of shrouding the advance.

The attack of the Canadian Corps was delivered in the angle formed by the two Roman roads: its front, in effect, formed the base of a triangle. On the extreme right, the 9th Brigade of the 3rd Division cleared Rifle, Holland, Vignette and Hamon woods adjacent to the Amiens–Roye road by 7.30 a.m. Within this time the villages of Demuin and Courcelles were also cleared with the assistance of tanks, and the 8th Brigade captured the village of Hangard, again with the help of tanks. A tank driver described his experiences:

> The mist was still dense, and it was most uncanny driving at speed towards an invisible object. I only had my compass to guide me... We soon reached the German support line, and as I straddled the bus across the main trench my machine-gunners got busy from both sides and caught several of the enemy scuttling for cover. We climbed right over and went blindly on, several times running into batches of Canadian infantrymen, who were getting ahead in places. Another German machine gun was firing very close to us, so I swung the bus and made straight for it.

Suddenly I noticed a brick wall right up against the nose of the tank, but as we had been through many of them before I did not hesitate, but just trod on the gas and charged straight through. A terrific rumble of masonry followed, and when the old bus regained level keel I opened my window and peered out. Gosh, we were inside a church, and had routed a machine-gun nest!

I drove out through the opposite wall, which had already been partly demolished by shell-fire, and then we noticed mixed up with the spasmodic rifle-fire the crack of light artillery not far ahead. It was either an anti-tank gun or a field gun working well forward. Its crew were certainly doing their stuff; they couldn't see the tank, or I doubt if they would have stayed on. There it was again – crack – and after a bit of manoeuvring we reached it. An 18-pounder field gun was facing us with its crew intact. Our machine guns loosed off at them, and as they turned to get away two of them dropped, and the next thing we saw was the Canadians dashing after them with their bayonets.[1]

The 1st Division in the centre of the attack employed its three brigades in sequence. The 3rd Brigade and a battalion of the 2nd Brigade were to gain the first objective; the 1st Brigade would then pass through it on the way to the second objective, and the 2nd Brigade would gain the final objective. Twenty-one tanks preceded the infantry, and the shock of their appearance, towering in the mist over their trenches, demoralised the defenders, who promptly fled, many half dressed. Nevertheless, once the tanks had passed, the oncoming infantry met some resistance; using the German method of infiltration, however, the leading waves pressed on, leaving any pockets of resistance to be mopped-up by the following waves. The village of Aubercourt was captured, and after a nest of machine guns in Morgemont Wood had been subdued by tanks, the resistance collapsed and the 3rd Brigade's objective was reached soon after 8 a.m. The 1st Brigade, following up at 8.30 a.m., had as its objective the village of Cayeux. By then the mist was beginning to clear, and joined by six tanks, the advancing battalions met heavy fire. Tanks assisted in smothering fire from four small woods and succeeded in reaching Cayeux ahead of the infantry. The brigade's objective was occupied by 11 a.m.

On the left of the corps front, the 2nd Division adopted the same method as that used by the 1st Division by deploying its three brigades in sequence. The 4th Brigade, supported by seventeen tanks, was to take the first objective, the 5th the second, and the 6th the final. A battalion of the 4th Brigade captured the village of Marcelcave by 7 a.m. but its neighbouring battalion was held up for a time by machine-gun fire from Morgemont and Cancelette woods until suppressed by two tanks. Seven tanks, for various causes, were put out of action. The 5th Brigade went forward at 8.20 a.m. with ten tanks and found the valley of Wiencourt 'full of infantry and heavy guns'. Two tanks rendered particularly valuable assistance by

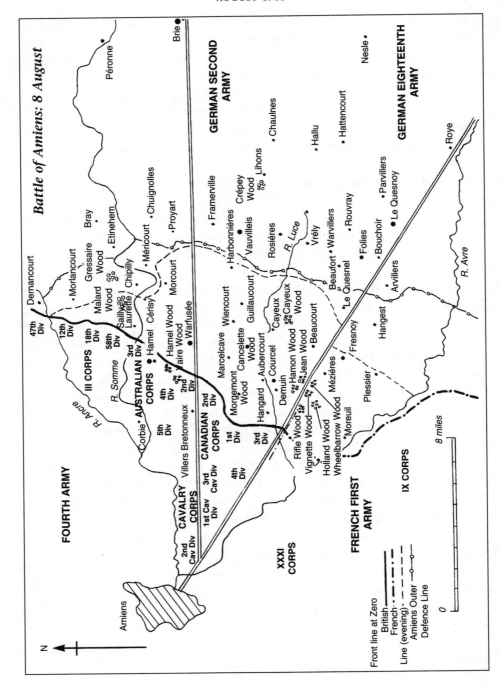

Battle of Amiens: 8 August

enfilading the valley from the south; elsewhere they roamed up and down raking the woods with fire and, in one instance, a solitary tank broke up an enemy assembly. Wiencourt was finally captured by 9.20 a.m. and farther east Guillaucourt was taken shortly before 10 a.m.

So far the Canadian attack had been remarkably successful. Its three divisions had all reached their second objectives by 11 a.m. and the remaining division, the 4th, was timed to go forward immediately after noon to the third objective. In the meantime, the 3rd Cavalry Division, together with a battalion of Whippets (sixteen to each of the cavalry brigades) was to pass through the infantry and press on to the third objective:

> By this time the mist had cleared and the whole Santerre plateau seen from the air was dotted with parties of infantry, field artillery, cavalry and tanks moving forward. Staff officers were galloping about, many riding horses in battle for the first time, prisoners in formed companies marching back with hardly more escort than the Canadian wounded whom they were carrying, whilst overhead the planes of the Royal Air Force were flying noisily to work. Indeed, at this stage there was more noise of movement than firing, as the heavy batteries, almost wheel to wheel, with their muzzles cocked to the highest elevation, were no longer in action; for the infantry had gone so far that it was no longer possible for them to shoot.[2]

The Canadian Cavalry Brigade with fourteen Whippets (two had broken down) entered Beaucourt, but its wood to the east was full of infantry and guns and impenetrable by cavalry, and an attempt to reach le Quesnel (the third objective) was thwarted by heavy fire. The Whippets attached to the 7th Cavalry Brigade were unable to keep up; 'It was soon evident that when not under fire the cavalry was too fast for the Whippets, and when under fire was unable to follow them.' Nevertheless, the 7th Brigade had more success than the Canadian Brigade: a squadron charged Germans bringing up machine guns to the southern edge of Cayeux Wood, and another squadron entered the wood and captured twelve machine guns and a battery of field guns. Advancing farther, they were stopped just short of le Quesnel, but with this exception, the 3rd Cavalry Division had reached the third objective of the Canadian Corps. Nevertheless, in the words of the Official Historian, 'having no orders from Cavalry Corps to go farther, although Fourth Army orders clearly directed that the cavalry should push forward from the old Amiens Outer Defence Line with the least possible delay, there the 3rd Cavalry Division stayed'.[3]

It was now the turn of the remaining division, the 4th, to press forward from the second objective, and it had begun its move up at 5.20 a.m. when it was joined by thirty tanks. The tanks were to advance to the third objective and to deposit infantry machine gunners; then fifteen tanks would return to precede the infantry. Things, however, did not go well: the tanks advanced at 1.30 p.m., but of the ten tanks moving forward to le Quesnel, nine were put out of action by field guns, and only four tanks reached the third objective. The 11th and 12th Brigades on the left of the Amiens–Roye road were more successful, reaching the third objective late in the afternoon. Farther north, the 2nd Brigade of the 1st Division overcame scattered resistance to reach their objective, as did the 6th Brigade of the 2nd Division. Thus the Canadian Corps had achieved its objective of the old Amiens Outer Defence Line except on the extreme right where the German garrison in le Quesnel still held out, no doubt encouraged by its performance in stopping tanks.

The task of the French First Army, south of the Amiens–Roye road and on the Canadian right, was to keep pace with the Canadian advance. After the French had delivered a preliminary bombardment, XXXI Corps advanced at 5.05 a.m. and made good progress. Moreuil was captured, and further south IX Corps crossed the Avre. Mézières was taken in the afternoon, where the advance halted, waiting for the artillery barrage. Preparation for this had begun at 4.30 a.m., but it was an hour later before the advance restarted in front of Plessier, and two hours later against Fresnoy; but enemy opposition had increased in this time and Fresnoy was not captured until 9.30 p.m. XXXI Corps had been instructed that its front 'must reach Arvillers this evening without fail', but this was now out of the question. Although initially the French advance had gone well, it was lagging well behind the Canadians by the afternoon. Had Arvillers been reached in the evening, or Fresnoy captured in the afternoon, the German position in le Quesnel would have been untenable. Haig's diary for 8 August records that after visiting Rawlinson, 'I called at HQ First Army at Conty. Debeney was much distressed and almost in tears because three battalions of his Colonial Infantry had bolted before a German machine gun. I told Debeney that the British advance would automatically clear his front. Meantime, to do his utmost to join hands with the British at Roye...'[4]

North of the Amiens–St Quentin road, the attack of the Australian Corps was to be delivered by four divisions: the 2nd and 3rd were to take the first objective, and the 4th and 5th would pass through them to the second – an advance at its greatest of 8,000 yards. Four battalions of tanks plus an armoured car battalion were allotted to the corps, together with the 1st Cavalry Brigade. The 7th and 5th Brigades of the 2nd Division, preceded by twenty-three tanks, advanced behind the barrage, meeting only light resistance, and reached their objectives by around 7 a.m. The 9th and 11th Brigades of the 3rd Division, attacking with the Somme on their left, were hindered by thick fog and could not keep up with the barrage. Tanks performed useful work attacking woods and nests of machine guns, and the enemy was so disadvantaged by the fog and the surprise of the attack that many surrendered with alacrity. Both brigades reached their objectives by 7.15 a.m.

At 8.20 a.m. the 5th and 4th Divisions began their passage through the 2nd and 3rd Divisions:

Crossing what was yesterday's No Man's Land, we saw a few of our dead who had fallen in the advance to the German front line. This position had been badly strafed by our barrage, and many dead Germans lay in their trenches. Beyond these we moved over undulating field ground. Here again were many German dead, and apparently they had been shot down in hurried retreat... German battery positions had been overrun and many gunners lay around their pieces. Every gun had been chalked with the name of the battalion that had captured it. One battery had dug-in its guns in cunning fashion in a gully to the right of Warfusée–Abancourt. The guns were covered with bomb-proof roofing, and fired from openings just above ground level. A tank had passed over the coverings of each gun, and the gunners were now either shapeless masses of flesh in the débris or were lying outside, shot by rifle bullets. One of them had been run over by a tank, and his body lay pressed as flat as a wafer and to a surprising length. We found the infantry of the 2nd Australian Division consolidating a trench system. One officer told us that the Germans were caught by the suddenness of the attack and showed very little fight.[5]

Both brigades of the 5th Division had a comparatively easy task in their advance to the second objective; in fact, progress was so fast that they were in danger of overrunning the barrage. The tanks accompanying the 8th Brigade suffered some losses from German field guns, but the combination of tanks and infantry soon overcame opposition, and the objective was reached shortly after 10 a.m. The armoured car battalion accompanying the 8th Brigade made a unique contribution. Finding the St Quentin road clear, the cars caught up with the retreating Germans, causing havoc among them with machine-gun fire. Some cars reached Framerville (nine miles from the front line), and surprised a German corps headquarters at breakfast; they shot up the Staff, and returned with detailed plans of the Hindenburg Line position. The 1st Cavalry Brigade also had something of a field day: although two squadrons were baulked in their attempt to reach Harbonnières, the main body of the brigade bypassed the village to the north and reached the old Amiens Outer Defence Line where the leading squadron came across 'a train with a large railway gun ... as it was trying to steam away from Proyart [when] it assisted the left squadron in killing or capturing its occupants; it then went on, capturing three field batteries...'[6]

With its 12th and 4th Brigades, the 4th Division attacked through the 3rd. The ground to be covered was seamed with gullies to the extent that tanks were unable to provide much assistance. The 12th Brigade met strong resistance from Morcourt, but this was eventually overcome by artillery fire, and the brigade arrived at its objective at 10.20 a.m. The task of the 4th Brigade was to capture Cérisy and Morcourt, but almost immediately the battalion detailed to capture the former village came under heavy fire from Chipilly across the river in the III Corps sector.

Despite this handicap both villages were eventually captured and the second objective achieved. Nevertheless, as will be seen later, the failure of III Corps to capture Chipilly was to have a significant effect on subsequent operations south of the Somme.

Thus the morning had gone well for the Australian Corps. It had gained its objectives except opposite Chipilly: its casualties had been light, and it had taken nearly 8,000 prisoners and 173 guns. It had now to reach, and consolidate, the third objective against counter-attacks.

The objective of III Corps on the extreme left of the Fourth Army's front was originally planned by Rawlinson to be the old Amiens Outer Defence Line running between the Somme and Dernancourt on the Ancre; but because of adverse ground conditions the corps commander (Lieutenant-General Sir R. Butler) did not believe that the objective could be reached on the first day.

> The line of advance from the British front trenches was full of obstacles. Immediately in front of the line, and on the river bank was the village of Sailly Laurette, the garrison of which, if not immediately overcome, would be able to enfilade the whole advance as the troops crossed No Man's Land. A mile and a half east of Sailly lay Malard Wood, covering both slopes of one of the gullies; while half way between the Malard Wood valley and the final objective on the cliff of Chipilly Ridge, lay a second gully, badly enfiladed from Chipilly village and completely overlooked from the Ridge itself. Heavy going all the way, up hill and down dale, through features eminently suited to machine-gun defence, culminating in a breathless scramble up a steep slope to meet an enemy who would probably defend it to the last; a total advance of about two and a half miles: altogether no light task for a single division [The 58th].[7]

The objective was later scaled down to the line of the Somme above Méricourt coinciding with the second objective of the Australian Corps.

Quite apart from the difficult nature of the ground to be covered, there were other factors that did not augur well. The four divisions of III Corps (from right to left, 58th, 18th, 12th and 47th) had all been involved in the March retreat and had suffered heavy casualties. These had been mostly replaced by young recruits, but the losses in experienced officers and NCOs were irreplaceable in the short term. Moreover, as earlier referred to, the 58th and 18th Divisions had been attacked on 6 August, and although the ground lost had been partially recovered on the next day, the enemy expected that a further attempt would be made and, in consequence, surprise was forfeited. The main attack was to be delivered on the right by the 58th Division, while the 18th Division would attack in the centre, the 12th Division on its left. Each division would employ three brigades which would leapfrog one another in two phases.

At 4.20 a.m. the leading waves of the 58th and 18th Divisions moved off behind a creeping barrage. At first all appeared to go well: on the extreme right the 174th and 175th Brigades reached their first objective east of Malard Wood, the enemy in Sailly Laurette was overcome with the help of two tanks and, pushing on, contact was made with the Australians. In the centre, the task of the 36th and 55th Brigades of the 18th Division was to gain the first objective, but the former brigade, loaned from the 12th Division, had replaced the 54th Brigade because of its losses on 6 August, and arrived knowing 'nothing of the ground except from what could be learned from the map...' The remainder of the ground lost on 6 August was soon recovered, but further progress became difficult because of increasing opposition. The timely arrival, however, of reinforcements from the reserve brigade (53rd), swept aside resistance and the first objective was reached. Nevertheless, an attempt to continue to the second objective was thwarted by fire from Gressaire Wood, forcing a withdrawal to the first objective. The 173rd Brigade of the 58th Division had followed the 174th Brigade into Malard Wood, but came under heavy fire and found it impossible to advance without further support.

> While this was happening the barrage had moved forward ... at the scheduled hour on to Chipilly Ridge, but ... only a few small parties were available to follow it and of these probably none reached the Ridge. The Huns on the Ridge were holding up by machine-gun fire the Australians on the south of the river, and they failed to reach the high ground from which the position was to be outflanked. Unfortunately aerial reports to Divisional Headquarters persisted that the Ridge was in our hands, and this mistake led to serious casualties in the afternoon. The 2/2nd Londons were ordered to advance at 3 p.m. but owing to the false report artillery support was denied them. In these circumstances the attack, although pushed forward ... with great gallantry, was inevitably withered by enemy machine-gun fire from Gressaire Wood.[8]

Farther north, in a subsidiary attack, the 35th Brigade of the 12th Division was successful in reaching its objective, despite stout resistance, but the main attack of III Corps had failed to reach its second objective. The Official Historian noted: 'With well trained troops and more experienced company leaders it should have gained complete success.' This comment seems a little severe bearing in mind the problems that had beset III Corps before, and on the day of, the assault. The ground over which the attack was made was the most difficult on the entire Fourth Army front, thus limiting the performance of tanks (only thirty-six were provided in contrast to the generous allocation to the two neighbouring corps), an attack was not unexpected by the enemy, and senior officers at battalion and company level suffered severe casualties during the advance.

Despite the set-back experienced by III Corps, the results of the day had been very satisfactory. An advance had been made of over seven miles (at its greatest), and casualties had been light at just under 9,000. Over 15,000 prisoners had been taken, and the official German Monograph admitted to estimated losses of between 27,000 and 28,000 all ranks. Nevertheless, tank casualties had been severe (only 145 remaining operational for the next day), and the RAF, concentrating on bombing the Somme bridges, had met determined opposition from enemy aircraft. According to the Official History, 'no vital damage was done to the bridges' but forty-four planes were shot down and fifty-two damaged beyond repair. In his *Memoirs*[9] Ludendorff described 8 August as 'the black day of the German Army', and it might be supposed that this was because of the extent of the Allied advance. In these terms, however, the German had merely suffered a tactical set-back – no vital strategic point had been threatened. On 20 November 1917 the British, employing an armada of tanks, had broken through the formidable Hindenburg Line near Cambrai to a depth of five miles, but within less than a fortnight the Germans had counter-attacked and recovered most of the ground they had lost. But the morale of the German Army in August 1918 was not that of November 1917, as Ludendorff lamented:

The report of the Staff officer I had sent to the battlefield as to the condition of those divisions which had met the first shock of the attack on the 8th perturbed me deeply. I summoned divisional commanders and officers from the line to Avesnes to discuss events with them in detail. I was told of deeds of glorious valour, but of behaviour which, I openly confess, I should not have thought possible in the German Army; whole bodies of our men had surrendered to single troopers or isolated squadrons. Retiring troops, meeting a fresh division going into action, had shouted out things like 'Blackleg' and 'You're prolonging the war', expressions that were to be heard again later. The officers in many places had lost their influence and allowed themselves to be swept along with the rest... Everything I had feared, and of which I had so often given warning, had here, in one place, become a reality. Our war machine was no longer efficient.[10]

Rawlinson decided on the afternoon of the 8th that the offensive should be continued on the next day, and his three reserve divisions (32nd, 17th and 63rd) began their move up to join, respectively, the Canadian, Australian and III Corps. Late in the afternoon, however, and for reasons that are still unclear, the release of the 32nd Division was countermanded. As a result, orders for the resumption of the Canadian attack at 5 a.m. the next day had to be changed: the 3rd Canadian Division would have to be used again, and 'fresh orders would have to be got out, and, as the wires forward were none too reliable, these orders would have to go by dispatch rider and motor car, so that in the congested state of the roads it would be impossible to maintain the 5 a.m. start. Finally, 10 a.m. was fixed by Lieutenant-General Currie [the Canadian Corps comander] and even this ... proved optimistic.'[11] The difficulties of communication in open warfare experienced during the March retreat were now returning to hamper the August advance. The vital arteries, the two Roman roads, were now choked with traffic: columns of prisoners moving westwards, columns of infantry moving eastwards, walking wounded, tanks, batteries of artillery and all forms of wheeled transport. Where telephone lines were available, they could not be used for reasons of security, and operational orders had to be entrusted to runners, dispatch riders or cyclists. It was not unusual for these to be delayed because the bearers lost their way, or the recipients were difficult to find.

There was no mist on the morning of the 9th, and at 4.30 a.m. a battalion of the 4th Canadian Division advanced on le Quesnel, the last remaining Canadian objective of the previous day. Its task was now eased by Fresnoy, on the other side of the Amiens–Roye road, being in French hands, and within an hour, after overcoming fierce resistance, the battalion occupied the village. The stage was now set for a further advance, but although the day had started well with the capture of le Quesnel, the rest of the day's operations were to be marred by delays, uncoordinated zero hours and a degree of confusion. Rawlinson's orders for the Fourth Army were an advance to the line Roye–Chaulnes–Bray–Dernancourt. The objective of the Canadian Corps was Roye–Hattencourt–Hallu, and as flank protection, the Australian Corps was to advance on Lihons-Chuignolles. The objective of III Corps was a line 'east of Etinehem-Demancourt'; Roye was the objective of the French First Army. The cavalry's role was to 'operate on the right of the Fourth Army in such a manner as to gain the objectives allotted to the Canadian Corps and to facilitate the advance of the French First Army'.

The Canadian advance, originally timed for 10 a.m., was to be by the 3rd, 1st and 2nd Divisions, but the move of the former division down the Amiens–Roye road was delayed by the time taken in reconnaissance, and in consequence it was after 2 p.m. before the advance parties moved east of le Quesnel. The late start meant that the village of Bouchoir was the farthest point reached – over six miles short of Roye. The French First Army, despite Foch's telephoned instructions to Debeney, that it must 'push forward XXXI Corps, drums beating, on Roye, without losing a moment and preventing any delay or hesitation', had little effect. The French advance began at 8 a.m., making only slow progress, but eventually reached Arvillers, more or less in line with the Canadian 3rd Division.

The 1st Division, on the left of the 3rd, was to capture the villages of Beaufort and Rouvroy with an advance timed for 11 a.m., but the supporting artillery was not ready and zero hour for the 1st Brigade was postponed until 1.15 p.m. Beaufort was captured, and with the assistance of Whippets, Folies was reached, but further movement eastwards immediately encountered heavy machine-gun fire. This was eventually subdued by Whippets, but the advance was halted some 400 yards short of Rouvroy. The 2nd Brigade was obliged to move off without the protective barrage: the artillery had not been informed of the postponement of the zero hour and fired the barrage at 11 a.m. Notwithstanding this disadvantage, the brigade pressed on to Warvillers and Vrély,

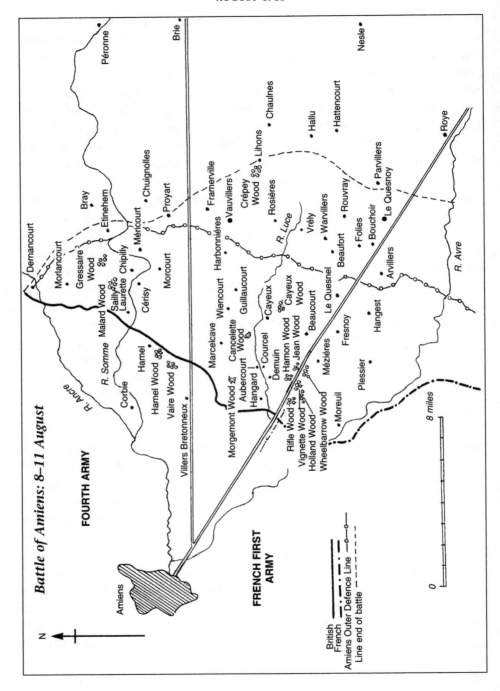

Battle of Amiens: 8–11 August

N

FOURTH ARMY

FRENCH FIRST ARMY

British
French
Amiens Outer Defence Line
Line end of battle

0   8 miles

capturing the former village by 4.30 p.m. albeit incurring severe casualties. The 6th Brigade of the 2nd Division accompanied by five tanks reached Rosières at 1.30 p.m. There was hard fighting in the village, and three hours elapsed before the brigade could move on to a line just beyond the Méharicourt–Rosières road.

It was not to be expected that the Canadian Corps could achieve in an afternoon what had originally been planned to take a full day, and it would seem that this was due in large measure to the change of mind by Fourth Army regarding employment of the 32nd Division and the consequent dislocation caused to the assault plans. Another factor just beginning to emerge was that the Canadians were on the verge of the old British front line of February 1917. Progress across the Santerre plateau had so far been eased for both tanks and infantry by the virtual absence of trenches and shell-holes, but the portents for further progress across the devastated areas of 1916 and 1917 were ominous.

It will be evident that the attack of the Australian Corps, sandwiched between the Canadian Corps on its right and III Corps on its left, would have to conform to the plans of its neighbours. Accordingly, Monash (the Australian Corps commander) proposed to use his 5th Division (followed later by the 1st and 2nd Divisions) to support the Canadians on his right, meanwhile delaying any advance on his left until III Corps made some progress north of the Somme. Zero hour was fixed for 10 a.m., but delays in communication that had bedevilled the Canadian Corps were now beginning to affect the Australian Corps. Orders for the move-up of the 1st Division were issued at 3.40 a.m. and conveyed by a car and a dispatch rider, but it was to be five hours before the division was on the move to Harbonnières, its rendezvous point. Meanwhile the 15th and 8th Brigades of the 5th Division crossed the Amiens Outer Defence Line and made some progress, although its six tanks were all put out of action by anti-tank gun fire from Vauvillers. A German retirement followed the arrival of the advanced battalions of the 1st and 2nd Divisions, and by 3.30 p.m. the 2nd Brigade of the 1st Division had reached within 1,200 yards of Lihons, its objective. Nevertheless, the Australians had suffered severe casualties in fighting their way across open country, and only two tanks survived from the thirty-six that had been allocated for the assault.

Across the Somme, III Corps had the task of reaching the line north-west of Etinehem, and along the high ground east of Morlancourt to Dernancourt. The cumulative effect, however, of the German attack on the 6th, the counter-attack on the 7th, and the main assault on the 8th, had seriously reduced its strength. The corps commander sought, and received, permission from Fourth Army headquarters to use the 131st Regiment of the American 33rd Division. The orders for 9 August were for the 58th and 12th Divisions to attack at dawn, passing through and taking over the front of the 18th Division in the process. The objective of the 58th Division was to outflank Gressaire Wood, and that of the 12th Division to capture

Morlancourt. When accomplished, the divisions would then pass on to the Amiens Outer Defence Line. The 131st Regiment was to be attached to the 58th Division for the operation, but as it was some six miles north of Villers Bretonneux, there was no possibility of it being ready for a dawn assault. The main operation was therefore postponed until 5.30 p.m., but before then the 58th Division was to detach a special force to attack the trouble spot of Chipilly.

The subsidiary attack on Chipilly was made at 4.15 p.m. by two battalions. At first they met heavy fire in enfilade but the village was eventually captured by 8 p.m. with the assistance of an Australian patrol and a company from the 131st Regiment. At 5.30 p.m. III Corps launched its main attack:

> The assembly proceeded as rapidly as possible, though time was short and the barrage could not open until all patrols were in. The Americans, who were rushed up from the rear, had to double nearly a mile to reach their assembly position at Malard Wood, but by a few minutes after zero every unit was moving forward... Our barrage opened up well on time but the shells fell harmlessly in Chipilly Valley instead of on the Ridge, which again became a hornets' nest of Hun machine-gunners.[12]

The three battalions of the American 131st Regiment came under furious machine-gun fire in attempting to clear Gressaire Wood, but undeterred by their losses they reached their objective. On their left, the 175th Brigade of the 58th Division met strong opposition, but by 8 p.m. were within a few hundred yards of their objective. On the extreme left, the 37th Brigade of the 12th Division, although initially meeting resistance, had a comparatively easy task in capturing Morlancourt.

Compared with 8 August, the outcome of operations on the 9th had been disappointing. As already mentioned, it would have been optimistic to expect that the objectives set could have been gained in half a day, and not even that in the III Corps sector. Initially the problem stemmed from the late start of the Canadian Corps because of the counter-order regarding the use of the 32nd Division, and this affected the timing of the attack of the Australian Corps. Moreover, the situation was aggravated by the time taken to transmit orders, many by hand because of the unreliability (and insecurity) of the signalling system. Thus the objectives set for the 9th remained to be accomplished on the 10th, and orders were issued from GHQ to this effect. The sector occupied by the Australian Corps, however, was enlarged to cross the Somme up to the Corbie–Bray road, and the 58th Division (excluding the American 131st Regiment) was sent into reserve.

The advance had now reached part of the area devastated by the Germans in their withdrawal to the Hindenburg Line in early 1917, and part of the old Somme battlefield. A wilderness of shell-holes, trenches, woven with wire entanglements, some intact and, over all, the grass and weeds had sprouted several feet high; a perfect area for machine-gunners. During the day the enemy had been reinforced by seven divisions, with the same number en route. The implications were that, in the event of determined enemy resistance, it could mean a virtual return to trench warfare; this, in the past, would have called for the traditional preliminary bombardment, but circumstances were now very different. It is not clear how much thought was given to the problems of crossing the old battlefields; possibly it was believed that the enemy, with the signs of hasty retirements and given the decline in his morale exhibited on 8 August, would not make a stand until he had retreated to a barrier such as the Hindenburg Line. Seemingly it was now a question of pursuit.

As on the previous day, there was a promising start when a brigade of the 3rd Canadian Division advanced at 4.20 a.m., captured le Quesnoy and moved on westwards to Parvillers. This, however, was to be virtually the only real success for the Fourth Army on what was to prove to be another disappointing day. The objective of the Canadian Corps (now including the 32nd Division) was the line of the railway from Roye–Hattencourt–Hallu. The right, advancing at 8 a.m., at first met little resistance, but soon came under machine-gun fire from the old trench area. The tanks suffered heavy losses from anti-tank fire, and progress of the infantry became slower until it was ultimately stopped on the old British front line. It was more successful on the left where a successful creeping barrage smothered machine-gun fire, and by the early evening the advance had reached its objective. It was evident, however, that enemy resistance was stiffening to the extent that two counter-attacks were mounted, although these were beaten off. An attempt to use cavalry to seize the high ground north of Roye and to occupy Nesle failed: 'Little came of the execution of these orders except casualties, as horsemen cannot charge entrenchments.'[13] The ground was also unsuitable for Whippets.

The Australian Corps fared little better. The objective of the 1st Division was the capture of Lihons and Chaulnes, but the attack was expected as the preparations for it had been observed. Zero hour was 8 a.m. but the advance immediately met strong opposition, and the division was seriously delayed by the need to clear Crépey Wood where the enemy mounted a fierce resistance and, once it had been taken, even a counter-attack. North of the Somme, two battalions of the 131st Regiment reached the old Amiens Defence Line, but an attack along either side of the Somme by two Australian brigades failed, although Etineham was evacuated by the enemy.

Haig now realised that the Amiens offensive had lost its momentum, and the time was approaching for a blow elsewhere. He proposed that the main operation should be an advance against Bapaume, with subsidiary operations against La Bassée and Aubers Ridge by the First Army, and against Kemmel by the Second Army. On the 10th he met Foch, who had other ideas. Whilst agreeing to the preparation of operations 'in the general direction of Bapaume and Péronne' and to the subsidiary operations, he directed that the action of the British Fourth and French

Armies 'should be continued eastwards in the general direction of Ham...' and 'the march of the French Third Army ... directed on Lassigny–Noyon in order to exploit the advance of the French First Army...' Haig, notwithstanding Foch's belief that the enemy was demoralised, was not happy, however, to continue the attacks eastwards from Amiens. He pointed out 'the difficulty of the undertaking unless the enemy is quite demoralised, and we can cross the Somme on his heels'. (It is somewhat ironic that Haig was now reluctant to accept that the Germans were demoralised when he had been insistent in putting this view forward in 1917.) Nevertheless he gave orders for the Amiens attack to be continued, and he instructed the Third Army to 'carry out raids and minor operations in order to ascertain the enemy's intentions on the Albert–Arras front, and take immediate advantage of any favourable situation which the main operations may create, and push advanced guards in the general direction of Bapaume'.

The formal orders issued by Rawlinson on 10 August were for the Fourth Army to 'press on to the Somme between Ham (exclusive) and Péronne and establish bridgeheads on the right bank of the river'. No significant progress, however, was made on the 11th, and after a discussion with Haig, Rawlinson's diary entry reads:

> I have stopped the attack, and told the corps to rest and reorganise. We shall renew the attack on the 15th, deliberately, with as many tanks as we can collect. The country over which we shall be working is seamed with old trenches which will be full of machine-gun nests, so I fear we shall have a high casualty list.[14]

It is not clear whether Rawlinson believed that preparations could be made for another assault in a mere four days' time; if he did, he was being uncharacteristically optimistic. His divisions were tired and, in lack of significant reinforcements, would have to be thrown into battle once again. There would not be enough time to observe the locations of enemy artillery to commence counter-battery fire, and there was no possibility of collecting a sizeable tank force. 'By 10 August the number of effective tanks was down to eighty-five, of which twenty-five were to receive direct hits during the day. On the 11th only thirty-eight, each in dire need of overhaul, went back in. On 12 August the last six were engaged and before the day was out the Tank Corps had been withdrawn in its entirety.'[15] Although the Battle of Amiens had come to an end on 11 August, it seemed, on the face of it that, as in previous offensives, the initial success achieved had faltered against stiffening enemy resistance, raising the daunting prospect either of having to defend the ground gained against counter-attacks, or having to prepare for the resumption of the attack. The reality, however, was far more propitious than could have been imagined. On the 10th Ludendorff had met the Kaiser at Avesnes and told him 'that we had suffered a severe defeat', and 'that the martial spirit of some divisions left much to be desired...' Nevertheless he was determined 'not to yield a foot of ground without a tenacious battle...'[16] The Kaiser's response was 'I see that we must draw up a balance sheet, we are on the brink of solvency. The war must be ended...'[17] At the meeting Ludendorff offered his resignation, but this was not accepted.

Foch issued an Instruction to Haig and Pétain on the 12th. He considered it vital to exploit the penetration already achieved, but thought that nothing was to be gained from uniform pressure all along the front: better to concentrate attacks on important points to increase the enemy's disorganisation. The operations he had in mind by the Fourth Army were the seizure of the important road junction at Roye (together with the French First Army), the capture of the Amiens–Brie road and the clearance of the enemy from the loop of the Somme at Péronne. These results could be 'increased to vast proportions by an extension of the attacks to the two flanks of the battle now in progress, on the one hand to north of the Somme, and on the other hand to east of the Oise'. These would be undertaken by the attack of the British Third Army in the general direction of Bapaume–Péronne, and of the French Tenth Army in the direction of Chauny and the Chauny–Soissons road 'in order to force the enemy to abandon the whole of the hilly and wooded massif between Noyon, Guiscard and Tergnier'.

Haig had a meeting with Pershing on the 12th from which it emerged that Pershing might have to withdraw the five American divisions training with the British Army. Haig was disappointed:

> I pointed out to him that I had done everything to help and equip these units of the American Army, and to provide them with horses. So far, I have had no help from these troops (except the three Battalions which were used in the battle near Chapally [Chipilly] in error)... All I wanted to know was definitely whether I could prepare to use the American troops for an attack (along with the British) at the end of September against Kemmel. Now I know I cannot do so.[18]

In the event, three divisions were withdrawn between 19 and 24 August to join the American First Army, but two remained with the British until the end of the war.

Following the meeting, Haig attended a conference at Fourth Army headquarters with Rawlinson, Debeney and Byng to discuss the continuation of the Amiens offensive on the 15th. The proposed offensive by Byng's Third Army was also discussed (provisionally fixed for 20 August) and a formal operation order for the attack on the Moyenneville–Ablainzevelle front (some 8 miles south of Arras) was issued next day:

> These operations should be carried out subsequent to a successful attack by the French First Army and the British Fourth Army on the front Roye–Chaulnes ... and, in conjunction with these operations, aim at throwing the enemy back to and beyond the line Bapaume–Péronne.[19]

The planned resumption of the Amiens offensive on the 15th, however, was causing concern to both Rawlinson and Debeney. On the 13th Rawlinson had met

Currie (Canadian Corps commander), who believed that an attack would be very costly, and supported his contention with photographs of the heavily wired German defences. For his part, Debeney argued that the attack should be postponed until the 16th because of the strength of the enemy position and ammunition problems. Rawlinson's diary for the 14th recorded:

> I went over to D. H. [Haig] at 10 a.m., with maps and photographs of the objectives for the attack which had been arranged for tomorrow. I pointed out to him that we were up against a regular trench system with masses of uncut wire, and I considered that to take it on with our present resources in guns and tanks would be to risk heavy losses and possible failure. I suggested that it would be far better and cheaper to hold the enemy to his ground, on my front, by wire-cutting and bombardment until the Third Army is ready to put in a surprise attack, and then to press simultaneously with that attack. This he entirely agreed to, and I left him with maps and photographs to show to Foch.[20]

Accordingly, Haig informed Foch of his decision to postpone the attack which brought an immediate reaction in a letter from Foch who disagreed with the subordination of the Amiens attack to that of the Third Army: 'Very much to the contrary, the attack of the First and Fourth Armies should be hastened as much as possible, and followed as rapidly as possible by that of the Third Army.' There was now a conflict of views which could not be solved by exchanges of letters and telegrams. Consequently, Haig went to see Foch who pressed him to continue the advance on Chaulnes and Roye. Haig's diary records:

> I declined to do so because they could only be taken after heavy casualties in men and tanks. I had ordered the French First and the British Fourth Armies to postpone their attacks, but to keep up pressure on that front so as to make the enemy expect an attack on this front, while I transferred my reserves to my Third Army (Byng), and also prepared to attack with the First Army (Horne) on the front Monchy–le–Preux–Miraumont. F. now wanted to know what orders I had issued for attack: when I proposed to attack. Where, and with what troops?

After giving Foch details of his instructions to Byng and Horne, his diary continued:

> I spoke to Foch quite straightly and let him understand that *I was responsible to my Government and fellow citizens for the handling of the British forces.* [Haig's emphasis][21]

Foch promptly climbed down and accepted Haig's proposals, but shortly afterwards he withdraw the French First Army from Haig's control. Pershing, however, who was now planning his own offensive, demanded the three American divisions, and Haig immediately wrote to Foch pointing out that his front would be reduced by about 18,000 yards if the transfer took place. To compensate for this, Foch arranged for the French First Army to extend its front northwards to around Lihons, thereby releasing the Canadian Corps. The American divisions were withdrawn on the 25th, and take-over of the Canadian front was completed by the 27th.

Whether Haig was right to refuse to continue the offensive after 11 August, despite the urgings of Foch, can only be conjectured, but he was strongly persuaded to do so by Rawlinson. Ludendorff wrote in his *Memoirs*: 'The situation [on the 14th] was uncommonly serious. If the enemy continued to attack with even ordinary vigour, we should no longer have been able to maintain ourselves west of the Somme.'[22] Even so, the Fourth Army was tired, with no prospect of substantial reinforcements, and its tank losses had been severe.

On the 19th Haig went to see Byng and expressed dissatisfaction with the latter's plan for the forthcoming attack. Haig was already aware from his Intelligence Branch that there was only one German division in reserve on Third Army front, and only ten fit divisions in reserve between the Oise and the sea. Moreover, Byng had earlier told Haig that the Germans were falling back opposite the centre of the Third Army front. With this in mind, it seemed to Haig that Byng's planned advance in his centre of about 6,000 yards failed to grasp the tactical possibilities, and he directed him to capture Bapaume as rapidly as possible and prevent the enemy destroying bridges and roads. On the same day he reported to Foch that the Third Army offensive would begin on the 21st, when the First Army would deliver a heavy bombardment on enemy defences to delude him as to the frontage of the attack. The Fourth Army would resume operations north and south of the Somme on the 22nd and 23rd respectively.

The jaws of the Allied armies were now beginning to close on the great German salient. On the 20th, the French Tenth Army had attacked north-westwards on a twelve-mile front from west of Soissons to Ribécourt, achieving an advance, in places, of 3,000 yards. Ludendorff considered the 20th to be 'another black day. Again we suffered heavy and irreplaceable losses.' Foch wrote to Haig:

> The enemy has everywhere been shaken by the blows already dealt him. We must repeat these blows without losing any time, and to increase their effect we must use every division that can be put into line without delay. Therefore I assume that the attack of your Third Army, postponed already until 21 August, will be launched on that day with the utmost violence, carrying along with it the divisions of the First Army lying next to it and your Fourth Army in its entirety. After your brilliant successes of 8th, 9th and 10th, any hesitation on their part would not accord with the situation of the enemy and the moral ascendancy we have obtained over him.[23]

Indeed, the mood in the German High Command was bleak. Ludendorff, in his *Memoirs*, described the conference at Spa:

On the 13th there was a discussion between the Chancellor, the Field-Marshal [Hindenburg], Secretary of State von Hintze and myself, in the Field-Marshal's room at the Hotel Britannic. I reviewed the military situation, the condition of the Army and the position of our Allies, and explained that it was no longer possible to force the enemy to sue for peace by an offensive. The defensive alone could hardly achieve that object, and so the termination of the war would have to be brought about by diplomacy... The Field-Marshal said nothing about the state of feeling at home; he took a more optimistic view of the military situation than I did. Secretary of State von Hintze drew, from what he had heard, the logical conclusion that peace negotiations were essential... The following morning there was a conference presided over by His Majesty... The Emperor was very calm. He agreed with the Secretary of State von Hintze and instructed him to open up peace negotiations, if possible, through the medium of the Queen of the Netherlands.[24]

Notes

1. Bacon, A. W., *I Was There*, Vol. 3, Amalgamated Press (London, 1938–9)
2. Edmonds, Brigadier-General Sir James, (comp.), *Official History of the War: Military Operations France and Belgium*, Vol. IV, HMSO (1947)
3. *Ibid.*
4. Blake, Robert, (ed.), *The Private Papers of Douglas Haig 1914–1919*, Eyre & Spottiswoode (London, 1952)
5. Williams, H. R., *The Gallant Company: An Australian's Story of 1915–1918*, Angus & Robertson (Sydney, 1933)
6. Edmonds, *op. cit.*
7. Grimwade, F. C., *The War History of the 4th Battalion The London Regiment (Royal Fusiliers)* Regimental Headquarters (London, 1922)
8. *Ibid.*
9. Ludendorff, General, *Concise Ludendorff Memoirs 1914–1918*, Hutchinson (London, 1933)
10. Ludendorff, General, *My War Memoirs 1914–1918*, Hutchinson (London, 1919)
11. Edmonds, *op. cit.*
12. Grimwade, *op. cit.*
13. Edmonds, *op. cit.*
14. Maurice, Major-General Sir F., *The Life of General Lord Rawlinson*, Cassell (London, 1928)
15. Smithers A. J., *A New Excalibur*, Grafton Books (London, 1988)
16. Niemann, A., *Kaiser und Revolution* (Berlin, 1922)
17. *Ibid.*
18. Blake, *op. cit.*
19. Edmonds, *op. cit.*
20. Maurice, *op. cit.*
21. Blake, *op. cit.*
22. Ludendorff, *op. cit.*
23. Foch, Marshal, *The Memoirs of Marshal Foch*, Heinemann (London, 1931)
24. Ludendorff, *op. cit.*

Left: General Henri-Philippe Pétain. (Philip Haythornthwaite)

Right: General Sir Henry Wilson, Chief of the Imperial General Staff. (Philip Haythornthwaite)

Left: General Sir Hubert Gough. (Philip Haythornthwaite)

Below: British Mark IV tank crushing German wire entanglements. (Philip Haythornthwaite)

Above: Field Marshal Sir Douglas Haig and his Army commanders at Cambrai on 11 November 1918. Front row: General Plumer (Second), Haig, General Rawlinson (Fourth). Second row: Generals Byng (Third), Birdwood (Fifth) and Horne (First). (IWM Q 9690)

Below: Captured German A7V tank. (Philip Haythornthwaite)

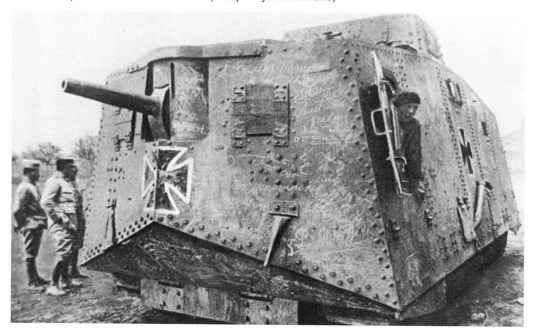

Above left: General John Pershing, Commander of the American Expeditionary Force. (Philip Haythornthwaite)

Above: Marshal Ferdinand Foch. (Philip Haythornthwaite)

Left: Hindenburg and Ludendorff at Avesnes. (Philip Haythornthwaite)

Above: American troops advancing, Gondrecourt, 16 August 1918. (IWM HU 71786)

Below: Australian troops waiting under the barrage minutes before moving out to attack Mont St Quentin, 1 September 1918. (IWM E (AUS) 3142)

Above: Canadian infantry waiting in a dry stretch of the Canal du Nord to go forward near Moeuvres, 27 September 1918. (IWM Q 9637)

Below: Part of the St Quentin Canal near Bellenglise where crossing was effected by the 46th Division on 29 September 1918. (IWM Q 9510)

Above: British troops going forward to meet the German advance in Picardy, March 1918, near Mailly-Maillet. (IWM Q 8619)

Below: 18pdr British field guns in action in the open near Albert during the German offensive, 28 March 1918. (IWM Q 8648)

2/Lt PETSCHLER R.E.

Your only duty is to blow up No 4 Bridge, in the event of the enemy being in possession of the Bridge-head - i.e., that there are none of our troops who can prevent him getting over.

Two things are most important :-

(a). That the enemy should not cross by the Bridge.

(ii). That it is not blown up unnecessarily.

You are personally responsible for the carrying out of these orders.

Captain.
Brigade Major.
89th Infantry Brigade.

/3/1918.

Above: Instruction to 2nd Lieutenant Petschler, RE, to blow No. 4 bridge at Ham.

Below: Battle of the Lys. Collected stragglers lining the railway near Merris, 12 April 1918. (IWM Q 8688)

9

The Approach to the Hindenburg Line

T he Third Army attack was to be undertaken, from right to left, by its three corps: V Corps (21st and 38th Divisions); IV Corps (37th, 42nd and the New Zealand Division); and VI Corps (Guards, 2nd and 59th Divisions), in all comprising eight divisions with five in reserve. One hundred and fifty-six tanks had been allocated for the attack, and ten RAF squadrons; its artillery had been augmented by transfers from the Fourth Army. The ground over which the attack was to take place was between the Somme battlefield of 1916 and the Arras battlefield of 1917 and was comparatively free of shell-holes and trenches. As tanks were to be employed, there would be no preliminary bombardment, and zero hour was fixed for 4.55 a.m. The main thrust of the attack was to be in the Third Army's centre between Moyenneville and Ablainzevelle when, if all went well, V Corps on the right would advance.

All the notable battles of 1918 seemed inevitably, at their outset, to be shrouded by fog, and the opening of the Third Army attack on 21 August was no exception.

> There was no artillery preparation as a prelude to this battle – only a curtain of fire due to come down and precede our advancing waves at zero hour – so that there was a very real lull before the storm.
>
> The night had been exceptionally calm. With battle at hand it assumed as usual an ominous silence. And quite right too – the day had something to reveal. Only an occasional shell came to disturb the almost perfect calm that reigned, and served but to intensify the stillness. Even the men spoke little, and then in whispers, like people in church, with death at the altar. From 4.30 onwards the time went leaden-footed. Glancing at my watch became a continuous and methodical performance... At seven minutes to five only the distant pup-pup-pup of a machine gun could be heard... Six minutes to five and one felt the proximity of the hour like a near presence. Suddenly a gun, like the mighty slamming of a door in a sleeping house, broke the stillness... Every one of the myriad guns crowding the area took up the signal and belched forth fire and noise. The battle had begun... I went a short distance with the company and, saying good-bye, stood and watched the men as they were quickly mixed with the mist.[1]

While the fog shielded the infantry of VI Corps, it was difficult for tanks with their limited range of vision, and a number lost their way. Nevertheless, the fog hampered the defenders, and by noon VI Corps had secured most of the line of the Albert–Arras railway, its second objective, apart from a few hundred yards. But by then the fog had cleared and the position reached soon came under artillery and machine-gun fire. It was then that exploitation should have taken place with the assistance of tanks and cavalry, but none had appeared. The problems experienced by tanks in the fog are graphically described in a diary by a Tank Corps section commander. His objective was the village of Courcelles:

> Soon everything was ready to move off and at 5.20 a.m. all engines were started and the last five minutes I spent giving final directions to my officers. As the daylight got stronger the ground mist seemed to get thicker, and at the time the barrage started there was a thick fog which made it extremely difficult to find the way.

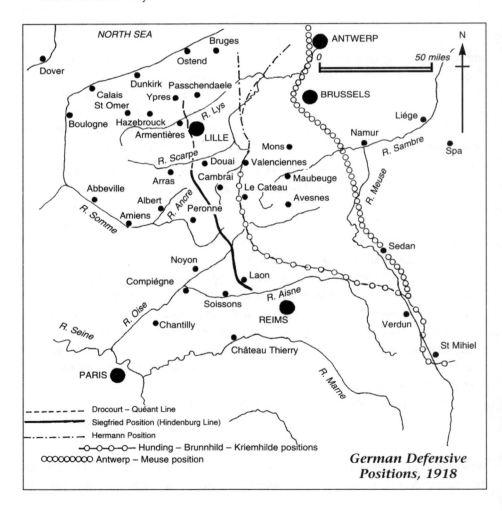

German Defensive Positions, 1918

He decided to travel in the leading tank (*Odette*) 'as it would have been quite easy to lose sight of all my section had I endeavoured to keep in touch with every one and I thought better to be sure of one than lose sight of the lot...' After the tank had some problems in climbing out of a deep ditch, he decided to walk outside

> as I wanted to use my pocket compass as I knew the one inside the tank was out of adjustment. Soon we crossed the old front line and got in touch with the infantry second wave, but pushed on ahead as we were already late and the leading wave was already well ahead, but it was very difficult to make much headway and several times we found ourselves going in the opposite direction to our objective...

Eventually a runner appeared who was able to direct him to where the infantry was being held up by machine-gun fire:

> After a short consultation with the infantry captain we estimated the whereabouts of the machine-guns and proceeded accordingly. This time I decided that walking in front would be rather a fool game, so after giving brief directions ... I followed behind. We had not got far when the sound of bullets hitting the tank announced that we had been seen and were being sprayed by way of a welcome. Now our 6-pounder got into action and returned the welcome with interest.[2]

Farther south, the advance of IV Corps had started well. The three leading divisions arrived on their first objective in good time. The two reserve divisions, whose task was to pass through to the second objective, should have been supported by field guns, but these were delayed in being brought up because of shell-fire. Denied the cover of an effective creeping barrage, the two divisions could make no significant progress towards the Albert–Arras railway. Some parties did reach the railway but were forced to withdraw, and the few tanks that also succeeded were knocked out.

On the extreme right, V Corps had the difficult task of crossing the Ancre:

> This river had been canalised at a higher level than the marshy floor of the valley, and the banks having been damaged by shelling, most of the valley, to a width of three hundred yards, was flooded, and the main stream was indistinguishable; in fact the Ancre had become a stretch of marsh and water covered by a tangle of fallen trees, branches and reeds, with wire – almost unnecessarily – added to make it a more difficult obstacle.[3]

V Corps had no specific objective other than to prolong the advance of IV Corps on its left by about a thousand yards near Beaucourt, and exploit any success by crossing the Ancre between Hamel and Miraumont. Zero hour at 5.45 a.m. was almost an hour later than for the two neighbouring corps. A brigade of the 38th Division captured Beaucourt shortly after 6.30 a.m. but then came under heavy machine-gun fire which delayed the river crossing until 3.30 p.m. Farther south, brigades of the 21st and 38th Divisions managed to cross the Ancre under cover of fog, but were forced to withdraw once it had lifted.

Although the centre of the Third Army had gained an appreciable amount of ground and had either reached its second objective, or were within a few hundred yards of it, it had not been quite as successful as that of the Fourth Army on 8 August. This attack had come as a complete surprise to the Germans, but although the attack of the Third Army was apparently unsuspected, mounting Allied pressure had forced the realisation that they must expect further attacks and plan accordingly, as a German account reveals:

> At 5 a.m. on the 21st August a mighty rolling barrage in thick fog opened the fight between Hamel and Moyenneville. Soon after the British divisions and squadrons of tanks began to advance, and the German troops, according to plan, evacuated the 3,000 to 4,000 yards' wide forward zone. The enemy attack expended itself in the first stage and under the fire of the German batteries and machine guns, stuck fast at the Miraumont–Courcelles railway and at the Ancre.[4]

Byng decided to devote the 22nd to making preparations for a further advance, although Haig, according to his diary, was not pleased: 'The Third Army is halting to-day. I cannot think this is necessary. I accordingly issued *an Order* directing *the offensive to be resumed at the earliest moment possible.*'[5] (Haig's emphasis)

On the 22nd the Fourth Army began its assault north of the Somme. The main attack was to be made by III Corps using the 37th and 12th Divisions in the centre of the attack, with the 18th Division and the 3rd Australian Division covering the flanks: cavalry was to follow up to exploit success. Zero hour was 4.45 a.m., and according to the *Official History*, 'The Germans were uneasy and evidently expecting attack on the 22nd and were assisted by the bright light of a waning moon.' The Australian division led the advance on the right, by-passing Bray, and reached its final objective north of the village shortly after 8 a.m. The 47th Division, however, was less fortunate. Its leading brigade lost direction in the fog and consolidated its line short of the Happy Valley, its objective. The supporting brigade, advancing from this position, met strong opposition and only a few parties reached the intermediate objective where it established touch with the Australians. An attempt by squadrons of cavalry to push through Happy Valley met wire and machine-gun fire and had to withdraw. The advance of the 12th Division was more successful. The village of Méaulte was quickly captured with the help of four tanks, and the final objective was gained by 8.30 a.m. Soon after 2 p.m. the Germans mounted a counter-attack on the junction of the 12th and 47th Divisions, but this was ultimately repulsed. The 18th Division on the far left succeeded in entering Albert, although the German garrison still held the east of the town. During the night a number of trestle bridges were erected over the Ancre, and by 10 a.m. on the 23rd Albert had been cleared of the enemy.

On the same day two divisions of the Australian Corps, accompanied by tanks, captured Chuignolles and Chuinges, the final objective, in the afternoon. It was now evident that the main German resistance was from machine-gunners and artillery: the infantry often offered only a token resistance before retiring. Byng's plan for the 23rd was to build on the success of the advance made by VI Corps on the left of the Third Army front two days earlier by a preliminary operation preparatory to an advance against Hamelincourt-Héninel, and his corps was reinforced by three divisions (52nd, 56th and 57th). Haig's telegram on the 22nd, however, addressed to all his Army commanders made it clear that he was expecting something more than the limited operation planned by Byng. His message exhorted his commanders 'to turn the present situation to account, the most resolute offensive is everywhere desirable. Risks which a month ago would have been criminal to occur, ought now to be incurred as a duty.'[6] In consequence, Byng revised his plan: all his three corps would advance along the entire Third Army front in a pincer movement to outflank the strongly held Irles–Achiet le Grand position. On the right, V Corps was to pass Thiepval from the south and VI Corps would capture Gomiecourt in a night operation; if the latter were successful, IV Corps would advance on Achiet le Grand and then combine with VI Corps in an easterly advance.

Zero hour for the Gomiecourt operation was before dawn at 4 a.m. It was a complete success: the village was captured by the 3rd Division within an hour. The remaining divisions of VI Corps advanced an hour later with the objective of the line Hamelincourt–Boyelles–Boiry Becquerelle. Despite opposition from machine-gun fire, the Guards Division captured Hamelincourt by 8 a.m., and the 56th Division took Boyelles and Boiry Becquerelle. This success brought further orders to advance: the Guards Division to cross the River Sensée, and the 56th and 52nd Divisions to advance on Sapignies, Béhagnies and Ervillers. Once again, the main opposition was from machine-guns, and although a Guards battalion succeeded in crossing the Sensée and reaching the objective of Hally Copse, the remainder of the brigade remained west of the river. Elsewhere on the Third Army front the attack by IV and V Corps was also successful: Irles and Achiet le Grand were captured by IV Corps, although the three attacking divisions suffered severe casualties from machine-gun fire, and V Corps, in a limited operation, captured Usna and Tara hills on the Albert–Bapaume road.

Thus, as a consequence of Haig's pressure, the Third Army's advance had been very satisfactory. A considerable amount of ground had been gained and over 5,000 prisoners rounded up. The French First Army, which had taken over the sector held by the Canadian Corps, had made no move since then: 'weakened and delayed by the extension of its front towards the north, it was not yet in a condition to relaunch an attack'. Nevertheless, over the last three days the French Third and

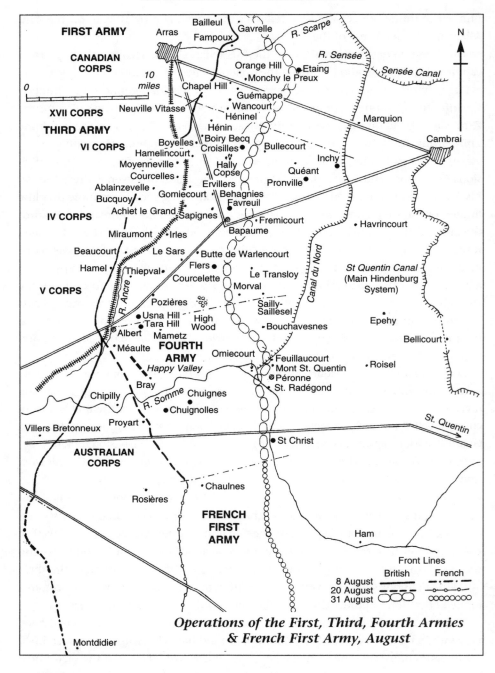

**Operations of the First, Third, Fourth Armies
& French First Army, August**

Tenth Armies had made good progress, although enemy resistance was stiffening, and a fresh attack begun on the 23rd by the Tenth Army on the Soissons front had realised 'only insignificant gains'.

The German regimental histories speak of disaster on 23 August:

> The day was a catastrophe for the regiment. It cost its good old, stock. All three battalion staffs, all company commanders, all medical officers, the greater part of the excellent telephone detachment, and more than 600 men: and in the period 8th to 22nd August we had already lost 300 men. Only two officers and 42 other ranks, mostly of the II Battalion, in addition to the regimental staff, escaped.[7]

The Fourth Army continued its attack on the following day (24th). Bray was captured by the 3rd Australian Division, and the assault of the 47th and 12th Divisions was designed to capture the final objective beyond Happy Valley. The opening barrage was described in a letter to his wife by a regimental commander in the 47th Division:

> I watched the opening of the barrage. How often have I tried to describe to you that grandest and most spectacular of all the shows ever staged by man! the crash of a thousand guns bursting suddenly out of the silence of the night: the continued roar: the rapid intermittent flicker on the clouds: the trembling earth beneath you – while you listen anxiously for the rattle of the enemy's machine guns – that nasty sickening sound which you are just able to distinguish amid the din, and which tells you that he is not taking it lying down.

A gap existed for a time between the two divisions as a result of persistent machine-gun fire and the situation became precarious, particularly as the enemy appeared to be preparing a counter-attack:

> I found things none too grand. The Brigade on our left had been held up, with the result that a dangerous gap existed between their right and ourselves. For some hours the position at this point remained critical, and several times it was reported that enemy counter-attacks were threatened.
>
> My own personal view was that nothing was farther from the enemy's mind than counter-attack. The viciousness of his shelling – all from heavy artillery and trench mortars – though it was by some taken to be in preparation for an attack, suggested to me that it was more likely to be covering a withdrawal – indeed, that he had already withdrawn his field guns...[8]

The delay caused Rawlinson to cancel the combined attack by III Corps and the Australians which had been timed for 4 p.m.

Farther north the Third Army had a very successful day. Its centre and right wing, advancing on both sides of the Albert–Bapaume road, took Thiepval Ridge, which had taken nearly four months to capture in 1916, and Pozières, the scene of desperate fighting by the Australians in August 1916. The New Zealand Division even reached the outskirts of Bapaume, but was unable to hold the position because its left flank was exposed. The advance was slower on the left wing by reason of strong opposition from Croisilles, although Henin village was captured.

> The enemy opposition throughout the day had been offered almost entirely by scattered machine guns. The riflemen seemed to have no desire to fight. Many of the machine guns, as later discovered, were a hundred to a hundred and fifty yards ahead of the main line, outside any wire, skilfully concealed by camouflage on wire netting. Unless these guns happened to be struck by the barrage, they were able to remain in action all day. Thus it was that night and early morning attacks in poor visibility succeeded and daylight advances had failed.[9]

The advance of both Armies continued on the 25th. The centre and right of the Third Army captured Courcelette, le Sars and the Butte de Warlencourt (the limit of the 1916 Somme offensive), and reached Avesnes, a suburb of Bapaume. The left wing, however, was now butting against the Hindenburg Line and little progress could be made. It appeared that the Germans facing the Fourth Army were retiring and Rawlinson instructed his corps commanders to give them no rest. Good progress was made in the early hours, aided by thick fog, but this was slowed once the fog thinned, and the advance came under artillery and machine-gun fire from enemy rearguards. Nevertheless, III Corps advanced over two miles.

The French 10th Army gained a little ground north of Soissons on the 25th. The First and Third Armies did not move, although Fayolle, while admitting that neither Army was ready to undertake a general offensive, instructed them to 'prepare and carry out ... local actions to improve their positions...'

Although the Fourth Army and the centre and right of the Third Army were making satisfactory progress, the left of the Third Army was approaching the Hindenburg Line defences where strong resistance was expected. Haig had told Horne (First Army) on 15 August to prepare an attack on the Drocourt–Quéant Line which, if successful, would outflank that section of the Hindenburg Line facing the Third Army. Both Armies prepared for combined movement on 26 August. The Third Army's objectives were, on the right, Flers; in the centre, Bapaume and Favreuil, and on the left, Croisilles. The First Army's immediate objective was the capture of Chapel Hill and Orange Hill and, if achieved, exploitation eastwards towards Wancourt, Guémappe and the hilltop village of Monchy le Preux. Only V Corps of the Third Army made any progress, capturing Mametz and High Woods. The other corps met stout resistance, particularly around the strongpoints of Bapaume and Croisilles. Nevertheless, the Canadian Corps of the First Army achieved a signal success in capturing Chapel and Orange Hills, and pressing on took Monchy, Guémappe and Wancourt: an advance at its greatest of nearly four miles.

This success accelerated OHL's decision not only 'to abandon to the enemy the devastated battle area north and west of the Somme', but, in the north, the Lys salient as well. A fortnight earlier the German view had been 'that it would be fatal to limit ourselves to the pure defensive; well planned counter-attacks must be undertaken...' This belief, however, was not now accepted by the Staff of the German Crown Prince's group of Armies

who had come to the view that we were thrown on the defensive for good and all. In a letter (to General Ludendorff) on the 26th August, it was said that we must, in any case, reckon on the long continuation of the enemy offensive, and with strong fresh attacks against strategically or politically important sectors of the front. To the large-scale offensive plan of the enemy 'we must oppose well-thought-out defensive measures... The enemy has naturally the intention of destroying our reserves. We can escape this only by accepting attack solely where the ground offers favourable conditions for defence. When this condition is not present, we must retire sector by sector according to a definite plan... It must find its end in a strong permanent position...'[10]

The permanent position in mind, facing the British, was the Hindenburg Position. In his reply, Ludendorff, while agreeing with this approach, added, 'I regard, in any case, the retirement into the jumping-off positions of last March – the Hindenburg Position – as the very farthest we can go in consideration of the unfavourable rein-forcement position.' The retirement was made on the night of 27/28 August to a line from Noyon to Nesle, and thence, following the line of the Somme, to the north-west of Péronne.

On the 26th Foch wrote to Haig in glowing terms:

Things are going very well with you. I can only admire the resolute manner in which you press the business forward, giving no respite to the enemy and constantly increasing the scope of your action. It is the persistent widening and intensifying of the offensive – this pushing vigorously forward on care-fully chosen objectives without over-preoccupation as to alignment or close liaison – that will give us the best result with the smallest losses, as you have so perfectly understood. No need to tell you that the Armies of General Pétain are about to recommence their attacks, using similar methods.[11]

According to Haig's diary entry for 27 August:

I took the opportunity of sending Foch a letter. I urged him to put the Ameri-cans into battle at once in order to enable an important advance to be made without delay, concentrically, viz., against Cambrai, against St Quentin, and against Mézières from the South. I also wrote to General Pershing who had thanked me for dispatching the American Divisions to him so promptly, and said that I hoped events would justify his decision to withdraw such a large force of American Divisions (over 150,000 men) from me at the height of battle. For the present, I am convinced that if they had taken part in this battle, they would, owing to the present tired and demoralised state of the Germans on this front, have enabled the Allies to obtain immediate and decisive results.[12]

Between the end of May and August, the number of American troops in France had risen from 650,000 to nearly one and half million, but many were still undergoing training. They had yet to be involved in a major offensive operation, but some units had rendered valuable service on the Marne in stemming the German Aisne offensive in June, and they had also taken part in the British offensive at Amiens in August. At the end of August Pershing agreed that the two divisions in the British zone should remain and be used by Haig in offensive operations, but henceforth he never deviated from his aim to form an independent American Army which would fight as such, rather than being mixed piecemeal with the troops of his Allies. This, as will be seen later, would soon lead to controversy.

One of Foch's objectives outlined at his meeting with the three commanders-in-chief on 24 July was the freeing of the Paris–Nancy railway by the reduction of the German salient at St Mihiel in the French sector east of Verdun where the bulk of the American divisions were positioned. At the time, Pershing considered that his forces were not yet organised to mount an offensive, although he stressed that they were eager to do so. On 30 August, Foch addressed a Note to the three commanders. He referred to the favourable developments that had taken place since 24 July and underlined the importance of exploiting the situation to the utmost. To this end, the British and the French Armies would continue their advance, and 'The American Army and the right of the French Armies, operating on the Meuse and westwards [would] attack in the general direction of Mézières' (some 70 miles north of St Mihiel). Foch, however, modified the original St Mihiel operation so that it would go no further than cutting off the salient at its base, leaving 'considerable Allied forces ... available for the principal operations in the direction of Mézières'. He was thus adopting Haig's proposal. Foch also referred to an attack to be carried out at a later date by a Franco-American force between the Meuse and the Argonne.

The next three days (27-29 August) saw clear signs of a German retirement, particularly in the Third and Fourth Armies' sectors. The German plan was a defence line pivoting on Quéant through Fremicourt, le Transloy and Morval to Péronne where the north–south stretch of the Somme created a natural obstacle. During the German retirement to the east bank of the Somme, the strongpoints of Croisilles and Bapaume were abandoned. Farther north the advance of the First Army to the Drocourt–Quéant Line had started well but came to a halt against uncut wire. The German retirement enabled the French First Army to advance. Roye at last was captured, and Debeney was instructed to 'keep contact with the right of the British Army [and] advance its right and centre in the general direction of Ham'. The French Third Army joined in the advance and captured Noyon, but the Tenth Army hardly moved.

Although Ludendorff had called 8 August 'the black day of the German Army', the reality was, as the British Official Historian pointed out, that 'August was the black month of the German nation'. The ending of the weary stalemate on the Western Front brought about by the sweeping German successes achieved on the Somme in March, and on the Aisne in May, had lifted the Army's and the nation's hopes, and it seemed that a victorious end to the war was at last in sight. But in August the tide had turned, and the taste of the Dead Sea fruit had turned to ashes. The nation's mood was sombre: 'For fifteen days the public saw the stations blocked and the lines encumbered with endless hospital trains and cattle trucks packed with wounded... The Kaiser, the Ministers, the political parties, the newspapers, the people, the military chiefs, abandoned themselves to destiny, vanquished in advance in their hearts.'[13] German soldiers going on leave were shocked to find their families on the brink of starvation: the effect of the blockade instigated and continued by the Royal Navy since August 1914 had brought about a slowly tight-ening throttle-hold on food supplies which grew even tighter once the United States had entered the war. This reduced the food available to much less than subsis-tence level, and the mood of soldiers returning to the front was bitter. Disaffection spread particularly when they were joined by released prisoners of war from Russia who believed, wrongly, that they were under no obligation to fight again.

Another detachment of reinforcements had arrived in the meantime. Half of them were boys that appeared to be hardly 16, others, old men who looked quite sick. Being the latest and probably the last to arrive they were able to describe the state of turmoil Germany was in that we had never suspected, since the newspapers told nothing of conditions at home. The new men told us amongst other things that the present male population of Germany consisted only of cripples, deserters and war profiteers; the people were starving, and even the babies underfed, that our navy was mutinous, the Austrian army not to be depended on and the wish for peace uppermost in everyone's minds.

Replacements that had come from the Eastern Front had fraternised with the Russians and were full of Bolshevistic ideas. Sullen and defiant, these men went about their duties showing open disapproval. It was only [Lieutenant] Baunacker's forceful personality that prevented trouble. Watching them I could well understand the rumours, that dissatisfaction was spreading all through the German army, and the famous discipline going to pieces.[14]

Haig issued orders on the 29th to the First, Third and Fourth Armies for the following day. The main attack was to be delivered by the First Army against the Drocourt–Quéant Line: the other armies to 'co-operate by vigorous action with the object of holding the enemy on their respective fronts'. Some progress was made by the Third Army on the 30th and the First Army advanced nearly two miles. The Australian Corps of the Fourth Army was already up to the Somme but its crossing presented a formidable obstacle:

> It was in fact a marsh over a thousand yards in width, studded with many small islets overgrown with rushes through which the stream threaded its way by numerous channels: the marshy parts were waist deep and the water channels too deep to be waded; along the western side runs the canal. To cross this reach and the canal a very large number of bridges would be required, and it was evident that the enemy had destroyed some of them. Ultimately it was ascertained that every bridge had been blown to pieces.[15]

On the same day Monash, the Australian Corps Commander, held a conference with his divisional commanders to discuss plans for the capture of Péronne. A frontal attack would be bound to incur severe casualties, and he decided to outflank the position from the north and seize the key feature of Mont St Quentin by a surprise attack. This is a hill some 140 feet high a mile north of Péronne and dominating the Somme reaches both to the north and south. If successful, it was considered that Péronne would fall. In his diary for 30 August, Rawlinson wrote: 'The 2nd and 3rd Australian Divisions are determined to get hold of Mont St Quentin and Péronne. If they can do it quickly I shall be delighted, but I doubt the Boche giving up such an important position without a stiff fight.' Attempts to construct bridges across the Somme during the night were mostly frustrated, but a bridgehead was eventually established at Omiecourt, some two miles west of Mont St Quentin.

On the next day the Australian Corps attacked Mont St Quentin and achieved a conspicuous success. At 5 a.m. the 5th Brigade, consisting of no more than seventy officers and 1,250 other ranks – four 'battalions' but, in total, little more than a battalion at full strength – began its assault:

> The advance began at 5 a.m. It was a dull morning, and still quite dark. The two right battalions advanced with as much noise as possible, a ruse which secured the surrender of the enemy lying out in advanced outpost positions. A nest of seven machine guns was rushed and captured without any loss to us.
>
> At the appointed hour, our artillery opened up on selected targets, the ranges being lengthened from moment to moment in sympathy with the advance of the infantry. Although during the advance a great deal of machine-gun fire was encountered, all went well. The centre and left battalions gained

a footing respectively in Feuillaucourt and on the main hill, but the progress of the right battalion was arrested by heavy machine-gun fire from St Denis...

The centre battalion had by 7 a.m. passed through the ruins of Mont St Quentin and had crossed the main road from Péronne to Bouchavesnes. It had now to receive the full brunt of a determined counter-attack, at a moment when it was still disorganised and breathless from its difficult assault. The battalion was therefore withdrawn across the road and established itself in an old trench system to the west of it.

In this position it beat off five successive counter-attacks, inflicting most severe losses on the enemy.[16]

These counter-attacks were delivered by the elements of five German divisions, including a Prussian Guards division, who had instructions to hold the position at all costs. It was not until the following day that the 6th Brigade, passing through the 5th Brigade, finally secured the summit of the hill. The way was now open for an attack on Péronne itself. Farther north the Third Army made no significant progress, and the First Army, poised before the Drocourt–Quéant Line, experienced tangible evidence of the enemy's resolve to hold on to the line by a counter-attack which, although initially successful, ultimately failed.

The Australians gained another important success on the following day (1 September). Advancing at 6 a.m. in drizzling rain, they captured the village of St Radégonde in forty-five minutes, and a battalion of the 14th Brigade reached the moat (a 'wide wet ditch') surrounding Péronne:

Word came through that the 54th Battalion had gained a foothold in the town of Péronne. This was achieved only by the utmost heroism. Small parties rushed across foot-bridges raked with machine-gun fire, in which many were killed, but the few who lived to reach the bridgehead attacked the German machine-gunners and cleared a way for other parties to cross the foot-bridges. Once a hold was gained on part of the town, it was exploited to the utmost, and the Germans were rooted out of cellars and other cover. Two NCOs of this battalion were afterwards awarded the Victoria Cross for their bravery and example in this fighting. Only the stoutest of troops could have gained an entry in face of the obstacles of the ramparts and moat and the determined garrison.[17]

The centre of the town was gained by 8.40 a.m. and, apart from a suburb in the north-east, Péronne was now in Australian hands. Meanwhile the Third Army captured Morval and Sailly Saillisel, and the First Army made a successful limited advance in preparation for the assault on the D–Q Line to take place on the following day. On 29 August Haig had received a telegram from Wilson marked 'H.W. Personal':

Just a word of caution in regard to incurring heavy losses in attacks on Hindenburg Line as opposed to losses when driving the enemy back to that line. I do not mean to say that you have incurred such losses, but I know the War Cabinet would become anxious if we received heavy punishment in attacking the Hindenburg Line without success.

Haig was indignant, noting in his diary:

It is impossible for a C.I.G.S. to send a telegram of this nature to a C. in C. in the Field as a 'personal' one. The Cabinet are ready to meddle and interfere with my plans in an underhand way, but do not dare to say openly that they mean to take the responsibility for any failure though ready to take the credit for every success! The object of this telegram is, no doubt, to save the Prime Minister (Lloyd George) in case of any failure. So I read it to mean that I can attack the Hindenburg Line if I think it right to do so. The C.I.G.S. and the Cabinet already know that my arrangements are being made to that end. If my attack is successful, I will remain as C. in C. If we fail, or our losses are excessive, I can hope for no mercy. I wrote to Henry Wilson in reply. What a lot of wretched weaklings we have in high places at the present time![18]

Construction of the Hindenburg Line (known to the Germans as the Siegfried-Stellung) had begun in September 1916 in case of a withdrawal on the Somme. In the event, this became a reality early in 1917. Except for the section between Neuville Vitasse (about three miles south-east of Arras) and Quéant, and from there to Drocourt, it was not a line as such but a defensive zone in considerable depth extending to the neighbourhood of Vailly on the Aisne (seven miles east of Soissons). The D–Q line was known to the British in 1917 as the 'D–Q Switch' and thought to be a reserve position in the event of the loss of Vimy Ridge. The section of the Hindenburg Line extending from west of Quéant to Neuville Vitasse had already been outflanked by the capture of Monchy le Preux, and the D–Q Line remained as a northerly extension. It comprised

a front system and a support system, each with two lines of trenches provided with concrete shelters and machine-gun posts and very heavily wired. The front line was mainly on the crest or on a forward slope, the support system on a reverse slope. It was without the depth of the Hindenburg Position; but the Buissy Switch, connecting with the Hindenburg Support, served as a retrenchment.[19]

The task of assaulting the D–Q position on 2 September was given to the Canadian Corps in co-operation with XVII Corps (Third Army), while XXII Corps secured the left flank. The attack was to be centred on the D–Q position astride the

Arras–Marquion road, and carried out by the 1st and 4th Canadian and 4th (British) Divisions, supported by two companies of tanks. Zero hour was 5 a.m. and the two Canadian Divisions met only token resistance from the defenders who promptly surrendered in considerable numbers. The two trenches of the front system were soon captured and the advance continued on to the support system where, for a time, it was held up by machine-gun fire. This was eventually overcome and the Buissy Switch was reached; here resistance stiffened, particularly at the southern end, and fighting continued for the rest of the day. Resistance at the northern end of the Switch, however, was much lighter; many Germans surrendered, and the advance continued beyond, capturing the village of Dury in the process. The 4th (British) Division on the left flank of the attack took both D–Q systems without much too much difficulty, but were unable to pass beyond the support line because of machine-gun fire from Etaing. XVII Corps, on the right of the Canadian Corps, captured three-quarters of a mile of the Hindenburg Line as far as the D–Q line and were close to Quéant. The other three corps in the Third Army gained most of their objectives, and the Fourth Army completed the capture of Péronne. A commentary on the quality of German resistance on 2 September is given in the war diary of Brigadier-General Hon. A. M. Henley:

> The surprising part to me both at Villers and before at Miraumont, is the number of prisoners. You will see in the Hun communiqués that he covers his retreat with rearguards of M.Gs, [machine-guns] and that is just what you would think if you saw and heard the fight. All his fire seems to come from M.G.s, and yet there are these frequent considerable bags of infantry in exposed position[s]. If they knew how to use their rifles they could produce a most withering volume of fire, but I can only conclude that they don't understand the weapon, and this is borne out by the promptitude with which they throw them away. The ground everywhere is littered with Bosche rifles and steel helmets.[20]

The French First Army, 'owing to stout resistance of the enemy' made only slight progress. The Third Army did not move, but the Tenth Army gained some ground north of Soissons. It was the successes of the British Armies – not emulated by the French Armies – and particularly the penetration of the D–Q position, that caused OHL to order an immediate retirement to behind the Sensée and the Canal du Nord and, farther south, to the Hindenburg Position, 'and the whole great salient won in March 1918 to be abandoned'. Moreover, orders were given to complete the evacuation of the Lys salient won in April. Crown Prince Rupprecht (commander of the northern group of German Armies), who was returning from sick leave, noted in his diary: 'In Nürnberg the inscription on a troop train was to be read: "Slaughter cattle for Wilhelm & Sons". Public feeling, for that matter, is not only very bad in Bavaria, but also in north Germany.' The Kaiser's reaction to the loss of the D–Q position was one of near hysteria: 'It means nothing more or less than that we have lost the war.' The Bavarian Official History recorded:

> The German divisions just melted away. Reinforcements, in spite of demands and entreaties, were not forthcoming... The general and continuing crisis in the situation made it impossible to afford units the necessary rest and change...The rations remained meagre and unvaried. In these circumstances, the troops deteriorated both spiritually and physically. For the most part they were worn out.[21]

The First Army issued orders on the evening of the 2nd for the Canadian Corps to continue its advance to the Canal du Nord, and XVII Corps 'to encircle Quéant and Pronville from the north'. During the evening, however, Canadian divisional commanders told Currie that because of heavy casualties there would be difficulties in making a further advance without adequate preparation. In consequence the First Army's orders were cancelled, but at dawn of the next day it was discovered that the enemy had withdrawn from the entire front of the Canadian Corps down to V Corps of the Third Army. It was now a question of pursuing a retreating enemy. The 4th (British) Division captured Etaing, and the Canadians were able to advance up to the high ground overlooking the Canal du Nord where they came under artillery and machine-gun fire. XVII Corps found Quéant and Pronville had been evacuated; Inchy was taken, but its approach to the canal also came under heavy fire. The other corps in the Third Army advanced against little opposition until it, too, came within range of fire from the canal. There was little activity on the front of the Fourth Army which, in any case, was planning to force a passage across the Somme at St Christ, combined with an advance from Péronne. As a result of the German retirement, GHQ issued an order to the effect that the operating principle was now 'to press the enemy with advanced guards with the object of driving the enemy's rear guards and outposts, and ascertaining his dispositions... No deliberate operation on a large scale will be undertaken for the present. Troops will, as far as possible, be rested...'

Between 21 August and 3 September the Third and First Armies had extended the attack begun by the Fourth Army on 8 August. The latter Army had advanced seven miles on its right and fourteen on its left, and the Third and First Armies had moved forward fifteen and twelve miles respectively. According to the Official History: 'At least nineteen additional German divisions had been thrown in on the front of the Fourth Army, and at least seventeen on that of the Third Army and the Canadian Corps of the First Army. These enemy reinforcements were about the same number as the total of British divisions which they sought to stop.'

On 21 August Winston Churchill, then Minister of Munitions, came to see Haig. According to Haig's diary:

He is most anxious to help us in every way, and is hurrying up the supply of '10-calibre head' shells, gas, Tanks, etc. His schemes are all timed for 'completion in next June!' I told him we ought to do our utmost to get a decision this autumn. We are engaged in a 'wearing out battle' and are outlasting and beating the enemy. If we allow the enemy a period of quiet, he will recover, and the 'wearing out' process must be recommenced. In reply I was told that the General Staff in London calculate that the decisive period of the war cannot arrive until next July.[22]

The mood in the War Cabinet for most of July had been one of pessimism. On 25 July Wilson had produced a memorandum entitled 'British Military Policy 1918–1919'. The memorandum had ranged over the Western Front and all the other theatres, but so far as the Western Front was concerned, Wilson considered that, despite the failure of the German attack at Reims begun on 15 July, enemy reserves were still substantial. An attack on the British front in Flanders as well as between Montdidier and Noyon was still a probability, but he thought it doubtful whether the Germans would make more than one further attack 'on a grand scale' in 1918. Should this occur, it might either be 'fought to a standstill' or, in the event of a successful attack on the British front, result in the abandonment of the Channel ports. If the Germans were stopped, it would involve a series of limited operations designed to push them back from 'vital strategical objectives', followed ultimately by the 'culminating military effort'. He then posed the question: 'When is this decisive effort to be made? That is to say, will it be possible to accomplish it in 1919 or must we wait until 1920?' After discussing all the possibilities, both on the Western Front and elsewhere, he answered his own question by taking 1 July 1919 'as the date by which we should complete our preparations for the decisive struggle'.

The memorandum was discussed at a meeting of the Imperial War Cabinet on 1 August. Wilson's diary records:

At the meeting of Prime Ministers ... Lloyd George was very captious about my paper, saying that no calculation had been made about losses for the coming 12 months, and so on... Practically all the Prime Ministers ... and Milner, are of opinion that we cannot beat the Boches on the Western Front, and so they go wandering about looking for laurels. Hughes [Australian Prime Minister] sees clearer than others, and sees that we must beat the Boche army if we want a real peace.[23]

Foch met Haig on 4 September and gave him a Directive dated the 3rd which had already been sent to Pétain and Pershing. He referred to the success of the Allied offensive from the Aisne to the Scarpe which, he considered, should now be widened to include all Allied forces 'following convergent directions from favourable parts of the front'. To achieve this, the British Army, supported by the left of the French Army, was to continue in the direction of Cambrai and St Quentin, and the centre to force the enemy beyond the Aisne and the Ailette. The American Army was to bite off ... as soon as possible, the St Mihiel salient in order to free the Paris–Avricourt railway, and then develop an offensive in the direction of Mézières a fortnight later.

The events of August might have given the impression that it was only the British Army that was making any substantial progress on the Western Front. This, up to a point, would have some validity. The American Army had not taken any significant part, the Belgians none at all, and whereas the French Tenth and Third Armies were making progress north of Soissons, the First Army had barely kept contact with the British Fourth Army on its left. It has to be borne in mind, however, that the French had suffered severe losses in the fighting on the Aisne and the Marne between May and July, whilst, from the French viewpoint, the British Army had had time to recuperate after the failure of the German offensives in March and April. The Belgians could not take on any significant rôle unless it was combined with an offensive by the British Second Army on its right, and a large proportion of the American Army still needed to develop its organisation and continue training. Foch, however, visited Pershing on 30 August to discuss future American operations. Foch had proposed that after the St Mihiel operation, the Americans should join with the French Second Army in an attack between the Meuse and the Argonne, and with the French Fourth Army in an offensive in Champagne. Pershing objected on the grounds that 'the American people and the American Government expect that the American Army shall act as such and not be dispersed here and there along the Western Front'. Foch had then asked whether Pershing wished to take part in the battle, to which Pershing replied, 'Most assuredly, but as an American Army and in no other way.' Foch replied, 'That means it will take a month. We must start on 15 September.' The next day Pershing wrote to Foch agreeing that an attack in the Mézières direction might produce decisive results, but added:

> There is one thing that must not be done and that is to disperse the American forces among the Allied Armies... I do insist that the American Army must be employed as a whole, either east of the Argonne or west of the Argonne, and not four or five divisions here and six or seven there.[24]

Nevertheless, he agreed to carry out the St Mihiel operation, and at a further meeting with Foch on 2 September it was agreed that the American Army would operate under its own commander on the Meuse–Argonne front in an attack on 25 September.

By 10 September it was apparent that the enemy was retiring on the Fourth Army front with the ultimate intention of making a stand behind the ramparts of the

Hindenburg Position; but the Germans hoped to delay, if not thwart, any attack on the position by a series of defensive lines in front of it. To breach the main Hindenburg Position would require a period of preparation because, for the time being, it was no longer a question of pursuing a retreating and demoralised enemy. On 8 September, Foch issued an addendum to his Directive of the 3rd. The British Army was to take as an objective 'the line Valenciennes–Solesmes–Le Cateau–Wassigny' (the line of the German Hermann position varying between seven and twenty-five miles east of the Hindenburg Position). GHQ thereupon sought the views of his Army commanders on the enemy's dispositions, probable intentions and morale, together with 'their proposals and recommendations for deliberate offensive operations ... on the fronts of their respective Armies'.

Rawlinson (Fourth Army), in his reply, considered that the four enemy defence lines (mostly old British trenches) fronting the Hindenburg Position would have to be taken preparatory to the assault on the main position. He saw no great difficulty in this, but the fourth defence line, known as the advanced Hindenburg Position, on a ridge overlooking the main Hindenburg Line itself, had been strengthened since 1917 and could present a formidable obstacle if held with determination. He advocated, as the first step, an assault on the first three defence lines to be undertaken as soon as possible to throw the enemy off balance. Byng (Third Army) thought that the enemy's morale was low and that many, given the opportunity, would surrender. He proposed an attack east of the Canal du Nord which, if successful, could be exploited in an advance by the First Army. Plumer (Second Army) had proposed pushing the enemy back between Armentières and Ypres and recapturing Messines, but Foch wished to involve the Belgian Army and the British Second Army in a combined assault to gain the high ground east of Ypres. This was supported by Haig, and it was decided that the Belgian King (Albert) would command an attacking force of nine Belgian and two British divisions with exploitation by the Belgians and three French cavalry divisions. The ultimate objective was to drive the Germans back to the Dutch frontier. (This had been Haig's unrealised objective in July 1917.)

In early September, the left of the Third Army, now close up against the Hindenburg Position, did little more than carry out patrol activity, but its centre and right wheeled to conform with the forward movement of the Fourth Army, which made excellent progress. The Australians, against sporadic opposition, crossed the Somme at two places below Péronne, and III Corps achieved an advance of almost two miles. The Germans facing the French Armies were also retiring to the Hindenburg Position, giving up ground 'in front of the First and Third Armies, in front of the right of the Tenth, on the whole front of the Sixth and before the extreme left of the Fifth... In the face of this event, General Fayolle ordered that the pursuit should be begun and carried out with the greatest possible energy.'

On 6 September, Ludendorff attended at OHL where Hindenburg stressed the seriousness of the situation. General von Lossberg (Chief of the General Staff, Fourth Army) recorded the following account:

> He then left the further conduct of the conference to General Ludendorff. The latter impressed me as being in a very nervous state, completely different from his former determined manner. The troops came in for a good deal of condemnation from his mouth. He made the troops and their leaders responsible for the events of the past days, without recognising that his own faulty leading bore the main blame for what had happened... He then sketched the plans of OHL for the Hermann and Hunding–Brunnhild Position, also the Antwerp–Meuse Position. In my statement I reported that General von Boehn on his daily visits to the front with me had assured himself that the Hindenburg Position was much dilapidated, had very little wire, and that on account of the condition of the troops a lengthy resistance in it could no longer be expected. The construction of the Hermann Position had not yet been begun.[25]

It was then suggested that after the loss of the Hindenburg Position, the whole German front should immediately be withdrawn to the Antwerp–Meuse Position, which should be constructed without delay. Ludendorff, however, would not agree to this 'and stuck to his plan to construct the Hermann and Hunding–Brunnhild Position, and to go back to it after the loss of the Hindenburg Position'.

Ludendorff, after the strain of the August reverses, was now a sick man and undergoing psychiatric treatment. He suffered a severe set-back when the news reached him of the American Army's attack on the St Mihiel salient. The salient had been held by the Germans since September 1914 and threatened the entire region between Verdun and Nancy as well as blocking the main railway line from Paris to the east. The main attack was delivered by the American First Army with seven divisions (each twice the size of a French division) followed by three further American divisions and three French divisions. The Germans suspected that an attack was imminent and initiated a withdrawal. After a four-hour preliminary bombardment, commencing at 1 a.m. on 12 September, the infantry, accompanied by tanks, advanced and secured all their objectives by the afternoon: 16,000 prisoners were taken and over 400 guns, at a cost of 7,500 casualties. The attack came as a bitter blow to the Germans. Apart from the loss of the salient and the casualties suffered, came the realisation that the American Army had at last demonstrated that in a single day it could smash its way through a strongly held position and repulse counter-attacks.

It was now evident that the views held by Haig and Foch on the prospects for a decisive result on the Western Front were at variance with those held in London, which envisaged that no substantial progress could be made until at least July 1919.

Foch was determined to spare France another winter of war, and on 8 September Haig told Churchill that he considered 'the Allies should get a decision as soon as possible, This month or next, not next spring or summer as the Cabinet proposed.' On 10 September Haig had an interview at the War Office with the Secretary of State for War (Lord Milner):

> I had specially asked for this interview, and I stated that the object of my visit was to explain how greatly the situation in the field had changed to the advantage of the Allies. I considered it to be of first importance that the Cabinet should realise how all our plans and methods are at once affected by this change.
>
> Within the last four weeks we had captured 77,000 prisoners and 800 guns! There has never been such a victory in the annals of Britain, and its effects are not yet apparent. The German prisoners now taken will not obey their officers or their NCOs... The discipline of the German Army is quickly going, and the German Officer is no longer what he was. It seems to me to be the beginning of the end...
>
> Briefly, in my opinion, the character of the war has changed. What is wanted now at once is to provide the means to exploit our recent great successes to the full. Reserves in England should be regarded as Reserves for the French front...
>
> If we act with energy now, a decision can be obtained in the very near future...
>
> Lord Milner fully agreed and said he would do his best to help.[26]

The task of the Third and Fourth Armies was now to clear the outpost positions fronting the main Hindenburg Line in preparation for the main assault. On 12 September the left of V Corps, IV Corps and VI Corps attacked at 5.25 a.m. with the objective of gaining a line extending from north of Havrincourt through Trescault to Gouzeaucourt. Good progress was made at first, but enemy resistance soon hardened and a number of counter-attacks were mounted, but these were all repulsed. Havrincourt village was captured in the morning but the enemy launched a determined counter-attack in the early evening which was eventually beaten off. The village of Trescault offered strong opposition until it was finally taken. During the day, the Third Army, against stubborn resistance, had pushed forward almost a mile on a five-mile front and was close to achieving its final objective. On the 13th Haig agreed to Rawlinson's proposal to attack the outpost positions between le Verguier and Epéhy on the 18th. There was to be no preliminary bombardment as Rawlinson was hoping to obtain surprise, and because of the need to conserve tanks for the main assault on the Hindenburg Line, only twenty tanks would be employed which, with one exception, were not to go beyond the first objective.

At 5.20 a.m., in miserable conditions of heavy rain and mist, the assault began. On the right, the 6th Division of IX Corps could make no progress because of enfilade fire from the strong-points of Round Hill and Manchester Hill in the French sector which, according to the *Official History*, the French 34th Division 'made only a very half-hearted attempt' to capture. Fresnoy was entered but could not be held, which frustrated the attack of the right of the 1st Division, although elsewhere it reached its second objective despite a counter-attack. The Australian 1st and 4th Divisions, however, were much more successful: they by-passed le Verguier, leaving it be mopped up later, and tanks provided useful assistance in subduing machine-gun posts. By 10 a.m. they had gained most of the third objective overlooking the St Quentin canal, and in the process had taken over 4,000 prisoners and several guns and trench mortars. III Corps had the most difficult task – to capture the strongly held villages of Ronssoy, Lempire and Epéhy/Peizière

> and the area around them, which had formed part of the Battle Zone of March 1918. This was a maze of trenches... [For the enemy] it was of vital importance to retain this front, as it covered the tunnelled portion of the St Quentin canal, over which a tank attack could be made without meeting the then insuperable obstacle which the canal presented elsewhere.[27]

The attack of the 74th Division surprised the defenders, and Templeux le Guérard and the Quarries beyond were captured with many prisoners. The 18th Division took Ronssoy with the aid of three tanks, but the attempt to reach the second objective was frustrated by the arrival of a fresh German division. The objectives of the 12th and 58th Divisions were Epéhy and Peizière respectively. Epéhy was eventually captured, although the 12th Division suffered severe casualties, and Peizière fell to the 58th Division, but neither division could reach its first objective. Thus only the centre of the Fourth Army's attack had reached the third objective, the flanks failing to reach either the first or second of them. V Corps, on the extreme right of the Third Army, joined in the Fourth Army attack with the intention of securing its first and second objectives. In this it was successful, taking over 1,800 prisoners.

Between 19 and 26 September the main action took place on the front of the Fourth Army in order to advance the wings to conform with the position reached by the Australian Corps in the centre. The French First Army took on a more positive role by capturing the trouble-spots of Round Hill and Manchester Hill after methodical bombardments by British and French artillery, and by the 26th the right of the Fourth Army overlooked the St Quentin canal. On the left, III Corps had to overcome stubborn resistance and counter-attacks in its advance towards the second objective, which was gained in part on the 26th, but the third objective remained out of reach. Nevertheless, the Third and Fourth Armies now overlooked the Hindenburg Line itself and the defences beyond and were poised for the forthcoming assault. At 10.30 p.m. on the 26th the preliminary bombardment began for what was soon to prove the climactic battle of the war.

Notes

1. Carstairs, C., *A Generation Missing*, Heinemann (London, 1930)
2. Smeddle, Captain H., Papers of, held in the Department of Documents, Imperial War Museum, London
3. Edmonds, Brigadier-General Sir James, (comp.), *Official History of the War: Military Operations France and Belgium 1918*, Vol. IV, HMSO (London, 1947)
4. *Ibid.*, quoted from *Bavarian Official Account*
5. Blake, Robert, (ed.), *The Private Papers of Douglas Haig 1914–1919*, Eyre & Spottiswoode (London, 1952)
6. Edmonds, *op. cit.*
7. *Ibid.*, quoted from history of 232nd Reserve Infantry Regiment
8. Feilding, Lieutenant-Colonel R., *War Letters to a Wife: France and Flanders 1915–1919*, Medici Society (London, 1930)
9. Edmonds, *op. cit.*
10. Edmonds, *op. cit.*, quoted from General von Kuhl's official report to the *Reichstag Committee of Enquiry into the Loss of the War*
11. Foch, Marshal, *The Memoirs of Marshal Foch*, Heinemann (London, 1931)
12. Blake, *op. cit.*
13. Quoted in Edmonds, *op. cit.*
14. Meisel, F., Papers of, held in the Department of Documents, Imperial War Museum, London
15. Edmonds, *op. cit.*
16. Monash, General Sir J., *The Australian Victories in France in 1918*, Hutchinson (London, 1920)
17. Williams, H. R., *Comrades of the Great Adventure*, Angus & Robertson (Sydney, 1935)
18. Blake, *op. cit.*
19. Edmonds, *op. cit.*
20. Henley, Brigadier-General Hon. A. M. (42nd East Lancashire Division), 20. Papers of, held in the Department of Documents, Imperial War Museum, London
21. Edmonds, *op. cit*, quoted from *Bavarian Official History*
22. Blake, *op. cit.*
23. Callwell, Major-General Sir C., *Field-Marshal Sir Henry Wilson*, Vol. 2, Cassell (London, 1927)
24. Edmonds, *op. cit.*
25. Lossberg, General F., *Meine Tätigkeit im Weltkriege 1914–1918* (Berlin, 1939)
26. Blake, *op. cit.*
27. Edmonds, *op. cit.*

10

Attacking the Hindenburg Position

Haig informed Foch on 22 September that he was prepared to undertake the attack in the direction of St Quentin and Cambrai. It would take place in two stages: the First Army would capture Bourlon Wood, and at the same time the Third Army would advance eastwards to Le Cateau–Solesmes. The date chosen was 27 September. Two days later, the Fourth Army, protected on the right by the French First Army, would deliver the main attack against the Hindenburg Line. Apparently, however, the War Cabinet were not fully aware of Haig's intentions. Lord Milner had spent ten days in France, and on his return on the 23rd he told Wilson of his concern. The latter's diary records:

> Long talk with Milner this afternoon on his return from 10 days in France. He thinks Haig ridiculously optimistic and is afraid he may embark on another Passchendaele. He warned Haig that if he knocked his present army about there was no other to replace it. Milner saw many generals in France and they were all most optimistic.

Two days later his diary entry reads:

> Douglas Haig writes for Yeomanry, cyclists, motor machine-guns, lorries – anything to make him more mobile in the coming great attack. This is the first I have heard of this big attack, except that Bonar Law [Deputy Prime Minister] said yesterday that Hughes [Australian Prime Minister] had given him all details of the British-French-American attack.[1]

It would not only be a 'British-French-American' attack, it would include the Belgian Army and 'for the first time in the War all the Allied Armies on the Western Front from the Meuse to the sea [would be] on the move together...'[2] The British Army was to attack the Hindenburg Line and all its defences beyond; the Belgian Army, combined with the British Second Army, was to gain the high ground east of Ypres; and the French and American Armies were to launch a combined offensive in the Argonne. All these attacks would take place between 26 and 29 September. At this time the combined Allied strength on the Western Front amounted to 171 divisions whereas the German total was slightly less at 165. Nevertheless, as the Official Historian noted, 'the Allies enjoyed the advantage of high morale and complete confidence: the enemy had lost the initiative and was discouraged, his effectives were falling and through lack of reinforcements could not be replaced...'[3]

On the 26th, the American First Army, supported by the French Fourth Army, attacked the German positions on either side of the Argonne Forest. The ultimate objective was to cut the east-west railway, a vital German supply line, running through the important junction of Mézières. It was a strongly defended position on a front forty-four miles wide and some fourteen miles deep, divided equally between the French and Americans, with a thickly wooded forest at its centre. The forest was almost wholly in the American sector, which included several wooded hills, the largest of which was Montfaucon (1,200 feet), and backed by the Kriemhilde Stellung – a south-easterly extension of the Brunnhild Position. Pershing described the defences as 'fortified strongpoints, dugouts, successive lines of trenches, and an unlimited number of concrete machine-gun emplacements. A dense network of wire entanglements covered every position. With the advantage of commanding ground, the enemy was peculiarly well located to pour oblique and flanking artillery fire on any assailant attempting to advance within range between the Meuse and the Argonne. It was small wonder that the enemy had rested for four years on this front without being molested.'[4]

Nevertheless, it was Pershing's choice: he had opted for the Argonne front rather than Champagne on the grounds that no other troops than the Americans possessed the morale or offensive spirit to assault it.

The front, as a whole, was defended by twenty-four divisions with twelve in reserve, facing nine American divisions (each twice the size of a French division) with three in reserve, and twenty-two French divisions with a cavalry corps in reserve. The Germans had suspected that an attack on the Argonne front might be imminent, but did not believe that an American Army would be involved, because a substantial proportion of the Army was in the St Mihiel sector, some forty miles to the south-east. The logistical problems of placing 600,000 American troops in the Argonne sector in less than three weeks and, at the same time, displacing over 200,000 French troops, were immense, quite apart from assembling nearly 3,000 guns and ammunition.

The American artillery bombardment began at 11 p.m. on the 25th:

At the beginning of the battle most of the light and heavy guns [of the American Army] including corps and Army artillery material and supply trains, as at St Mihiel, were provided by the French, some by the British, and practically none from home. We had 189 light tanks, all of French manufacture, 25 per cent of which were handled by French personnel, but no heavy tanks could be obtained.[5]

At first all went well: the Americans advanced between two and four miles, the French slightly less. Montfaucon was captured on the 27th, but progress became slower as German reinforcements arrived. Nevertheless, the American advance achieved deeper penetration than the French, and although by the 28th the Americans were approaching the Kriemhilde line, they could make little further progress against strong opposition. American casualties were so heavy that the three leading divisions had to be relieved. After the success of the St Mihiel attack, the failure to

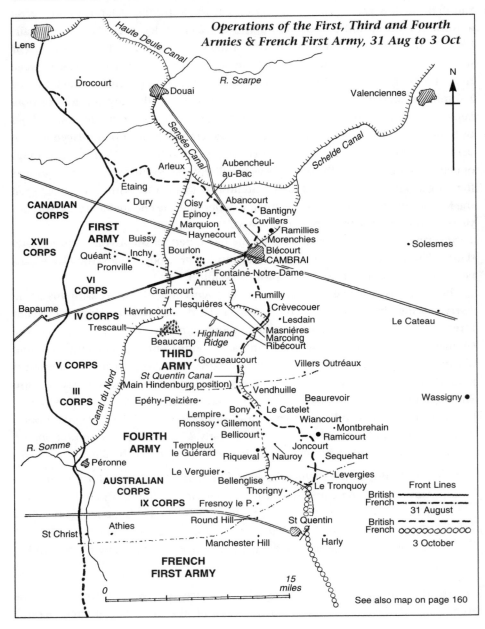

Operations of the First, Third and Fourth Armies & French First Army, 31 Aug to 3 Oct

N

Lens

Haute Deule Canal

Drocourt

Douai

R. Scarpe

Valenciennes

Sensée Canal

Aubencheul-au-Bac

Schelde Canal

Arleux

Étaing

CANADIAN CORPS

FIRST ARMY

XVII CORPS

· Dury

Oisy

Epinoy·

Marquion

Buissy

Haynecourt

· Abancourt

·Bantigny

Cuvillers

·Ramillies

·Morenchies

Quéant ·

·Inchy·

Bourlon

Blécourt

CAMBRAI

Pronville

VI CORPS

Graincourt

· Anneux

Fontaine-Notre-Dame

·Rumilly

Bapaume

IV CORPS

Havrincourt·

Flesquières

Crèvecouer

·Lesdain

Le Cateau

Trescault

· Highland

Beaucamp Ridge

Masnières

Marcoing

Ribécourt

V CORPS

III CORPS

THIRD ARMY

· Gouzeaucourt

St Quentin Canal

(Main Hindenburg position)

Épéhy-Peizière·

· Vendhuille

Villers Outréaux

Beaurevoir

Wassigny ●

Lempire·

Ronssoy· Gillemont

Bony ·

Le Catelet

Wiancourt

·Montbrehain

FOURTH ARMY

Bellicourt·

Templeux le Guérard

Riqueval · Nauroy

Joncourt

· Ramicourt

R. Somme

Péronne

Le Verguier·

Sequehart

AUSTRALIAN CORPS

Bellenglise

Thorigny ·

·Levergies

Le Tronquoy

IX CORPS

Fresnoy le P.·

Front Lines

British ——————
French —·—·—·—·
31 August

British — — — —
French ooooooooooo
3 October

St Christ·

Athies

Round Hill

Manchester Hill

St Quentin

Harly

FRENCH FIRST ARMY

0   15 miles

See also map on page 160

138

achieve greater penetration on the Argonne was a disappointment to Pershing who had hoped that by sheer weight of numbers he would force his way through the defences. The Argonne front, however, was of such crucial importance to the Germans that they were determined to offer the strongest resistance. Moreover, the Americans were handicapped by the speed at which their supply arrangements had had to be made, and by the availability of only three roads to the front: congestion was such that on one occasion traffic was blocked for twelve hours.

The first of the attacks to be carried out by the British Army planned on 27 September was to be undertaken by the First and Third Armies. The Canadian Corps of the First Army was to force the crossings of the Canal du Nord on a frontage of 2,500 yards and then fan out to almost 10,000 yards in order to secure a line between the Schelde and Sensée canals. The Canal du Nord was under construction at the outbreak of the war in 1914 and was only partially completed: large stretches were dry but on the extreme right of the First Army's front it was dry for only a short stretch of just over a mile from the Army boundary to Inchy. Beyond that point it contained water up to its junction with the Sensée canal. The Canadian Corps faced a series of obstacles in order to reach its ultimate objective of a line between Morenchies (on the Schelde) and Aubencheul au Bac (on the Sensée). It had to force the crossings of the Canal du Nord, then breach the Canal du Nord Line and its extension, the Marquion Line, immediately to the east of the canal, and then attack the Marcoing Line, some four miles farther east. Currie, the Corps commander, planned the attack in two phases, using two divisions in the centre and two on the flanks to establish a line beyond Bourlon Wood, after which all four divisions would advance to seize the bridges over the Schelde north-east of Cambrai. There would be no preliminary bombardment; the first phase would be under the cover of creeping artillery barrages combined with machine-gun barrages, and sixteen tanks would accompany the two leading Canadian divisions. XVII Corps (Third Army) on the extreme right was to co-operate with the advance of the Canadian Corps.

In the first phase, the 1st and 4th Canadian Divisions crossed the Canal du Nord without much difficulty, although heavy fire encountered from the Marquion Line caused severe casualties. Bourlon Wood and village were captured by the early evening. The 11th British Division arrived to pass through the 1st Canadian Division and, with the 3rd Canadian Brigade, captured the village of Marquion against little further opposition. In the second phase, the 1st Canadian Division captured Haynecourt, and its 2nd Brigade reached the Cambrai–Douai road, some three miles beyond the third objective. The 11th British Division captured Oisy and Epinoy, and the 56th British Division, advancing northwards on both sides of the Canal du Nord, met few problems and eventually gained contact with the 11th Division at Oisy at 2 a.m. on the following day. Only on the right of the First Army's sector was the third objective not attained because of problems experienced by XVII Corps.

Otherwise the attack of the Canadian Corps was a conspicuous success, achieving an advance, at its greatest, of some five miles; only the Marquion Line, on the Canal du Nord, had offered any serious resistance.

It was a different picture for the Third Army whose task was to keep pace with the first phase of the Canadian Corps attack. XVII Corps and a division of VI Corps had to cross the Canal du Nord in their attack on the Marcoing–Caintaing Line while the rest of VI Corps was to capture the Flesquières Ridge and clear the Hindenburg Support Line. IV Corps was to take Beaucamp and Highland Ridge. The ground to be covered, however, was seamed with old trenches, and in contrast to the experience of the Canadian Corps, the enemy was intent on making a stand. The 52nd Division of XVII Corps had few problems in crossing the canal, but were delayed by fire from a sugar factory west of Anneux. The 63rd Division, passing through, was again delayed by its attempts to capture Anneux and Graincourt (the second objective) which was not achieved until 4 p.m.

> Away to the left was the real trouble, for there the British advance was hung up before the village of Graincourt. It was being stubbornly defended, and the German garrison was inflicting heavy punishment on the British troops, whose dead lay thick about the ruins. Strong reinforcements of the Guards Brigade, however, were coming up, and I watched them attack afresh. They were well handled. The fire of several batteries was directed on the village, and the men went forward in artillery formation, until they had established a fire line, when they rose to their feet and charged. Many fell, but the attack was pushed home, and soon the men disappeared into the wrecked houses, after which the enemy machine guns fell silent, and batches of prisoners were marched out.[6]

The 57th Division should then have passed through to the third objective but failed to recognise signals to advance. In consequence it did not move off until 6 p.m. The four divisions of VI Corps also experienced problems. The Guards Division captured Flesquières and eventually reached its second objective but was then frustrated by a strong counter-attack by a fresh division. The 3rd Division captured Ribécourt against determined opposition, and the 62nd Division, which was to pass through, encountered the counter-attack that had stopped the Guards, and was driven back. The two divisions on the extreme right reached their second objective in spite of heavy casualties: ten out of the twelve tanks accompanying were knocked out almost immediately.

On the 28th the Third Army had a much more successful day. The 57th and 63rd Divisions of XVII Corps penetrated the Marcoing–Caintaing Line and reached the third objective of the previous day. Pushing on, they reached the Schelde canal, and although the bridges had been destroyed some parties managed to cross by means of the lock gates. VI Corps crossed the canal at Marcoing, capturing the village in the process. On the same day, the 3rd Canadian Division on the right wing of the First

Army was ordered to capture Fontaine Notre Dame and push on to the Marcoing Line. Fontaine was captured with little difficulty but the advance was temporarily halted by fire from the Marcoing Line. The line was penetrated, however, on the left and the advance reached the Cambrai–Douai road. As a result, the right wing of the Canadian Corps was now level with the Third Army's left wing.

On the same day (28th) the Belgian Army and the British Second Army launched attacks in the Ypres area extending from Clerken in the north to the Ypres–Comines canal in the south. The main objective of the Belgian Army was to gain possession of the Ypres Ridge extending from Staden through Passchendaele to the boundary at Broodseinde; here the Second Army would assault the continuation of the ridge as far as the Ypres–Comines canal, a mile north of Hollebeke.

These attacks were to take place over a battlefield of bitter memories. In 1917, it had taken the British Army four and a half months to reach Passchendaele, meanwhile suffering grievous casualties in appalling conditions and at a cost of a quarter of a million casualties. Now the same ground had to be crossed again. The fearsome artillery bombardments of 1917 had destroyed the fragile drainage system and left a wilderness of water-filled shell craters, decaying trenches, rusting wire entanglements and all the débris of a war that had passed by. It appeared a daunting proposition but, in contrast to 1917, the position was not held in strength (only five divisions), and the enemy's resolve to resist had all but disintegrated.

The main direction of the Second Army's attack was on the left, straddling the Ypres–Menin road. In the centre and on the right, X and XV Corps were 'to watch their opportunity and take every advantage of the enemy weakening on their front to press his retirement'. Attacking without a preliminary bombardment at 5.30 a.m., the four divisions (with two in reserve) of II and XIX Corps swept through sporadic opposition, gaining all their objectives by 4 p.m. and establishing a line from Broodseinde to Kortewilde on the Ypres–Comines canal. Farther south, patrols of X and XV Corps met stronger resistance, although some progress was made. The nine divisions of the Belgian Army advanced simultaneously after a preliminary bombardment of three hours. They overran four German lines of defence, captured Passchendaele and made contact with the left of the Second Army at Broodseinde, although Staden remained out of reach. Nevertheless, an advance of five miles had been attained, equalling the Second Army's progress. The success of the joint offensive forced the Germans to begin a withdrawal from the Wytschaete–Messines area, and Crown Prince Rupprecht recorded in his diary: 'The worst is that according to a report from the Fourth Army, the troops will no longer stand up to a serious attack.'[7]

At 6 p.m. on the 28th, Ludendorff saw Hindenburg:

I explained to him my views as to a peace offer and a request for an armistice. The position could only grow worse, on account of the Balkan situation

[Bulgaria was seeking an armistice], even if we held our ground in the West. Our one task now was to act definitely and firmly, without delay. The Field-Marshal listened to me with emotion. He answered that he intended to say the same to me in the evening, that he had considered the whole situation carefully, and thought the step necessary. We were also at one in the view that the armistice conditions would have to permit a regular and orderly evacuation of the occupied territory and the resumption of hostilities on our own borders... The Field-Marshal and I parted with a firm handshake, like men who have buried their dearest hopes, and who are resolved to hold together in the hardest hours of human life as they held together in success.[8]

Meanwhile the British Fourth Army was poised to launch its attack on the Hindenburg Line. The preliminary bombardment had begun at 10.30 p.m. on the 26th, fired by over 1,600 field, medium and heavy guns and howitzers. For the first time, a British version of mustard gas was directed at enemy artillery positions together with 'sustained shelling of strong-points and defended localities, as well as the entrances of tunnels and dug-outs, and telephone exchanges, to cut lanes in wire entanglements and demoralise the garrison by forcing them to keep under cover...' The position to be attacked was covered by the St Quentin canal, except for one stretch of some three miles between Bellicourt to just short of Vendhuille where the canal ran in a tunnel, and a similar stretch of about a mile at le Tronquoy. Thus the canal presented a natural and formidable obstacle and, moreover, the ground above the tunnelled stretch was strongly defended with several lines of trenches and thick belts of wire entanglements. Behind the front position, the Hindenburg Line itself, were two defensive lines – the Hindenburg Support and Reserve systems. The position was held by seven divisions which could be reinforced by six more in three days. Arrayed for the assault were IX Corps (nine divisions, including two American and three Australian), III Corps (two divisions), and XVIII Corps (three divisions plus the Cavalry Corps), together with three tank brigades.

As a preliminary operation before the main attack, the Preliminary Objective – a position overlooking the section of the canal in tunnel – had to be secured; but to reach the objective three enemy strongpoints would have to be overcome. Monash decided to give the task to the American 27th Division and the operation was launched on the 27th. At 5.30 a.m., on a misty morning which prevented aerial observation and, in consequence, artillery support, the 106th Regiment, supported by twelve tanks, began its assault and immediately met resolute opposition. Some of the strong-points were reached but could not be held, there were heavy losses in tanks, and in the face of determined counter-attacks the Americans were forced to withdraw to their start line. Unfortunately, some parties were still scattered between the start line and the objective, and this would have serious repercussions two days later.

When the news of the success of the Flanders attack reached Rawlinson, he recorded in his diary on the night of the 28th:

Today has been a record in the way of Allied successes on the Western Front. Under Foch's tuition and the lessons of over four years of war, we are really learning, and the synchronisation of the various attacks has been admirable. All three that have yet gone in have been very successful, and I am fully confident that mine, which starts at dawn tomorrow, will be no less victorious. With new troops like the Americans, one has, of course, anxious moments. For instance, today it was quite impossible to find out just where they were. Alarmist rumours came in from the front, and the evidence seemed to show that they were not on the Gillemont Farm line, where they should have been, but the airmen reported repeatedly that they were. It was just the same on the Somme. New troops never know just where they are... I feel pretty happy about the prospects as a whole, for, if the Americans are inexperienced, they are as keen as mustard and splendid men... D. H. [Haig] came to see me... He thinks we shall finish the war this year, and I hope he may be right, but it is no certainty.[9]

The task of IX Corps was to force the passage of the canal between le Tronquoy and the Riqueval Bridge, and the main thrust was to be spearheaded by the 46th (Midland) Division whose aim was to reach the first objective, after which the 32nd Division would pass through to the second. The west bank of the canal was strongly held, and the canal itself, some thirty-five feet wide, resembled the moat of a castle 'defended by belts of wire in the water and on the banks, and by flanking emplacements'. It was indeed a fearful obstacle, but the 137th Brigade of the 46th Division was to achieve not only the greatest success of the day, but one of the most notable feats of the war. After a stormy night, the seemingly inevitable ground fog had formed. At 5.50 a.m., and greatly helped by the impact of the preliminary bombardment on the canal defences, the brigade, 'in small parties and protected by the fog ... worked their way up to within a short distance of the enemy trenches, then, rising with a shout, dashed in with the bayonet, the enemy giving way in all directions and many of them making their way through the fog, in spite of considerable casualties inflicted by the artillery as they retired'.[10] Covered by a field artillery barrage 'described as one of the finest ever seen', and equipped with lifebelts from cross-Channel steamers, officers swam across the canal with ropes, followed by the infantry with the aid of collapsible boats, lifelines and rafts. The Riqueval bridge was seized intact just before it was due to be demolished and, after a pause, the advance was resumed at 7.30 a.m. with the 138th and 139th Brigades following up, capturing Bellenglise en route. The division gained its objective by 3.30 p.m.

The mist by then had completely cleared and the sight was one for which every commander worth the name had lived during the long years of war. As far as the eye could see, our troops were pushing forward; batteries were crossing the canal and coming into action; Engineers everywhere at work; large bodies of prisoners were coming in from all sides; and the men of the 32nd Division were advancing fast. The enemy were shelling the line of the canal and Bellenglise, but no one seemed to mind. It was indeed a breakthrough.[11]

The attack on the left was to be undertaken by the American 27th and 30th Divisions, after which the 3rd and 5th Australian Divisions would pass through to the first objective. On the extreme left, the 27th Division was still faced with the strong-points fronting the Hindenburg Main Line which the 106th Regiment had failed to capture two days earlier. Moreover, they were situated in an area where, as mentioned, doubt existed as to the plight of troops still scattered between the original start-line and the preliminary objective. This uncertainty had inhibited the delivery of the preliminary bombardment up until zero hour on the 29th, so that it was concentrated on the Preliminary Objective, thus falling beyond the strong-points. The same uncertainty also affected the positioning of the creeping barrage, compelling the 27th Division to advance without its protection. Furthermore, of the thirty-four tanks accompanying the division, twelve were soon knocked out, seven were ditched and ten wandered into an old British minefield. Despite these severe handicaps, the Americans struggled on in the face of fire from artillery and machine guns, eventually reaching a line just short of the Preliminary Objective. The 30th Division fared better. It crossed the Hindenburg Main and Support Lines, capturing Bellicourt and the southern end of the tunnel, and pushed on to Nauroy. The 27th Division's difficulties impacted on the 3rd Australian Division which, advancing in thick fog, came under heavy fire from the strong-points. These were eventually captured in the afternoon, but a section of the Hindenburg Main Line still remained in enemy hands, causing problems with enfilade fire. Capitalising on the success of the 30th Division, however, the 5th Australian Division crossed the front line of the Hindenburg Position and reached the line of the Bellicourt tunnel by 11 a.m. By then enemy resistance had strengthened, and the 15th and 8th Brigades, accompanied by twelve tanks and eight Whippets, renewed the attack at 3 p.m. All the tanks were soon put out of action, as were five of the Whippets. Advancing against machine-gun fire from the Hindenburg Support Line, the 15th Brigade passed through troops of the 30th Division to capture part of the Support Line, and the 8th Brigade came abreast of the 32nd Division (IX Corps).

Thus the results of the day had been one of mixed fortunes. The attack in the centre had been most successful, accomplishing an advance of over three miles and, in the process, penetrating both the Hindenburg Main and Support systems.

Progress of the advance on the left had been disappointing, and on the extreme right where the objective had been to 'exploit southward with a view to assisting the French First Army'. A limited advance had been made to the St Quentin–Bellenglise road, but the French contribution had been merely support by 'fire and demonstration'.

On the same day, the Third Army's attack continued along its entire front. Little was achieved on the right, but in the centre the New Zealand Division achieved a noteworthy success by gaining all its objectives. It forced the southern end of the Marcoing Line and advanced over two miles. Both VI and XVII Corps were equally successful, capturing the remaining portion of the Marcoing Line, seizing Masnières on the St Quentin canal, and establishing a bridgehead on the Schelde canal. Farther north, the Canadian Corps of the First Army gained some ground east and north-east of Cambrai. The line reached was only a mile from Cambrai, and it could only be a matter of days before the town fell.

Ludendorff learned on the 28th that Bulgaria was seeking a separate armistice. This news, coming on top of the reverses experienced on the Western Front and coupled with the knowledge that Austria-Hungary was seeking peace, brought Ludendorff close to physical collapse; there is some evidence that he suffered a genuine fit. In September 1915, Germany and Austria had decided to attack Serbia in order to free the railway communication with Turkey, and in this venture they were joined by Bulgaria who hoped to gain Serbian territory in Macedonia. A Franco-British force arrived in September to assist Serbia, and by the following July the Allied force totalled nearly 300,000 men (including Serbs) which was later increased to over half a million by the addition of Greek troops. In 1916 and 1917, the French and the Serbs mounted several abortive offensives, the mountainous country proving a formidable obstacle. The Germans had viewed the build-up of the Allied force with equanimity, regarding it as 'an enemy army, prisoner of itself'. It was bedevilled by conflicting international politics; moreover, the British War Cabinet was half-hearted about the campaign, having tried unsuccessfully to withdraw the six British divisions. In September 1918, however, the Allies launched a powerful offensive, and the Bulgarians, weary after three years of war, collapsed. There is a certain irony in the fact that what had always been regarded as a 'sideshow' should, in the ultimate, have had such a powerful effect on German morale.

Following the decision of Ludendorff and Hindenburg to seek an armistice, a fateful meeting was held at Supreme Headquarters at Spa on the next day (29th) in an atmosphere of foreboding. Apart from the Allied successes since 8 August and the deterioration in the Army's morale, there was the realisation that Germany's allies were now in acute difficulties. Bulgaria had sought an armistice on the 26th, Turkish forces were fast retreating before British pressure in Palestine, and the Austro-Hungarian army was close to collapse. Moreover, there was serious unrest in the Reichstag (German parliament). Ever since the days of Bismarck, Germany's first Chancellor, the Reichstag had lacked all power to control military affairs, which remained under the control of the Kaiser and the Chancellor. Since 1917, however, their influence had waned and control had passed to Ludendorff and Hindenburg, constituting, in effect, a military dictatorship, with the former the dominant force. Both had consistently refused to keep the Chancellor or von Hintze, and, for that matter, the Reichstag or the people, informed of the deteriorating military situation. Nevertheless, the privations of the civilian population were now such that liberal members of the Reichstag were demanding a change to democratic government, particularly as they knew that Austria had already made peace overtures.

The meeting was attended by Ludendorff and Hindenburg, Admiral von Hintze (Foreign Minister) and some General Staff representatives. Ludendorff reviewed the military situation, saying that an armistice was essential, 'our situation admits of no delay, not an hour is to be lost', and that the Reichstag should be informed. Von Hintze suggested that an armistice proposal should be made to the American President (Woodrow Wilson), based on the Fourteen Points he had announced as his terms for peace on 8 January 1918. He realised, however, that Ludendorff did not see an armistice as unconditional surrender, rather a breathing space to enable the German Army to withdraw from occupied territories and stand on the defensive in the Homeland. Von Hintze, who was dismayed at this approach, explained that 'such a sudden shift from the fanfares of victory to the dirges of defeat would work upon the army, the nation, the monarchy, and the Empire' and that 'along with the request for an armistice, indeed prior to it, there must exist a readiness for peace'. Ludendorff would not agree with this until it was pointed out to him that without 'readiness for peace' the Allies would undoubtedly impose unacceptable terms. Yet even then Hindenburg considered that any peace treaty should allow the German annexation of the coal-mining area of Longwy and Briey in France. Von Hintze then suggested that if 'revolution from above' was 'set going ... on the initiative of the Monarch, it should form a bridge to make transition from victory to ... defeat bearable by bringing into co-operation with the Government as many interested people as possible'. By this means the Kaiser would announce a change to democratic government which would then have the responsibility of deciding whether to continue the war or to make peace.

> After the discussion [Ludendorff recorded] we went at once to His Majesty who had come from Cassel to Spa. His Majesty was unusually calm. He expressed his concurrence with the proposal to approach President Wilson. In the afternoon, at Von Hintze's suggestion, an Imperial Proclamation was sent to the Chancellor [Hertling] who had arrived in the meanwhile for the introduction of the parliamentary system in Germany... Count Hertling thought himself unable to carry it out, and resigned. The search now began in Berlin

for the new Parliamentary Chancellor. It was a curious proceeding, in which the Sovereign abandoned all initiative.[12]

The peace programme of Fourteen Points announced by President Wilson to the American Congress in January 1918 called for freedom of navigation on the seas and the reduction of national armaments; and so far as Germany's strategic interests were concerned, the evacuation of Belgium, the occupied territory of France, including restoration of Alsace-Lorraine to France, all Russian territory, and the creation of an independent Polish state. The programme was publicly endorsed in Britain but, privately, the War Cabinet had serious reservations about some of the points, particularly freedom of the seas. It had made little impression in France. Not surprisingly, it had been coldly received in Germany where great hopes, at the time, were being placed on the forthcoming offensive. In the closing moments of his speech on the programme to the Reichstag, Chancellor Hertling had said: 'Our military situation was never so favourable as it is now. Our highly gifted Army leaders face the future with undiminished confidence in victory.'

The Chancellorship was offered to Prince Max of Baden, a cousin of the Kaiser, who arrived in Berlin on 1 October. He was briefed on the situation by Major von dem Bussche (OHL's liaison officer to the Reichstag), and when Major Bussche spoke to Reichstag party leaders on the following day, he told them that although the 'army was strong to stand against its opponents for months to come ... each day brings our opponent nearer his goal, and will make him less inclined to conclude a peace with us which is tolerable. Therefore no time must be lost.'[13] The Reichstag leaders, aware for the first time of the critical military situation, were appalled, and its leakage to the press caused public shock and a sense of betrayal.

After the Fourth Army's success in breaking through the Hindenburg Line on 29 September, it was not to be expected that an advance from a front of some eleven miles would achieve uniform progress along its entire length, particularly when hampered by the fortifications of the line. Indeed, the initial breakthrough itself might be considered something of a marvel. Rawlinson recorded in his diary on 5 October:

Had the Boche morale not shown marked deterioration during the past month, I should never have contemplated attacking the Hindenburg Line. Had it been defended by the Germans of two years ago, it would certainly have been impregnable and, with the Fourth Army as it is now, I would gladly defend it against any number of German divisions... I think it may be truly said that the attack of September 29, which finally broke the Hindenburg Main Line, was the culminating point of the great offensive on the Western Front. It now remains to follow up our success. The great difficulty is going to be getting the heavy guns and railways quickly enough over the broken country.[14]

On the 29th the Fourth Army issued orders for a limited advance on the next day with the objective of capturing the remainder of the Hindenburg Main and Support Lines, and Foch, who had visited Haig, ordered the French First Army to take Thorigny on the right of the British IX Corps. The British 1st Division, however, seized Thorigny on the morning of the 30th, and two brigades of the 32nd Division took Levergies and reached the outskirts of Joncourt where contact was made with the 5th Australian Division. On the left, the 3rd Australian Division was confronted with a strong German position in the village of Bony and, to add to its difficulties, was enfiladed by artillery fire from north of Vendhuille in the Third Army's sector. The enemy offered stubborn resistance to the Australian attempt to work up the Hindenburg Main Line and, for a time, there was an interlude of trench warfare, with fierce hand-to-hand fighting. Ultimately the division cleared a portion of the Line and reached the outskirts of Bony. On the extreme left, III Corps, advancing towards the large village of Vendhuille, found that it had been evacuated, but the enemy still remained on the eastern edge covered by the St Quentin canal, with a section of the Hindenburg Main Line in the rear. The western edge was mopped up, but no attempt was made to cross the canal.

Although the breach had been made on the 29th, progress between 30 September and 2 October was by means of somewhat piecemeal operations, and for the time being it was no longer possible to provide adequate artillery support because of difficulties in communication. Rawlinson's orders for 1 October were for IX Corps and the Australian Corps to press forward to the high ground from Joncourt to Sequehart 'with a view to securing passage for the advance of the Cavalry Corps'. During the night, however, the German Eighteenth Army was ordered to withdraw to a line between Preselles–Sequehart–Harly: in the process St Quentin was to be evacuated. The 32nd and 5th Australian Divisions entered Joncourt, but failed to hold Sequehart and Preselles in the face of a counter-attack. Nevertheless, the 32nd Division, pressing on from Joncourt, penetrated a section of the Beaurevoir Line (the Hindenburg Reserve System) and held on to it in spite of repeated counter-attacks. A brigade of the 5th Australian Division seized Estrées and, on the left, the 3rd Australian Division captured Bony and the Hindenburg Main Line to the north, and pushed up towards Le Catelet on the Hindenburg Support Line. Little progress was made on the following day, although the French First Army advanced to the west bank of the St Quentin canal but failed to secure a crossing.

Allied pressure continued elsewhere on the Western Front on 30 September. A German retirement to the east bank of the Schelde (St Quentin) canal enabled the Third Army to advance without serious opposition to the west bank, but attempts by patrols to cross were strongly resisted. The First Army made only limited progress. On 1 October the New Zealand Division (IV Corps) of the Third Army forced a crossing of the Schelde at Masnières and captured Crèvecouer; and two divisions of VI Corps took Rumilly at the second attempt. The Canadian Corps of the First Army experienced serious casualties in its attempt to capture the villages of Abancourt, Cuvillers, Bantigny and Blécourt. The last was held for a time, but a counter-attack drove the Canadians out. Nevertheless, although the objectives remained out of reach, the Canadians now overlooked Cambrai, where it was apparent that the enemy intended to make a stand.

The Fourth Army resumed operations on 3 October. IX Corps and the Australian Corps were to attack at 6.05 a.m., with XIII Corps on the left, in an attempt to force the Beaurevoir Line. This was the Hindenburg Reserve System constructed in 1917 which extended into the Third Army's sector. It was the penultimate German defensive line before the Hermann Position, and it was hoped that forcing it would assist the Third Army to secure passages across the St Quentin canal. The line consisted of 'two trenches with concrete emplacements every two or three hundred yards and with machine-gun nests scattered in depth behind it...' As mentioned, it had already been penetrated for a short distance east of Joncourt, and the main assault was entrusted to the 46th Division (IX Corps). At first the attack went well. The villages of Ramicourt and Wiancourt were captured and the western outskirts of Montbrehain, the final objective, were reached. From here it appeared that the enemy was in full retreat. Early in the afternoon, however, the Germans delivered a strong counter-attack and retook Montbrehain, forcing a withdrawal to a line covering Ramicourt. The 2nd Australian Division on the left eventually came up to Wiancourt and established contact with the 46th Division, but its intended assault on the village of Beaurevoir had to be postponed because of the possibility of a counter-attack. The 50th Division (XIII Corps), moving up on the extreme left, captured Le Catelet and Gouy, but the former village was lost in a counter-attack. Nevertheless, it had been a satisfactory day for the Fourth Army: the Beaurevoir Line had been penetrated along its entire length except for a short stretch of just over a mile on the boundary with the Third Army.

The attack was resumed on the next day (4th). Little progress was made by IX Corps mainly because of counter-attacks from the strong-point on Mannequin Hill, and lack of French support. The Australians also made negligible progress; on the extreme left the 25th Division (XIII Corps) managed to enter Beaurevoir village, but could not hold it in the face of strong opposition and heavy casualties. On the 5th, the 2nd Australian Division captured Montbrehain with the valuable assistance of tanks, and after two artillery bombardments on Beaurevoir the village was captured by the 25th Division in the early evening. Little assistance had been forthcoming from the French First Army which 'tried in vain to advance to the south, the east and the north of St Quentin'. On the morning of the 4th, Foch impressed upon General Fayolle 'the importance of the First Army supporting the right of the British Fourth Army at all costs', but Debeney 'demanded to be reinforced with more artillery'.

On the same day Haig issued orders for future operations by the Fourth, Third and First Armies with the preface:

The recent offensive operations of the Allies on the Western Front have met with success at all points. The enemy has lost heavily in men and material and has been compelled to use his reserves piecemeal to retain his line intact. He is now faced with necessity of maintaining a wide battle front with depleted reserves and dispirited troops.[15]

The orders went on to underline Haig's intention 'to strike the enemy a vigorous blow, and exploit success with mounted troops before a new defensive position can be organised'. To this end, the Third and Fourth Armies would deliver an attack on a wide front on 7 October (subsequently postponed to the 8th). The First Army was to secure a passage of the Schelde at Ramillies (three miles north-east of Cambrai) to protect the left flank of the Third Army's attack.

Meanwhile, events in Germany were moving towards a crisis. On 1 October, Ludendorff addressed his senior staff officers, telling them that 'OHL and the German army were finished, the war no longer to be won, unavoidable and final defeat was close at hand'.[16] The Bulgarians were now out of the war, Austria-Hungary and Turkey were close to collapse, and 'the troops could no longer be relied upon'. He feared an imminent Allied breakthrough, and with the possibility of revolution in Germany led by communist elements, an immediate armistice was essential. These statements reflected the fact that Ludendorff had completely lost his nerve; there was no question that the Allies could have achieved a strategic breakthrough at this stage. Hindenburg, however, was calmer: 'I am totally convinced that Germany with God's help will come through this difficult period.' The peace offer had not yet been sent to President Wilson although von Hintze telegraphed Supreme Headquarters to the effect that a new government would probably be formed that night (1 October) and, if so, the proposal could then be sent. Prince Max, the new Chancellor, refused to sign it, however, until the new government had been formed. At a meeting of the Crown Council on the next day, Prince Max said he was still opposed to making the peace offer as he believed that the German people would see it as a confession of defeat and lose the will to fight on. He insisted that OHL should put its demand in writing, whereupon Hindenburg handed him the following note:

OHL maintains the demand made on Sunday the 29th of September of this year for an immediate issue of the peace offer to our enemies... The German Army still stands firm and victoriously repels all attacks. The situation, however, is becoming more acute every day, and may compel OHL to take vital decisions. In these circumstances, the proper course is to break off the struggle in order to spare the German people and their Allies useless sacrifices. Every day's delay costs the lives of thousands of our brave soldiers.[17]

Prince Max subsequently telegraphed a series of questions in reply. How long could the army keep the enemy from crossing the German border? Did the Supreme Command expect a military collapse and would this mean the end of the power to defend Germany? Was the military situation so critical that an armistice and peace must be sought at once? All eminently sensible questions, but the reply from OHL evaded answering any of them, merely reiterating the demand 'for the immediate issue of the peace offer'. Accordingly, the request for an armistice dated 4 October was sent via Switzerland to Washington on the following day. The text ran:

> The German Government requests the President of the United States of America to take steps for the restoration of peace, to notify all belligerents of this request, and to invite them to delegate plenipotentiaries for the purpose of taking up negotiations. The German Government accepts, as a basis for the peace negotiations, the programme laid down by the President of the United States in his message to Congress of January 8, 1918, and in his subsequent pronouncements, particularly in his address of September 27 1918. In order to avoid further bloodshed the German Government requests the President to bring about an immediate conclusion of a general armistice on land, on water, and in the air.

Similar requests were made to President Wilson by the Austrian and Turkish governments.

It was significant that the peace offer was made to the American President and not to Foch as Allied Commander-in-Chief. Prince Max's reasoning was that as the British and the French had not formally accepted the Fourteen Points as a basis for negotiation, their acceptance by Germany would put her on the same high moral ground as the President, implying a dialogue between heads of state.

On 5 October, the Kaiser issued an Order of the Day to his forces:

> For months past the enemy has been striving against your lines with powerful efforts, almost without a pause. You have had to resist by fighting for weeks on end, frequently without rest, and to show a front to a foe vastly superior in numbers [sic]. Therein lies the immensity of the task which has been given you and you are fulfilling it. Troops from every province are doing their duty and, on foreign soil, are heroically defending the Fatherland... In the midst of the hardest fighting comes the collapse of the Macedonian front [caused by the Bulgarian armistice]. Your front is unbroken and will remain so. In agreement with my Allies I have decided to offer peace once more to our enemies; but we will only stretch out our hands to an honourable peace.[18]

Haig met Foch on the 6th, and his diary records:

He [Foch] had a Paris morning paper opened out on the table in front of him in which in large type was printed a note from Austria, Germany, and Turkey, asking for an armistice at once, and stating their readiness to discuss conditions of peace on the basis of President Wilson's 14 Points. 'Here' (said Foch) 'you have the immediate result of the British piercing the Hindenburg Line. The enemy has asked for an armistice.' His opinion is that the enemy should be told to retire to the Rhine as a guarantee of good faith, before any negotiations are begun. I explained to Foch the position on the British front and said that if we get sufficient artillery and ammunition forward we proposed to attack tomorrow morning on the front from Cambrai to the right of our Fourth Army... Foch said he was very pleased with all we had done, and was in complete agreement with what I proposed to do now.[19]

Foch then turned to the situation on the Meuse–Argonne front, expressing his disappointment with the American attack west of the Meuse. He had broached the subject of the transfer of American divisions elsewhere, but Pershing would not agree, 'saying that he would win through if left alone'.

It was increasingly apparent that the Germans were retiring, but with what ultimate object was not clear. There was a strong possibility that retreat to the Hermann Position was intended where it was assumed that a stand would be made, and therefore in the path of the British Third and Fourth Armies. Despite the enormous losses suffered by the Germans since March, an appreciation of their strength at the beginning of October revealed that there was a total of 194 divisions on the Western Front. Of this total, 80 divisions faced the British Army on a front of 120 miles, whereas the balance of 114 divisions was spread over 285 miles. Thus on a division per mile basis, the Germans were more closely distributed against the British Army than elsewhere.

On 8 October, the Fourth Army resumed operations in conjunction with the Third Army on its left and the French First Army on its right. Zero hour was 5.10 a.m. and good progress was made in the centre and left, but initially there were problems on the right adjoining the French First Army because of enfilade fire from Cèrise Wood in the French sector. The wood was eventually captured by a brigade of the British 6th Division, and some forward movement was now possible, particularly as the French XV Corps then arrived. The American 30th Division did well in sweeping aside all opposition and occupying Prémont – some four miles from its start line. There was an attempt to use cavalry in exploitation, but no suitable gaps could be found.

Zero hour for the Third Army was earlier, at 4.30 a.m. Apart from the general objective of Le Cateau–Solesmes on the Hermann Line, some twenty miles away, it was important that its advance should keep pace with that of the Fourth Army on its right. One particular difficulty was that the northern end of the Beaurevoir Line remained to be forced and, as a preliminary operation before the main assault, two divisions (38th and 21st) of V Corps carried out a night attack at 1 a.m. On the right, the former division was held up by strong wire entanglements until three tanks arrived to force a passage, allowing the infantry to follow through and capture the village of Villers Outreaux. The 21st Division on the left had less difficulty and reached its first objective by 2.30 a.m. Thus in the V Corps sector the Beaurevoir Line had been quickly overrun, and the two divisions achieved an advance of nearly three miles, seizing three villages and two woods in the process.

The main assault was now launched. The 37th and New Zealand Divisions of IV Corps had about three miles of the last fragment of the Beaurevoir Line to cross, and both divisions had first to penetrate belts of wire. Those facing the 37th Division had been insufficiently cut, but once again tanks arrived to crush a path. The New Zealand Division pushed on, capturing the villages of Lesdain and Esnes – the latter village beyond its objective. It was at Esnes that a surprising development occurred. The Germans launched a strong counter-attack led by two captured British tanks, but these were knocked out by fire from tanks and the attack was repelled. IV Corps achieved a similar advance to that of V Corps and captured 1,400 prisoners. In the centre, VI Corps had a much more difficult time. At first the advance of the 3rd Division went well but then came under heavy machine-gun fire, and at 8.30 a.m. it was faced with a counter-attack led by five captured British tanks supported by infantry and fire from artillery and machine-guns. This resulted in a withdrawal until two British tanks appeared which engaged and disabled the enemy tanks. The 2nd Division was similarly counter-attacked. One enemy tank was knocked out by British tanks, and two others engaged by a trench mortar battery; one was captured and the other withdrew. This unexpected resistance for a time halted the advance, but at 6 p.m. a combined attack by both divisions was completely successful. The advance of the remaining corps (XVII) had the object of encircling Cambrai, and its second and final objective was gained by noon. It too, however, was counter-attacked by four captured tanks which succeeded in disabling three British tanks, but ultimately two enemy machines were destroyed, in one instance using captured German field guns, and the others made off.

The successes gained on the 8th by the Third and Fourth Armies came as a severe blow to Ludendorff, and during the night of the 8th/9th a retreat began to the Hermann Position which 'existed for the most part on paper', and Cambrai was evacuated. With the fall of the final remaining section of the Beaurevoir Line, the last established German defensive position had been breached, and it was now a matter of pursuit.

The Fourth Army continued its advance on the 9th and made steady progress against weakening resistance. The cavalry on the right of the advance found little opportunity to push forward because of wire, but on the left, where there was less wire, they were more successful. The Fort Garry Horse of the Canadian Cavalry

Brigade charged Gattigny Wood and despite many losses drove the enemy out. (It was the Fort Garry Horse that had gained the only cavalry success at the Battle of Cambrai in November 1917.) Afterwards cavalry captured Honnechy, and later the Canadian Cavalry Brigade secured Reumont. Notwithstanding the German retirement, the left of the French First Army was some three miles behind the line reached by the Fourth Army. The Third Army met even less resistance. All its four corps not only realised their set objectives but went beyond: V Corps advanced over seven miles, some parties actually reaching the River Selle, but found it strongly held. The First Army attacked at 1.30 a.m. On the right, the Schelde canal was crossed without opposition. As Cambrai had already been evacuated, the rearguard leaving at 2.30 a.m., the Canadian Mounted Rifles reached the railway about two miles to the east of the town by noon and established contact with XVII Corps (Third Army). Farther north, the only opposition to the Canadian Corps was from rearguards and all objectives were attained. In Flanders there had been no progress by the Belgian and British Second Armies.

On the 9th Haig received a telegram from Lloyd George which, after amendment, read:

> I have just heard from Marshal Foch of the brilliant victory won by the First, Third and Fourth Armies and I wish to express to yourself, Generals Horne, Byng and Rawlinson and all the officers and men under your command my sincerest congratulations on the great and significant success which the British Armies, with their American brothers in arms have gained during the two past days. The courage and tenacity with which the troops of the Empire, after withstanding the terrific enemy onslaught of the spring of this year, have again resumed the offensive with such decisive results is the greatest chapter in our island history. The smashing of the great defensive system erected by the enemy in the west and claimed by him to be impregnable is a feat of which we are justly proud and for which the Empire will always be grateful.

In a letter to his wife enclosing copies of a number of congratulatory telegrams he had received, Haig wrote:

> The Prime Minister shows the least understanding of the great efforts made by the whole of the British Army. He speaks of the 'success' of the last 'two days'. In the papers I see that some friend of his has altered the word to 'few days'. Then, as the message originally reached me, no mention at all was made of Horne and the First Army, when the Canadian Corps were actually in Cambrai, and have had such hard fighting for Monchy [le] Preux, the Drocourt–Quéant line etc.[20]

Even more surprising was that the telegram omitted any mention of the successes of August and September. Duff Cooper, in his biography of Haig, criticised Lloyd

George for basing his message on information received from Foch, with the implication that 'he wished to make it plain that Foch, not Haig, was winning the war, and that Haig, like other subordinate commanders and his American brothers in arms, was only to be congratulated when Foch was kind enough to say he had done well'.[21] It is not entirely clear, however, whether the telegram was actually drafted by Lloyd George. According to Wilson's diary for the 9th, recording a discussion in Paris, 'Foch gave Haig and our Armies great praise, so I got a telegram of congratulation to Douglas Haig from Lloyd George.'

Haig wrote to Foch on the 9th suggesting that as the Fourth, Third and First Armies were approaching the Selle, the advance should continue in a north-easterly direction towards the line Maubeuge–Valenciennes, thereby severing the German lateral line of communication between Valenciennes and Mézières, and eventually combining operations with his Second Army and the Belgians. He also suggested that six American divisions should be transferred to him to take part in the suggested operation. Foch, however, at a conference on the next day, turned down Haig's suggestion of a north-easterly operation. He rejected the proposal to transfer American divisions, no doubt in the belief that Pershing would refuse. Haig was given a Directive which, in effect, placed the main burden of future operations on the British Armies:

Today, the 10th October, three convergent operations are in the course of exploitation:

1. that of Belgium [including the British Second Army]
2. that of Solesmes-Wassigny [British]
3. the Aisne-Meuse [American-French] The most profitable to exploit, thanks to the success of the British Armies, is Solesmes–Wassigny. It is therefore to be pursued in the greatest possible strength, in order to develop it as progress is made to Avesnes–Mons.

The Fourth Army continued its advance on the 10th towards Le Cateau and the Selle. Progress was rapid until the line of the Selle was reached, but an attempt to push cavalry forward in exploitation produced no tangible result. The Official Historian noted:

The total losses of the Cavalry Corps during the 8th, 9th and 10th October had been 7 officers and 77 other ranks killed, and 41 officers and 479 other ranks wounded or missing. It had captured over five hundred prisoners, 10 guns and 60 machine guns; but the cavalry had done nothing that the infantry, with artillery support and cyclists, could not have done for itself at less cost: and the supply of the large force of horses with water and forage had gravely interfered with the sending up of ammunition and the rations for the other arms, and with the allotment of the limited water facilities.[22]

The line of the Selle was held in strength, but the river itself south of St Souplet did not present much of an obstacle. Between there and Le Cateau, however, it 'was normally only 15 to 18 feet wide and 3 to 4 feet deep, but at the time was swollen by rain...' Moreover, there were wide marshes on either bank. According to German regimental histories, the Selle formed part of the Hermann Position, but no signs of defences were visible other than a few trenches.

The Third Army's advance to the Selle met little serious resistance until, on the right, the leading battalions of the 37th and New Zealand Divisions came up to the river. Some parties from both divisions eventually managed to cross the river at Briastre by means of improvised foot-bridges, but without flank support they were forced to withdraw, leaving posts on the eastern bank. Only a small advance was made by the Canadian Corps of the First Army with the object of keeping in step with the Third Army.

For the time being, it appeared that the German retirement on the fronts of the Fourth, Third and First Armies had come to a halt. Haig met his three army commanders on the 11th to discuss future operations. In accordance with Foch's Directive, his advance would be easterly, and he ordered that the principal effort should be made by the Fourth Army which was to establish itself on the line Le Cateau–Wassigny, the boundary with the French and, in co-operation with the French First Army, push forward strong advanced guards to the Sambre and Oise canal. The Third Army was to establish itself on the line of the Selle and secure the crossings, with its left flank protected by the First Army. The combined offensive was not to take place before the 14th – the date of the renewed offensive in Flanders. Although it was realised that the delay would give time for the Germans to strengthen their defences, it was necessary to improve communications. Ammunition and rations had to be brought up, but on the Fourth Army front the railway (originally the main line between St Quentin and Cambrai) had been much damaged by the Germans in their withdrawal, and roads and bridges had been similarly damaged. Thus the reconstruction of the railway and improvements in railhead distribution were urgently needed. As will be seen later, supplying the rapidly advancing Armies would soon present formidable problems.

President Wilson's reply to Germany's appeal for an armistice arrived in Berlin on the 9th and Prince Max and his new Cabinet met Ludendorff and Hindenburg to consider its terms. The reply had been signed by Robert Lansing, the Secretary of State, and sought 'the exact meaning of the note of the Imperial Chancellor'. Did it mean that the German Government accepted the terms laid down in the President's address to Congress on 8 January? The President believed that he could not be free to propose an armistice 'to the Governments with which the Government of the United States is associated against the Central Powers so long as the armies of those Powers are upon their soil', and that 'the good faith of any discussion would depend upon the withdrawal of forces from invaded territory'. It also enquired whether the German Chancellor was speaking 'merely for the constituted authorities of the Empire who have so far conducted the War'. Ludendorff's immediate reaction was that 'from the military standpoint, it demanded a condition precedent to the conclusion of any armistice the evacuation of the occupied territory in the West. We were quite prepared for this.' At the meeting, however, he expressed the view that

> Wilson's note still allowed us to hope that we should obtain a peace that would not amount to destruction. Prince Max also wanted to hear the views of other high officers on the situation. Only [OHL], however, had a view of the whole position ... [and] I refused his request. The Field-Marshal and I had alone to bear the responsibility... It was now time, at last, to ascertain definitely whether the German people would fight on, if the negotiations with the enemy did not lead to an acceptable peace. Preparations had to be made. The Press had given us a favourable view of the possibility of continuing the fight.[23]

As President Wilson's reply had been drafted without any consultation with the Allied governments, the terms were considered at a conference between the British, French and Italian Governments at Versailles on the 9th. It was decided that it called for a response on the stated conditions for an armistice; and after expressing appreciation of the 'lofty sentiments that had inspired the reply' and agreeing that a preliminary condition was the evacuation by the enemy of all invaded territories, the Conference considered that the condition for the conclusion of an armistice was not sufficient:

> It would not prevent the enemy from taking advantage of a suspension of hostilities to place himself, at the expiration of an armistice not followed by peace, in a better military situation than at the moment of the interruption of hostilities. They might be enabled to withdraw from a critical situation, to save their stores, to reform their units, to shorten their front, to retire without loss of men upon new positions which they would have time to select and fortify.
>
> The conditions for an armistice can only be fixed after consultation with the military experts and in accordance with the military situation at the actual moment when negotiations are entered on.

Prince Max replied on the 12th to the effect that the government 'accepted the propositions laid down by President Wilson in his address of January 8th, and in his subsequent addresses as the foundation for a permanent peace of justice' and was prepared to evacuate the occupied territories. The reply concluded with the assurance that the German Government represented the views of the majority of the Reichstag and the German people. On the same day, however, a German submarine torpedoed and sank the *Leinster*, an Irish Mail steamer, with great loss of life. It aroused a storm of indignation in America and Britain, and hardened the tone of President Wilson's second Note dated the 14th. After making it clear that the German Government would have to discuss armistice conditions with the Allied commanders, it went on to deplore the fact that at the time the German Government was proposing peace 'its submarines are engaged in sinking passenger ships at sea', and that in their enforced withdrawal 'the German Armies are pursuing a course of wanton destruction ... in direct violation of the rules and practices of civilised warfare...The power which has hitherto controlled the German Nation is of the sort here described. It is within the choice of the German Nation to alter it.' The Kaiser may have read a suggestion that he should abdicate in this last demand, and he told Prince Max, 'You must use it to arouse the entire people to rally round their Emperor in defence of their sacred heritage, just as the government must stand shoulder to shoulder behind him. This impudent intervention in our political affairs must be properly exposed to all.'[24]

Notes

1. Callwell, Major-General Sir C., *Field-Marshal Sir Henry Wilson*, Cassell (London, 1927)
2. Edmonds, Brigadier-General Sir James, and Maxwell-Hyslop, Lieutenant-Colonel R., (comp.), *Official History of the War: Military Operations France and Belgium*, Vol. V, HMSO, 1947
3. *Ibid.*
4. Pershing, J. F., *My Experiences in the World War*, Stokes (New York, 1931)
5. *Ibid.*
6. Reitz, Lieutenant-Colonel D., *Trekking On*, Faber (London, 1933)
7. Diary of Count Rupprecht
8. Ludendorff, General, *Concise Ludendorff Memoirs 1914–1918*, Hutchinson (London, 1933)
9. Maurice, Major-General Sir F., *The Life of General Lord Rawlinson*, Cassell (London, 1928)
10. Priestley, R. E., *Breaking the Hindenburg Line: The Story of the 46th (North Midland) Division*, T. Fisher Unwin (London, 1919)
11. *Ibid.*
12. Ludendorff, *op. cit.*
13. *Ibid.*
14. Maurice, *op. cit.*
15. Edmonds, *op. cit.*
16. Asprey, R. B., quoted in *The German High Command at War*, Little, Brown & Co. (London, 1993)
17. Edmonds, *op. cit.*
18. *Ibid.*
19. Blake, Robert, *The Private Papers of Douglas Haig 1914–1919*, Eyre & Spottiswoode (London, 1952)
20. *Ibid.*
21. Duff Cooper, A., *Haig*, Faber (London, 1935)
22. Edmonds, *op. cit.*
23. Ludendorff, *op. cit.*
24. Asprey, *op. cit.*

11

The Beginning of the End

Between 11 and 14 October, the latter being the date proposed for the attack by the Second Army, the Fourth Army made only slight improvements to its position in preparation for its assault on the Selle line. The operations of the Third Army, accomplished against strong resistance, were confined to pushing up to the River Selle; some footing was gained on the eastern bank, but no progress could be made beyond. Farther north, the centre and right wings of the First Army made good headway against sporadic resistance including, on one occasion, a German counter-attack led by six tanks. The right wing almost reached the Selle by the 13th, and the centre and left wing made good progress, particularly after it was found that the Drocourt–Quéant line had been evacuated. The right wing was handicapped, however, by the need to cross not only the River Sensée but also several canals; nevertheless, by the 14th its advance had reached a position overlooking the important town of Douai from the west.

Ever since the withdrawal of the enemy in August from the head of the salient won in the April Lys offensive, the Fifth Army, sandwiched between the First and Second Armies, had not undertaken any set-piece offensive, merely pursuing the retreating enemy, until at the end of September its front extended from Loos in the south to a point some two miles west of Armentières in the north. Armentières (in the Second Army's sector) had been evacuated on the night of 1/2 October, and on the latter date it was learned that the Germans were carrying out a further retirement to the Haute Deule canal. Once again it was a matter of following up a retreating enemy, and considerable progress was made up to the 4th 'over flat, low-lying, nearly waterlogged country', mainly against opposition from rearguards. Some further gains were made over the following days, and by the 14th the advance had reached the Haute Deule canal.

The Second Army renewed its Flanders offensive on the 14th in conjunction with the Belgian and French Armies on its left. Foch had wanted it resumed earlier, but it had been delayed by 'the state of the roads and the disorganisation of the supply services in the Belgian and French sectors of the front'. The Second Army had used the interval to harass the enemy by frequent bombardments and feint attacks, and had no doubt been encouraged by the GHQ Intelligence Summary dated 14 October:

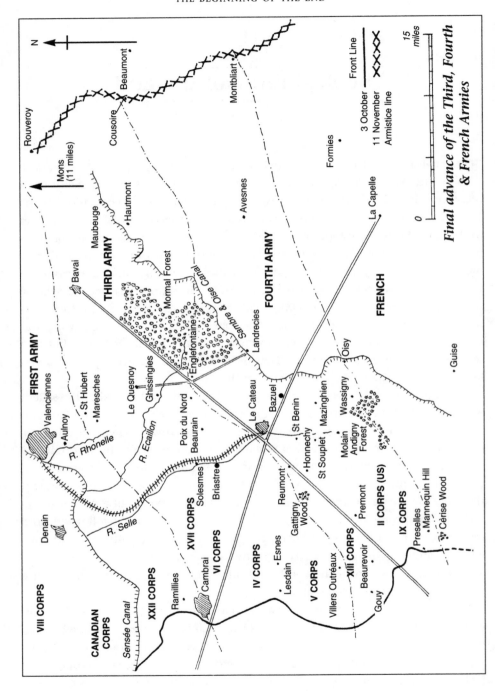

Final advance of the Third, Fourth & French Armies

From the mass of evidence received from agents it appears that the evacuation of material from the Belgian coast is now well advanced, and the absence of any serious work on defences shows that the enemy will not fight to retain this region indefinitely. The clearance of Lille also would appear to be nearly complete, and it is probable that the enemy intends an early retirement to the line of the Schelde...[1]

The Second Army's task was to protect the right flank of the Belgian and French advance where the main rôle had been given to the French XXXIV and VII Corps, flanked on either side by Belgian divisions, who were to seize Roulers and press on to Thielt and Ghent. Plumer's orders for his Second Army were for XX, XIX and II Corps to advance to the River Lys (XV Corps was already there) and, given success, establish bridgeheads on the south side of the river. Zero hour was 5.35 a.m. No tanks would be employed and there would be no preliminary bombardment, only a creeping barrage. The attack was reasonably successful against occasionally strong resistance from fortified farmhouses and pillboxes, and by the end of the day all the objectives, except on the extreme left, had been reached, and the Belgians had kept abreast. The line of the Lys had not been reached, however, and the attack was resumed on the next day (15th). XV Corps on the right crossed the Lys and entered Comines which had been evacuated, and X Corps found that Menin had also been evacuated although the bridges across the Lys had been destroyed. On the left, XIX and II Corps, in spite of strong resistance, reached the line of the Courtrai–Roulers railway, although the Franco-Belgian force farther north had failed to keep pace. Progress was maintained over the next four days. Tourcoing, Roubaix and Courtrai were entered, and by the 19th the entire front of the Second Army had crossed the Lys. The Germans were also retiring on the Franco-Belgian front, enabling the Belgians to enter Ostend on the 17th and Zeebrugge and Bruges two days later.

By the 16th, the Fourth Army had completed its preparations for forcing the passage of the Selle. On the eve of the battle, Rawlinson wrote to Colonel Wigram (Assistant Private Secretary to the King):

For the last week we have been stuck up against Le Cateau and the valley of the Selle, which the Boche has fortified to some extent, and, what is more inconvenient, has dammed at many of the mills and bridges, causing inundations which limit the front on which attack is possible. However, I am having a go at his position tomorrow (17th), with some seven divisions in line, and I have no doubt that we shall penetrate, and give the enemy another nasty knock... All are in good heart, and quite determined to reply to the Boche squeal for an armistice by hammering on his now partly demoralised army. In the line before my Fourth Army the enemy has brought up four new divisions in the last few days, and another is coming in tonight: but with the exception of these, they are all very much reduced in strength by recent fighting, and none have had more than ten days' rest, and some only three days'. We have an immense preponderance of artillery...[2]

The preliminary bombardment by more than 1,300 guns had begun on the 13th, delivering over 7,500 tons of shells on enemy battery positions, communications and assembly areas. The River Selle constituted about two-thirds of the battle area: between Le Cateau and St Benin its depth had been increased by damming and a passage could only be forced by bridging, but south of St Souplet the river did not present a serious obstacle. The town of Le Cateau was comparatively undamaged, and its houses and cellars could afford centres of resistance if the enemy intended to make a determined stand.

Zero hour on the 17th was 5.20 a.m., by which time thick mist had formed. IX Corps on the right was to advance in a south-easterly direction and form a defensive flank to guard against an enemy counter-attack from Andigny Forest on the boundary with the French First Army. With no river to cross, the advance initially went well, but some battalions lost direction in the mist and suffered fire from nests of machine guns that had been by-passed. At 11 a.m. there were signs that an enemy counter-attack was in readiness, but such was the excellence of the artillery support that 'all guns were turned on this target, and only one German succeeded in reaching the infantry position alive'.[3] By late in the evening IX Corps had reached its first objective, apart from a small section on the left, and were established on a plateau overlooking the valley of the Selle. The American 27th and 30th Divisions, attacking in the centre, crossed the lower reaches of the Selle with the aid of planks laid on the abutments of the destroyed bridges, but tanks experienced considerable difficulties. The advance was delayed by the need to mop-up enemy resistance in the village of Molain and the barrage was lost. The Americans then came under heavy artillery and machine-gun fire and were forced to dig in less than a mile from their first objective.

On the left, the 50th Division of XIII Corps had the most difficult section of the river to cross, but under cover of the barrage and the mist several duckboard and floating bridges were thrown across, and the passage was achieved without much opposition. It was in this part of the front, however, that German resistance was most determined. Once the mist had cleared, an enemy counter-attack was launched, forcing the leading battalions to withdraw to the railway south of Le Cateau. The attack was repulsed, but further advance was blocked by strong resistance from the Railway Triangle. Artillery was brought up to shell the position but to no avail, and a second enemy counter-attack compelled another withdrawal. Farther north, the 66th Division attacked at the later zero hour of 8.05 a.m. The

South African Brigade, attacking from north of Le Cateau, crossed the Selle by means of foot-bridges, and although confronted by belts of uncut wire, which had to be cut by hand, it pressed on to its intermediate objective despite enfilade fire from houses in the town. A neighbouring brigade entered the town and, after some fierce house-to-house fighting, cleared most of the town by the early evening.

The attack was resumed on the next day (18th) with a slightly later zero hour (5.30 a.m.) for the Americans and XIII Corps: final timing, however, was left for IX Corps to decide because of the late termination to their advance on the previous day. The choice of a zero hour before dawn was unfortunate because the enemy was expecting a resumption at this time and immediately launched a heavy counter-bombardment. This effectively prevented both American divisions from gaining much ground until the early evening; but although it caused delay to the advance of XIII Corps, the village of Bazuel on the second objective was captured as well as the Railway Triangle, and Le Cateau was finally cleared. On the right, IX Corps escaped the counter-bombardment by moving off at 11.30 a.m. The attack was led by a battalion of the Black Watch who

> carried all before them, and in three-quarters of an hour the leading companies were in the outskirts of Wassigny. In the village itself very little resistance was forthcoming, as all the garrison were either asleep or eating. In one cellar, after a Lewis gunner had fired a drum of bullets into it, five officers and seventy-two other ranks surrendered; in another, five officers were discovered at luncheon.[4]

After consolidation, only isolated resistance was encountered and the corps reached its second objective by 2 p.m. and gained touch with the French First Army which had made good progress, clearing the entire Andigny Forest.

There was dense fog on the morning of the 19 October, and the advance of IX Corps met little opposition as during the night the enemy had retired to the east of the Sambre canal. The American divisions captured Mazinghien and were within half a mile of their second objective where they were ordered to stand fast and await relief. XIII Corps secured its second objective without too much difficulty in a limited advance. Thus, in three days, the Fourth Army had crossed the Selle along its entire front. In the process it had broken into the southern stretch of the Hermann Line, taking more than 5,000 prisoners and 60 guns and putting it in a good jumping-off position to assault the Sambre canal.

Elsewhere on the Western Front, the right of the French First Army 'succeeded in pushing an element (one company) on to the eastern bank of the Oise' as a preliminary operation to an advance directed at the line Sambre and Oise canal–Mormal Forest–Valenciennes. This position would bring the important railway junction of Aulnoye, a vital link in German lateral communications, within range of Allied artillery. The Tenth Army offensive that opened on the 19th gained a penetration of two miles on its first day. There had only been desultory action on the Meuse–Argonne front since 3 October. Pétain had suggested forming a separate army equally divided between the French and the Americans, but Pershing had refused. Instead the French 17th Corps was placed at Pershing's disposal on the 5th. On the 8th, a combined assault with two American divisions resulted in the gain of three-and-a- half miles of ground and the capture of 3,000 prisoners.

The enemy, however, was conducting an elastic defence and had been substantially reinforced, as the Americans found to their cost when attacking the Kriemhilde Line on the 14th. Very little was achieved at great cost: 'The rawer of the American troops exposed themselves as recklessly as the new British divisions on the first day of the Somme [1 July 1916]'[5] The lack of progress by the Americans on the right wing of the Allied advance caused Clemenceau to complain to Foch:

I have postponed from day to day writing you about the crisis existing in the American Army... You have watched at close range the result of General Pershing's actions. Unfortunately, thanks to his invincible obstinacy, he has won out against you as well as against your immediate subordinates... Our worthy American allies, who thirst to get into action and who are universally acknowledged to be great soldiers, have been marking time ever since their forward jump on the first day. Nobody can maintain that these fine troops are unusable; they are merely unused...

In his reply, Foch defended the Americans by describing the crisis as the sort from which all improvised armies suffer... But there is no denying the magnitude of the effort made by the American Army... From 26 September to 20 October its losses in battle were 54,158 men – in exchange for small gains on a narrow front, it is true, but over particularly difficult country and in the face of serious resistance by the enemy.[6]

On the 19th, Foch issued what was to be his last Directive:

1. The Flanders Group (including the British Second Army) to advance in the general direction of Brussels.
2. The other British Armies to advance to the south of the Flanders Group.
3. The French First, Tenth, Fifth and Fourth Armies and the American First Army to operate south of Froidechapelle–Philippeville line.

Thus the direction of the Flanders Group and the four British Armies would be towards the north-east, with the Franco-American assault pushing north-west-wards. For the time being, however, the British Fourth Army was to establish a defensive flank facing east to cover the advance of the Third and First Armies.

Meanwhile, there had been a meeting of the German War Cabinet on the 17th to consider the reply to be made to President Wilson's second Note. Ludendorff, who was present, claimed that army morale was much better, but 'these armistice negotiations are having very bad consequences, since my soldiers can't see why they should continue fighting if they have to give up Belgium and Alsace-Lorraine'. He admitted, nevertheless, that the situation was perilous, but 'it could be saved if we have reinforcements'. He was then told by the War Minister that '60,000 to 70,000 men were immediately available from the Home Army', whereupon Ludendorff said, 'If I have these reinforcements now, I can face the future with confidence, but I must have them immediately.' This was promised. Prince Max, however, wrote in his diary: 'The statement of the military stripped of its embroideries revealed the following: a reversal of fortune in our favour is inconceivable. The submarine war cannot bring it about. We have lost the initiative.' He believed that reinforcements would not affect the situation without an improvement in morale both in the army and at home. He was resolved that negotiations with President Wilson should continue, but if they were asked 'to accept dishonourable conditions to get an armistice, then the people must be called out to make a last stand'. In this event, he thought that Ludendorff would be a broken reed: 'In the course of the meeting I lost confidence in Ludendorff as a man. He ought to have looked at the situation ruthlessly in the face, without any regard for his own prestige.'[7]

The meeting continued on the next day, although Ludendorff was not present. The decision was made to discontinue the submarine war, and when Ludendorff was informed of this he telegraphed the Chancellor to express his disagreement:

> The question to be asked is, will the German people fight for their honour not only with words but actually to the last man, and thus ensure the possibility of recovery; or will they allow themselves to be driven to capitulation before making a supreme effort? By consenting to the abandonment of U-boat warfare as agreed in the Note, we enter the latter path.[8]

Prince Max then informed the Kaiser that he would resign before changing his mind on the submarine question: 'It gives me no pleasure to have to say so, but I am completely convinced that if I go, the Cabinet will fall to pieces, and then comes the revolution.'[9] It is probable that he had been strengthened in his decision by a letter from Crown Prince Rupprecht dated the 18th:

> Our troops are exhausted and their numbers have dwindled terribly. The number of infantry in an Active division is seldom as much as 3,000. In general, the infantry of a division can be treated as equivalent to one or two battalions, and in certain cases as only equivalent to two or three companies...The morale of troops has suffered seriously and their power of resistance

diminishes daily. They surrender in hordes, whenever the enemy attacks, and thousands of plunderers infest the district round the bases. We have no more prepared lines, and no more can be dug...We cannot sustain a serious enemy attack, owing to a lack of all reserves. If we succeed, by retreating behind the serious obstacle of the Meuse, in shortening our front considerably, we can hold out there under favourable circumstances for one or two months... I do not believe there is any possibility of holding out over December, particularly as the Americans are drawing about 300,000 men monthly from beyond the ocean... Ludendorff does not realise the whole seriousness of the situation. Whatever happens, we must obtain peace before the enemy breaks through into Germany; if he does, woe on us![10]

The reply to President Wilson's Note was sent on the 25th. The Chancellor accepted the condition that the armistice should be arranged by military advisers, but asked the President to approve no demand 'that would be irreconcilable with the honour of the German people and with paving the way to a peace of justice'. He intended to halt the sinking of passenger ships, assured the President that Germany would observe humane rules of civilised warfare and concluded by promising that a Bill would be introduced to make decisions on war and peace subject to the Reichstag's approval.

Wilson (CIGS) had telegraphed Haig on the 13th that there were reports of an armistice and that the American President had been informed that 'the terms must be laid down by the Allied Naval and Military Representatives. This point has not yet been reached, and until it has ... the operations now going on should be continued with all the vigour you consider safe and possible.'

Haig visited the War Office on the 19th and saw Wilson:

He considers that 'the Germans should be ordered to lay down their arms and retire to the east bank of the Rhine'. I gave my opinion that our attack on the 17th inst. [by the Fourth Army] met considerable resistance, and that the enemy was not ready for unconditional surrender. In that case, there would be no armistice, and the war would continue for another year![11]

They then had a meeting with the Prime Minister, Lord Milner and Bonar Law (Deputy Prime Minister), and Lloyd George asked Haig for his views on the terms that should be offered to Germany. Haig posed two questions. Was the enemy now so exhausted that he would surrender unconditionally? In the event of a refusal, could the Allies continue to press him so vigorously during the winter months that his retirement would be so rapid as to leave him no time to destroy railways and roads? Haig answered his own questions in the negative: 'The German army is capable of retiring to its own frontier, and holding the line if there should be any attempt to touch the honour of the German people, and make them fight with the courage of despair.' He then summed up the situation of the Allied Armies:

French Army: worn out and has not been really fighting latterly. It has been freely said that the 'war is over' and 'we don't wish to lose our lives now that peace is in sight'.

American Army: is not yet organised: it is ill-equipped, half-trained, with insufficient supply services. Experienced officers and NCOs are lacking.

British Army: was never more efficient than it is today, but it has fought hard, and it lacks reinforcements. With diminishing effectives, morale is bound to suffer.[12]

According to his *War Memoirs*, the Prime Minister considered Haig's view of the military prospects to be 'unduly restrained':

He advised us that in his view it would be best to offer armistice terms which involved no more than the retirement of the enemy to his own frontiers, evacuating Belgium, France and Alsace-Lorraine, and returning the commandeered Belgian rolling stock and deported Belgian citizens. If Germany rejected satisfactory peace terms we could then resume the War in 1919 on enemy soil.

Mr Bonar Law pointed out that such terms really amounted to complete defeat, and that in the military situation which Haig described there was nothing which should compel the Germans to accept such terms...

We passed under review the military terms which Foch had suggested for an armistice, and the naval terms which our Admiralty demanded. These anticipated the main features of the Armistice ultimately imposed, and I pointed out that they amounted to abject surrender. I asked Haig what would be the effect on our Army if we insisted on such terms and the enemy refused them.[13]

Haig's response was that 'The British Army had done most of the fighting latterly, and everyone wants to have done with the war, provided we get what we want.' He urged that 'we only ask in the armistice for what we intend to hold, and that we set our faces against the French entering Germany to pay off old scores'. In his opinion, 'the British Army would not fight keenly for what is really not its own affair'.[14] The Prime Minister summed up: 'On the whole, the military advice we obtained did not encourage us to expect an immediate termination of the war. All our plans and preparations at that date were therefore made on the assumption of all our military advisers that the War would certainly not conclude before 1919.'[15]

Between 17 and 22 October, the operations by the First and Third Armies were concentrated on crossing the river Selle and the Haute Deule and Sensée canals. VIII Corps of the First Army crossed the Heute Deule canal on the 17th against little opposition and entered Douai which had been evacuated (including civilians) and 'a great part of which was burning'. The Canadian Corps forced the passage of the Selle, and both corps continued their advance on the next day, meeting only insignificant resistance, albeit fog, and the uncertainty of the enemy's whereabouts, proved something of a handicap. By the 19th, the Germans were retiring along the whole of the First Army's front, and the VIII and Canadian Corps pushed on against ever dwindling opposition except from long-range artillery. There was a combined advance by both the First and Third Armies on the 20th.

The greater part of the Third Army was still on the west bank of the Selle and its immediate task, after forcing a passage, was to establish a bridgehead on the high ground beyond. Zero hour was 2 a.m. on a damp and foggy night; it was hoped that the timing and the absence of a preliminary bombardment would achieve surprise. The Selle was crossed by foot-bridges, but on the right the main opposition came from the line of the railway which ran northwards from Le Cateau to Valenciennes along the eastern bank. This was eventually overcome, and the advance continued to its objective. On the left, the main obstacles were the river itself – some twenty feet wide and about four or six deep – and the village of Solesmes, which was strongly held. A battalion of the 62nd Division (VI Corps), however, waded across before zero hour, capturing Solesmes shortly after 7 a.m. Thereafter the advance of VI Corps continued without encountering strong opposition. By the end of the day, all the Third Army's objectives had been reached and a line established beyond the Selle. The First Army's attack was also successful although the enemy was not always prepared to withdraw without a struggle. The Selle was crossed on the right, but the advance was delayed until the evening because of strong resistance from the enemy position on the Le Cateau–Valenciennes railway. In the centre, the Canadians had a difficult time in their attempt to capture the village of Denain, and further progress was checked until the Germans withdrew in the early evening. On the left, however, the advance of VIII Corps met no opposition.

There was little serious fighting on the two following days (21st and 22nd). The Third Army was making preparations for a renewed offensive on the 23rd, although the centre and left of the First Army followed up the German retirement to the Schelde canal. There was little French activity during this period. The First Army 'was practically stationary', and the Tenth Army, following up a German retirement, made little progress because of the 'waterlogged ground and intense machine-gun fire'. There was no significant advance on the Meuse–Argonne front.

The operations on the 23rd and 24th were designed to bring the Fourth, Third and First Armies into line facing east before the Hermann II Position. This ran four miles to the east of Hermann I along the Sambre–Oise canal, and then ran north, passing west of Le Quesnoy until it joined the Schelde canal at Valenciennes. Neither Hermann I or II were prepared defensive positions, the main dependence being on natural obstacles – Hermann I on the River Selle, and Herman II on the Sambre–Oise and Schelde canals. There were trenches (in poor condition) in the gap between the two canals, protected by two lines of wire entanglements, and machine-gun nests dug in the fields and orchards. 'Between the woods was pasture-land cut into innumerable small enclosures by high, thick hedges.' The hedges had been wired, and to some extent the ground to be covered resembled the *bocage* country of Normandy that had caused so many problems to the Allied forces in 1944.

The task of the Fourth Army, as mentioned, was to provide a defensive flank to the main operation which was to be undertaken by the Third Army. The Fourth Army now consisted of two corps (IX and XIII), the two American divisions constituting the American II Corps having been withdrawn into GHQ Reserve. The objectives set were: IX Corps, an advance of two miles to the Sambre canal, and XIII Corps, to secure the Landrecies–Englefontaine road, entailing an advance of five miles. Zero hour was 1.20 a.m. and although there was a bright moon, ground mist had formed by midnight. Twenty-three tanks were employed to provide assistance in clearing paths through the hedges, but poor visibility made it difficult for the infantry to find the gaps. Although progress was at first slow, causing the barrage to be lost, only patchy resistance was encountered and the advance gained almost all its objectives, albeit with heavy tank casualties, mainly due to ditching and mechanical problems.

The zero hours for the four corps of the Third Army had varied between 2.00 and 3.20 a.m. according to the distance from the start-line to the objective. On the right, V Corps overcame all resistance and advanced three-and-a-half miles to its objective, but attempts to push on were frustrated by fire from the village of Poix du Nord in the Hermann II Position. Elsewhere, the advance proceeded to the objectives without undue problems, although there was stubborn resistance from a strong-point in the village of Beaurain which was eventually overcome by mortar fire. The First Army was equally successful: the Canadian Corps entered the western suburbs of Valenciennes and reached the Schelde, and VIII Corps crossed the River Scarpe.

The attacks continued on the next day (24th). IX Corps, on the right of the Fourth Army, found that the enemy had retired to the eastern bank of the Sambre canal. In the centre, XIII Corps faced the irregular character of the Hermann II defensive position. First, the wire had to be penetrated; thereafter a breach of the defences was accomplished only by hand-to-hand fighting. At the end of the day, the Fourth Army had almost reached its final objective, and was within a mile of the great Mormal Forest. The right of the Third Army was also approaching the forest after forcing its way through Hermann II and, in the centre, was less than two miles from Le Quesnoy. XVII Corps, on the left, had problems crossing the River Ecaillon, and having lost the barrage ended just short of its final objective. The

Ecaillon, some twenty feet wide and four deep, also caused problems for XXII Corps of the First Army, but passage was forced by the infantry swimming or wading across. There was little movement by the Canadian and VIII Corps as they were already close up to the Schelde.

The results of the two days' fighting had brought the Fourth Army to the Sambre canal and the First Army to the Schelde canal – the last natural barriers before the Antwerp–Meuse position – and the Third Army was poised before the bastion of Le Quesnoy.

A German account of the fighting on the 23rd records:

On this day the British attacked north and south of Solesmes with strong forces... One diary remarks that it was the day of heaviest fighting since the great defeat of the 8th August with its direful results. On account of the dwindling strength of the divisions, the Second Army headquarters drew the attention of the Crown Prince Rupprecht's Group of Armies, as well as of OHL, to the fact that the Second Army had reached, near the Forest of Mormal, its last rearward position, and that, in view of the general condition of the troops, the defence of this great wooded area raised serious considerations. The Army Commander, therefore, recommended a general retreat to the Antwerp–Meuse position at an early date... During the afternoon of the 24th the Second Army received orders to continue to hold the present battle area, and if forced to retire only to do so fighting step by step.[16]

President Wilson's third Note was received in Berlin on the 23rd. It stated that the Allied Governments were agreeable to an armistice but on condition that hostilities would not be renewed. It went further:

The nations of the world do not, and cannot trust the word of those who have hitherto been the masters of German policy... The Government of the United States cannot deal with any but veritable representatives of the German people, who have been assured of a genuine constitutional standing as the real masters of Germany. If it must deal with the military masters and the monarchical autocrats of Germany now ... it must demand not peace negotiations but surrender.[17]

This uncompromising message meant, in effect, the abdication of the Kaiser and the resignation of Ludendorff and Hindenburg.

When Ludendorff was informed, his response was that it was 'an intolerable humiliation. There was only one solution: break off negotiations with Wilson and fight to the end.'[18] On the 24th a proclamation was issued from Supreme Headquarters, 'For the Information of all Troops'. It was signed by Hindenburg, although it is probable that it had been drafted by Ludendorff. It concluded:

170

Wilson's answer is a demand for unconditional surrender. It is thus unacceptable to us soldiers. It proves that our enemy's desire for our destruction, which let loose the war in 1914, still exists undiminished. It proves, further, that our enemies use the phrase 'Peace of Justice' merely to deceive us and break our resistance. Wilson's answer can thus be nothing for us soldiers but a challenge to continue our resistance with all our strength. When our enemies know that no sacrifices will achieve the rupture of the German front, they will be ready for a peace which will make the future of our country safe for the great masses of our people.[19]

This fateful proclamation had been dispatched without reference to the Government, causing a storm of protest in the Reichstag, and Prince Max asked the Kaiser to dismiss Ludendorff. According to the latter's *Memoirs*, he had decided to resign on the morning of the 26th, but had been dissuaded by Hindenburg on the grounds that he should not desert the Emperor and the army, and after 'an inward struggle' he consented. Almost immediately, however, they were summoned by the Kaiser:

The Emperor seemed wholly changed in comparison with the previous day. Speaking to me alone, he expressed himself particularly against the army order of the evening of the 24th. There followed some of the bitterest moments of my life. I said respectfully to His Majesty that I had gained the painful impression that I no longer enjoyed his confidence, and that I accordingly begged most humbly to be relieved of my office. His Majesty accepted my resignation.[20]

Hindenburg also offered his resignation which was not accepted. On the 27th the reply to President Wilson's third Note was sent: 'The German Government now awaits proposals for an armistice which shall be a first step towards a just peace such as the President has outlined in his proclamations.'[21]

There was a conference at Foch's headquarters on the 25th, attended by the three Commanders-in-Chief, to consider the terms for an armistice. Haig reiterated the views he had expressed to the War Cabinet on the 19th. He believed that the Germans could still withdraw to a shorter front and make a stand; that the British and French troops were exhausted; and that the American Army was lacking in experience. Pétain considered that the Germans should retire by stages 'so rapidly that they would be compelled to leave most of their material behind, and therefore should be incapable of further fighting'. Pershing took a much stronger line: he proposed the German evacuation of France and Belgium within thirty days; retirement to the east bank of the Rhine and the surrender of all submarines and submarine bases to a neutral power. Foch did not support Haig's contention that the Germans were still capable of making a stand:

Although we are not able to tell its exact condition, still we are dealing with an army which has been pounded every day for three months, an army that is now being beaten on every part of its front of 250 miles; an army which since the 15th July has lost a quarter of a million men in prisoners alone and over four thousand guns; an army which is, physically and morally, a thoroughly beaten army. Certainly the British and French Armies are tired; certainly the American Army is a young Army, but it is full of idealism and strength and ardour; it has won victories and is now on the eve of another victory; and nothing gives wings to an Army like victory.[22]

Meanwhile, in the last two weeks of October the Fifth Army continued its pursuit of the retreating enemy to the Schelde. In its path, extending along its entire front, was the Haute Deule canal; and situated only four miles from its left wing was the important manufacturing town of Lille, surrounded by a continuous line of fortifications designed in the seventeenth century by the famous military engineer, Vauban. As in the case of other large French towns, it was not to be shelled in order to protect civilians. On the 15th, however, the Germans carried out a further retirement along the entire Fifth Army front, thus enabling the Haute Deule canal to be crossed. On the right wing, I Corps was able to advance about two miles beyond the canal, and a further four miles on the next day. The left wing facing Lille made only slight progress, but on the 17th the Germans evacuated the town without offering any serious resistance. Little military damage had been done, but many private houses had been ransacked, and property 'wantonly broken up' by the retreating enemy:

> The survivors of the inhabitants looked fit but thin, with their clothes hanging loose about them, but, as a medical officer said, the weaker vessels had died under a régime of semi-starvation from which the town had suffered for just four years. The Germans, however, had the humanity to leave six days' supplies behind for the inhabitants.[23]

The pursuit was maintained over the next three days against only slight opposition, and the Army's left wing reached the Schelde. Efforts by the centre and right wing to close up to the canal encountered determined resistance. Attempts were made on the 21st and 22nd to establish bridgeheads north and south of Tournai, but were frustrated by heavy artillery fire. Thereafter there was little change in the position until the end of the month, and it was apparent that, for the time being, the enemy's retreat had come to an end, and a stand would be made on the Schelde.

Farther north, the objective of the Second Army had also been the Schelde but, unlike the Fifth Army, it had to contend with stubborn resistance from a hitherto unsuspected defensive system of heavily wired trenches, known to the enemy as the

Courtrai Switch, which extended from Helchin on the Schelde to east of Courtrai on the River Lys. The Army's attack opened on the 20th and had a comparatively easy passage on the right wing where XV Corps approached the Schelde. Little progress could be made on the left wing, however, because of stiffening opposition. On the 21st, X Corps joined XV Corps on the Schelde, but attempts to bridge the canal failed. On the left wing, XIX and II Corps made little progress over the next three days; the enemy even mounted several counter-attacks and retook some lost ground. A combined assault by XIX and II Corps, in conjunction with a French division, saw some gains, but the line reached was still four miles from the Schelde. Better progress was made during the 26th and 27th as the enemy began to retire to the east bank of the Schelde. Thus the Second, Fifth and First Armies were now poised before the Schelde, and orders were given for the following sequence of further operations: on 31 October, on the left, an attack by the Flanders Group of Armies (including the Second Army); on 1 November, a by-pass south of Valenciennes by the British Third and First Armies; on the same day, an assault by the American First Army and the French Fourth Army; and, finally, on 4 November, in the right centre, an attack by the British Fourth, Third and First Armies together with the French First Army.

On 31 October a concerted attack was launched by XIX and II Corps of the Second Army in conjunction with the French VIII Corps. The two British corps reached the west bank of the Schelde, and on their left flank, the French advanced five miles to reach the western bend of the Schelde. The Second Army, having reached the Schelde, could now be returned to Haig's command under a compromise agreement reached some days earlier; Foch, despite Haig's objection, had originally wanted it to remain in the Flanders Group because of the political value attached to the Belgian King re-entering Brussels in command of a group of Allied Armies.

At 5.15 a.m. on 1 November, XVII Corps of the Third Army, XXII Corps and the Canadian Corps of the First Army began their operation to move forward south of Valenciennes in order to outflank the town and also the line of the Schelde. On the right, XVII Corps crossed the River Rhonelle on foot-bridges, reached its objective, the village of Maresches, by 8.30 a.m., advanced beyond and was nearing St Hubert when the enemy launched a strong counter-attack led by four captured British tanks. This was directed not only against XVII Corps but also the 49th Division of XXII Corps, forcing a withdrawal. Two of the tanks were knocked out by field guns, but progress of both corps had been checked. An attempt was made to resume the advance in the early evening, but heavy machine-gun fire compelled a postponement until the next day. The advance of the Canadian Corps went well until it encountered machine-gun fire from the southern outskirts of Valenciennes. The 12th Canadian Brigade, however, succeeded in crossing the Schelde and entering the western outskirts of the town. The combined attack was resumed on the next day, and after a token resistance the enemy evacuated the town and withdrew from the Schelde. This withdrawal caused the abandonment of the offensive planned for 4 November, and once again it now became a matter of pursuit.

The American First Army and the French Fourth Army resumed their offensive on 1 November on the Meuse–Argonne front. The Americans, demonstrating that they had overcome the logistical and communication problems that had earlier beset their operations, broke through east of Buzancy, the 2nd Division advancing nearly six miles and outpacing the French on their left. Over the next three days, both Armies pursued a demoralised enemy; by the 5th the Americans had cleared the approaches to Beaumont on the Meuse and the French had crossed the Aisne.

Notes

1. Edmonds, Brigadier-General Sir James, and Maxwell-Hyslop Lieutenant-Colonel R., (comp.), *Official History of the War: Military Operations France and Belgium 1918*, Vol. V, HMSO 1947
2. Maurice, Major-General Sir F., *The Life of General Lord Rawlinson*, Cassell (London, 1928)
3. Edmonds, *op. cit.*
4. *Ibid.*
5. Falls, Cyril, *The First World War*, Longmans (London, 1960)
6. Foch, Marshal, Foch The *Memoirs of Marshal Foch*, Heinemann (London 1931)
7. Max, Prince of Baden, *Memoirs* (2 vols), Constable (London, 1928)
8. Edmonds, *op. cit.*
9. Max, *op. cit.*
10. *Ibid.*
11. Blake, Robert, (ed.), *The Private Papers of Douglas Haig 1914–1919*, Eyre & Spottiswoode (London, 1952)
12. *Ibid.*
13. Lloyd George, David, *War Memoirs*, Odhams (London, 1938)
14. Blake, *op. cit.*
15. Lloyd George, *op. cit.*
16. Edmonds, *op. cit.*
17. Max, *op. cit.*
18. Foester, W., *Der Feldherr Ludendorff* (Wiesbaden, 1952)
19. Ludendorff, General, *Concise Ludendorff Memoirs*, Hutchinson (London, 1933)
20. *Ibid.*
21. Max, *op. cit.*
22. Edmonds, *op. cit.*
23. *Ibid.*

12

The Collapse of Germany

The crisis in Berlin deepened with the news that the Austrian emperor had written to the Kaiser on 27 October expressing his determination to seek a separate armistice without waiting for the result of the current negotiations between Germany and President Wilson. This had been brought about by the success of the Italian offensive begun on the 24th. The plan was to cross the River Piave (the line reached after the retirement following the Caporetto disaster) and separate the Austro-Hungarian armies on the river from those in the mountains by an advance in a north-easterly direction. Italian, British and French troops had established a bridgehead by the 27th, and on the 30th reached the Austrian headquarters at Vittoria Veneto. Thereafter, the Austro-Hungarian troops melted away, and on the night of 2/3 November the Austrian command issued an order for the cessation of hostilities which came into effect on 3 November.

Demand was growing in Berlin for the Kaiser's abdication, and the Chancellor recognised that less harsh peace terms would not be possible while the Kaiser remained: his difficulty was finding the means to break the news to him. 'To whom could I now turn, who would be willing and fitted to speak to the Kaiser as a friend? I knew of no one in Berlin.'[1] He attempted to obtain an audience with the Kaiser who was at Potsdam, but was refused. On the 30th the Kaiser arrived at Supreme Headquarters at Spa, telling Admiral von Hintze, 'Prince Max's Government is trying to throw me out. At Berlin I should be less able to oppose them than in the midst of my troops.' The Chancellor tried unsuccessfully to persuade the Kaiser to return to Berlin with the plea, 'at any hour we may be confronted with decisions on which the fate of Germany depends, decisions that can only be made through the co-operation of Crown, Chancellor and Government'.[2] There was a Cabinet meeting on the 31st, but the members were divided on the question of abdication. After the meeting, the Chancellor decided that the Kaiser would have to abdicate voluntarily, otherwise it would be forced upon him with the possibility of it leading to civil war 'since there are millions in the country who would stand firmly behind His Majesty'.[3] The task of persuading the Kaiser to abdicate was finally given to Dr Wilhelm Drews (Prussian Minister of the Interior) who saw the Kaiser on 1 November. The Kaiser's account of the meeting was contained in a letter to a friend:

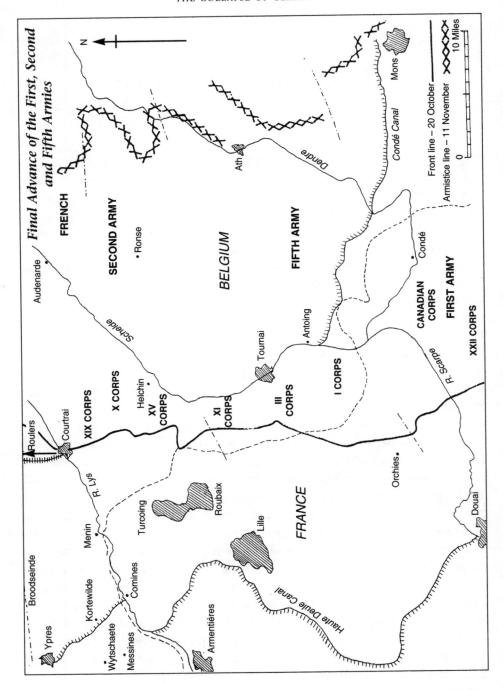

Final Advance of the First, Second and Fifth Armies

I said, 'How comes it that you, a Prussian official, one of my subjects who have taken an oath of allegiance to me, have the insolence and effrontery to appear before me with a request like this?' You should just have seen how that took the wind out of his sails. It was the last thing he expected, he made a deep bow on the spot. 'Very well then, supposing I did,' I said. 'What do you suppose would happen next, you, an administrative official? My sons have assured me that none of them will take my place. So the whole House of H [Hohenzollern] would go along with me.' You should have seen the fright that gave him, it again was the last thing he'd expected. He and the whole of that smart govt [sic] in Berlin. 'And who would then take on the regency for a twelve-year child, my grandson? the Imperial Chancellor? I gather from Munich that they haven't the least intention of recognising him down there. So what would happen?' 'Chaos,' he said, making another bow. You see, you only have to question such muddle-heads, and go on questioning them, for all their confusion and empty-headedness to become obvious. 'All right then,' I said, 'let me tell you the form chaos would take. I abdicate. All the dynasties fall along with me, the army is left leaderless, the front-line troops disband and stream over the Rhine. The disaffected gang up together, hang, murder and plunder – assisted by the enemy. That is why I have no intention of abdicating.'

At this point, the unfortunate Dr Drews managed to say that he was there under orders from the Chancellor, whereupon the Kaiser said, 'The King of Prussia cannot betray Germany etc. I have no intention of quitting the throne because of a few hundred Jews and a thousand workmen. Tell that to your masters in Berlin!'

On 29 October, GHQ issued orders for the renewal of operations: 'The Fourth, Third and First Armies will resume the offensive on or after the 3rd November [in effect, the 4th], with a view to breaking the enemy's resistance south of the Condé canal and advancing in the general direction of Avesnes–Maubeuge–Mons.' The French First Army was to co-operate by an advance towards La Capelle.

The Fourth Army was confronted along its whole line of advance not only by the Sambre canal (running north to south on the right, and south-east to north-east on the left), but also by the great Forest of Mormal where the Germans had felled some trees and, in the clearings created, positioned wire entanglements and barricades manned by machine-gunners. The canal was about six feet deep and seventy feet wide from bank to bank except at the locks. Virtually the whole frontage of IX Corps on the right was close up to the canal, and at 5.45 a.m. in thick mist the canal was crossed with varying degrees of difficulty on planks and floating bridges. Enemy resistance was generally slight, but the 2nd Division encountered heavy fire and suffered heavy casualties in its first attempt to achieve a crossing. So desperate were further attempts that no less than four Victoria Crosses were awarded, two posthumously; and it was here that the poet Wilfred Owen, a lieutenant in the Manchester Regiment, was killed. On the left, XIII Corps at first met with strong resistance in its advance towards the forest, but once the accompanying tanks had overcome the nests of machine guns, the opposition weakened, and by the evening an advance of nearly four miles had been recorded. The south-east to north-east stretch of the canal was crossed on the next day, and over the next two days the advance was hindered only by the incessant rain and patchy resistance from rear-guards. By the evening of the 7th, the position reached was nearly fifteen miles from the start-line.

The Forest of Mormal occupied a half of the Third Army's frontage, but before the troops could reach the forest, their path was barred by the town of Le Quesnoy:

> Above the Roman road to Bavai the 37th Division and the New Zealand Divi-sion had the severest struggle in the action. They had to advance by Ghissin-gies and the hills above the Ecaillon stream towards the old fortress town of Le Quesnoy. By this picturesque old walled city Englishmen came under the fire of cannon in the year of Crécy, and in 1711 the Duke of Marlborough ended his last campaign by its walls.[4]

The original plan was to take the town by envelopment rather than by a frontal assault, and an advance north and south of the town by battalions of the New Zealand Division (IV Corps) and the 62nd Division (VI Corps) met little opposition on their way to the objective. As fire continued to come from le Quesnoy, however, a message was dropped from British aeroplanes: 'You are completely surrounded, and our troops are far to the east of you. If you will surrender, you will be treated as honourable prisoners of war.'

> But the German commandant would not surrender. Two treating parties were sent in, each consisting of a New Zealand officer and two German officer pris-oners. Entering by a breach in the outer ramparts, they shouted the summons to surrender and the promise of honourable treatment. A few men accepted the offer and came out, but the German commandant resolved to stand in le Quesnoy to the last, hoping thereby to win more time for the withdrawal of the main German forces.[5]

There then ensued an action reminiscent of other wars and other days. New Zealand artillery breached the curtain wall, and in the afternoon the infantry scaled the sheer inner walls with the aid of ladders and cleared the machine-gun posts at the point of the bayonet: Le Quesnoy then surrendered. On the right, V Corps, assisted by tanks, successfully cleared a path through wired hedges and then pushed on through the forest. This proved to be less difficult than expected, and a line was established on the eastern edge of the forest in the early hours of the next day.

Although VI and XVII Corps on the left met stiffer opposition than their neighbours, this eventually weakened and by the end of the day the Third Army's objectives had been reached along its entire front. Progress, however, was slower over the next three days because of the appalling state of the roads and tracks caused by the continuous rain which seriously delayed the bringing up of artillery, ammunition and rations. Moreover, the rain had swollen the numerous small streams that seamed the area of the advance, where, in summer, they would have presented few difficulties.

XXII Corps and the Canadian Corps of the First Army met strong resistance south of the Condé canal (which connects Condé with Mons) through the period 4 to 6 November. It was not until the 7th that it was learned that the enemy was withdrawing, enabling the two corps to push on at a greater pace; but north of the canal, VIII Corps, at a halt before the Schelde, made no advance.

On the 4th, the left wing of the French First Army had established touch with the British Fourth Army at Oisy, but there was no movement by its right wing, or by the Fifth and Third Armies, although the American First Army continued to make progress. On the 5th, according to the French Official History, 'the enemy began a vast movement of retreat extending from the Meuse to Condé on the Schelde'. The left of the French First Army continued to keep pace with the British and, by the evening, the Americans had crossed the Meuse, its left wing within ten miles of Sedan. On the 6th, OHL ordered all the German armies to retire to the Antwerp–Meuse position.

Ludendorff had been replaced by General Wilhelm Gröner (formerly Chief of Staff of the Kiev Army Group) who arrived at Spa on 30 October. After assessing the situation he was summoned to Berlin on 5 November when he told the Cabinet: 'We can hold out long enough for negotiations. If we are lucky the time might be longer: if we are unlucky, shorter... But one thing must not be allowed to happen: the American Army – or any considerable portion of it – must be prevented from advancing north of Verdun.' On the next day, however, his forecast was even gloomier: 'We must now cross the lines with a white flag', and when asked when this should take place, he replied, 'It must be Saturday [9th] at the latest. He turned aside demands for the Kaiser's abdication, believing that if they persisted the army would fall apart and then, 'The wild beast in man will break out in the hands of disorganised soldiers pouring back into their native land... If the army remains unbroken, we should be offered better terms and have a better foundation for reconstruction.'[6] Gröner's unofficial solution to the problem, however, was that the Kaiser 'should go to the front, not to review troops or confer decorations but to look on death. He should go to some trench which was under the full blast of war. If he were killed, it would be the finest death possible. If he were wounded, the feelings of the German people toward him would completely change.'

Indeed, the shadows were fast closing upon Germany. On 30 October Turkey signed an armistice with the Allied powers. At the same time Admiral Scheer issued orders for the High Seas Fleet to put to sea in a last bid for glory, but the crews of six battleships refused. When the order was repeated, the crews mutinied and some were imprisoned. On 4 November there was a large demonstration by sailors in Kiel, and after an inflammatory speech by two socialists, they marched towards the prison singing the Internationale, but were dispersed by fire from a naval patrol. Two days later, the sailors and dock workers took over the naval base, and ships in the harbour ran up the red flag. Similar revolutionary organisations sprang up in Hamburg and Bremen, and within days had spread to other cities.

There was a series of meetings in Paris at the end of October and the beginning of November between the Prime Ministers of France, Britain and Italy and Colonel House (President Wilson's personal representative) to discuss the terms for an armistice. The sticking point was Clause 2 in the President's Fourteen Points relating to the Freedom of the Seas. This had always been opposed by the British Government because it appeared to imply that if Britain ever became involved in a future war, she would not be able to impose a blockade or apply economic pressure on an enemy unless the war was being fought under international covenants. House threatened that the United States would make a separate peace unless this clause was accepted, and Lloyd George and Clemenceau countered this by saying that, nevertheless, Britain and France would fight on. Lloyd George, however, eventually compromised by expressing his willingness 'to discuss the freedom of the seas in the light of the new conditions which have arisen in the course of the present war'. At the meeting of the Supreme War Council on 4 November, it was agreed that President Wilson should inform Germany that the Allies 'expressed their willingness to make peace with the Government of Germany on the terms laid down in the President's address to Congress on 8 January, 1918', but it was pointed out that Clause 2 relating to Freedom of the Seas was 'open to various interpretations, some of which they could not accept' and reserved to themselves 'complete freedom on this subject when they entered the Peace Conference'. They further stressed that compensation should be made by Germany 'for all damage done to the civilian population of the Allies and their property by the aggression of Germany by land, by sea, and from the air'.

President Wilson addressed a further Note to Berlin on 5 November quoting the text of the memorandum he had received from the Supreme War Council. He concluded by informing Germany that Foch was authorised by the Allied Governments to receive accredited representatives of the German Government and communicate to them the armistice terms. When the Note was received in Berlin on the 6th, General Gröner suggested, and the Chancellor agreed, that Matthias

Erzberger (head of the Catholic Party) should be the Government representative, and Erzberger left for Spa that day to join military members for the journey to France. In the hope that it would check the uprising, a statement was issued to the Press to the effect that the Allies had accepted the Fourteen Points and a German armistice team was already on its way.

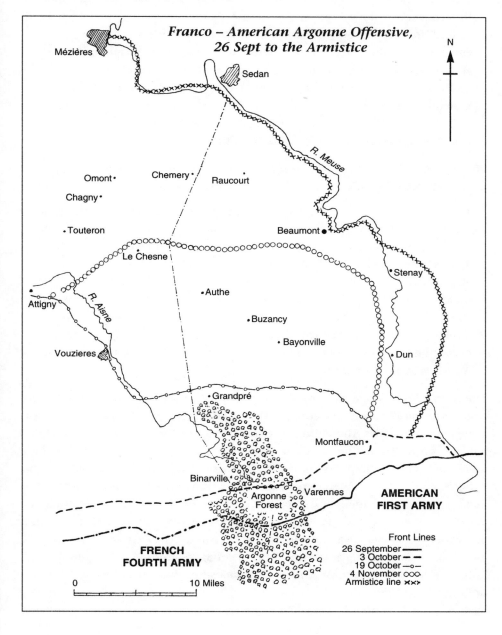

Franco – American Argonne Offensive, 26 Sept to the Armistice

Front Lines
26 September ——
3 October — —
19 October —o—
4 November ooo
Armistice line ×××

Notwithstanding the momentous events of the past few days, there was no slackening of the pressure being applied by the Allied Armies. For the British Armies, GHQ issued orders that on the 8th:

The Fourth, Third and First Armies should continue their present operations with the object of reaching the line Avesnes–Maubeuge–Mons road (for short the 'Avesnes road'): advanced guards and mounted troops should then be pushed forward beyond the road to keep touch with the enemy: every endeavour should be made to restore the rearward communication; the Fifth and Second Armies, in conjunction with the Flanders Group of Armies should on 11November carry out an operation to force the passage of the Schelde and then drive the enemy back over the river Dendre (15 miles east of the Schelde).

The Cavalry Corps (less 2nd Cavalry Division and one cavalry brigade) would operate under the orders of GOC Fifth Army.

The problem of supplying the advance was now becoming a major problem, particularly as it could be expected that the weather would worsen.

The ever-lengthening distances involved and the gradual deterioration of the roads as the weather grew worse, the demolitions more frequent and the traffic heavier, imposed a severe strain on the transport vehicles and their drivers. The mobile workshops found it almost impossible to deal with the abnormal amount of repairs due to bad roads and to excessive use. The infantry had by now got beyond the forward limit of lorries, reckoned at about thirty miles, and beyond that limit the divisional horse transport bringing up supplies, although reinforced from the ammunition columns, was beginning to feel the extra strain involved in the hilly country which the Armies were now entering.[7]

The Fourth Army reached the Avesnes road around noon on the 8th, but attempts to push forward encountered strong resistance including, in one instance, a determined counter-attack. The Third Army came up against even stronger opposition; a prisoner revealed that orders had been given to hold on at all costs, and not until late in the evening did patrols find that the enemy had retired. It was only on the extreme right that the Avesnes road was reached; nevertheless, in the centre, the large village of Hautmont was captured, and on the left, XVII Corps made an advance of four miles 'in very enclosed country, a labyrinth of small fields, hedged and wired, intersected by a number of small streams...'[8] The First Army had to cross an extensive coal-mining area with scattered cottages, pitheads and slag heaps – all potential defensive positions. Only slight opposition was encountered, however, until the afternoon when the leading battalions came under artillery fire. An average advance of about three miles was achieved, and the furthest point reached was only some seven miles from Mons. Rapid progress was made by the three Armies over the next two days because of an extensive enemy retirement, and on the Fourth Army's front cavalry squadrons penetrated nearly ten miles to the Belgian frontier. On the 9th, the Third Army entered Maubeuge, and on the 10th, the Canadian Corps of the First Army captured Mons, but only after overcoming stubborn resistance, particularly from machine-gunners.

It was a similar situation on the fronts of the Fifth and Second Armies. Both Armies had been held up west of the Schelde ever since the beginning of November where, although no serious attempt had been made to cross, probes by patrols to assess the defences had been vigorously resisted. Early on the 8th, however, patrols of the Fifth Army discovered that the Germans had abandoned their bridgehead west of Tournai–Antoing, enabling advanced guards to cross. The portion of Tournai west of the canal was entered, but the enemy still held the eastern bank. On the Second Army front, patrols accomplished a crossing of the Schelde at four locations, but on the 9th the enemy retired on the entire fronts of both Armies, and over the next two days the advanced guards of both Armies made lengthy advances without meeting any serious opposition.

The French Sixth Army on the left of the British Second Army had also been halted on the Schelde, but the enemy retreat on the 9th enabled the French to push advanced guards across the river. Thereafter the advance proceeded against little resistance, and by the 10th was level with the Second Army. On the Meuse–Argonne front, the Americans had advanced twenty-four miles between 1 and 7 November on either side of the Meuse, the French on their left capturing Mézières and Charleville. There then began a race to capture Sedan, a centre of immense significance to the French for it was from the same beleaguered town, in September 1870, that the French Emperor Napoleon III had ridden to surrender to the Prussians. Pershing, with a somewhat insensitive regard for French feelings, had planned for it to be captured by his I Corps, but ultimately the French were allowed the courtesy to be the first to enter.

Soon after midnight on the 7th, a wireless message was sent to Foch informing him that the German Armistice Commission was about to leave and requesting details of the meeting place. Foch replied:

> If the German plenipotentiaries desire to meet Marshal Foch and ask him for an armistice, they will present themselves to the French outposts by the Chimay–Fourmies–La Capelle–Guise road. Orders have been given to receive them and conduct them to the spot fixed for the meeting.

The Commission consisted of Erzberger, General von Winterfelt (formerly military attaché in Paris), Count Alfred von Oberndorff, Vanselow, a naval captain and several assistants. They arrived in a fleet of cars at La Capelle in the evening, and spent the night in a château on the Aisne. On the morning of the 8th they were taken by train to a siding in the forest of Compiègne (originally constructed to enable a railway gun to shell Noyon), and at 9 a.m. they were ushered into a Wagon Lits saloon coach. Soon afterwards Foch entered with General Weygand, Admiral Sir R. Wemyss (First Sea Lord) and two British naval officers.

Marshal Foch asked the German delegates the purpose of their visit.

Herr Erzberger replied that the German delegation had come to receive the proposals of the Allied Powers looking to an armistice on land, on sea and in the air, on all the fronts, and in the colonies.

Marshal Foch replied that he had no proposals to make.

Count Oberndorff asked the Marshal in what form he desired that they should express themselves. He did not stand on form; he was ready to say that the German delegation asked the conditions of the armistice.

Marshal Foch replied that he had no conditions to offer.

Herr Erzberger read the text of President Wilson's last Note, stating that Marshal Foch is authorised to make known the armistice conditions.

Marshal Foch replied that he was authorised to make these known if the German delegates asked for an armistice.

'Do you ask for an armistice? If you do, I can inform you of the conditions subject to which it can be obtained.'

Herr Erzberger and Count Oberndorff declared that they asked for an armistice.[9]

Weygand then read the armistice terms, the principal conditions being:

1. Evacuation of occupied territory including Alsace-Lorraine within fourteen days: evacuation of the left bank of the Rhine within thirty-one days, and 5,000 guns, 25,000 machine guns and 1,700 aeroplanes to be handed to the Allies.
2. Surrender of all submarines, and internment in neutral or Allied ports of ten battleships, six battle-cruisers, eight light cruisers and fifty destroyers.
3. Renouncements of treaties of Brest-Litovsk and Bucharest.
4. All valuables and securities removed from invaded regions to be returned.

Foch demanded that the terms be accepted or rejected within seventy-two hours, and a reply received before 11 a.m. on the 11th. The Germans pleaded for an immediate cessation of hostilities on the grounds that 'Bolshevism may gain ground over the whole of Germany and threaten France herself'. Foch was unmoved, saying:

At the moment when negotiations for an armistice are just being opened, it is impossible to stop military operations until the German delegation has accepted and signed the conditions which are the very consequence of those operations. As for the situation described by Herr Erzberger as existing among the German troops and the danger he fears of Bolshevism spreading in Germany, the one is the usual disease prevailing in beaten armies, the other is symptomatic of a nation completely worn out by war. Western Europe will find means of defending itself against this danger.[10]

The delegates then dispatched a courier to Spa with the full terms of the Allied demands.

Meanwhile insurrection was rapidly spreading in Germany. A general strike had been called in Berlin, and revolutionary councils were being set up in city after city. In some places where troops had been ordered by the authorities to use force, they joined the rebels. On the previous day, the Chancellor had telephoned the Kaiser in an endeavour to persuade him to abdicate: 'Your abdication has become necessary to save Germany from civil war and to fulfil your mission as a peacemaking Emperor to the end. The blood that is shed could be laid at your door.' The Kaiser, however, was obdurate: he refused to abdicate or leave Spa except to lead his army to Berlin to restore order. The Socialist Democratic leaders (Ebert and Scheidemann) warned the Chancellor that the Government would collapse if the Kaiser refused to abdicate, raising the spectre of civil war.

At Spa on the morning of the 9th, Hindenburg was briefed on the state of the army, and also the latest news from Berlin where revolution appeared to be imminent. He then went to see the Kaiser in company with Gröner. Hindenburg was too overcome with emotion to read his report, leaving it to Gröner to inform the Kaiser that he no longer had an army: 'The army will march home in peace and order under its leaders and commanding generals, but not under the command of Your Majesty, for it no longer stands behind Your Majesty.' The Kaiser angrily demanded a statement signed by all his generals confirming that the army no longer supported him: 'Have they not taken the military oath to me?' Gröner replied, 'In a situation like this the military oath is a mere fiction'[11], and even Hindenburg said that he could not vouch for the trustworthiness of the army. This, coming from such a staunch royalist as Hindenburg, was a bitter blow to the Kaiser. The final blow came from a report from over thirty senior officers who had been brought to Spa and questioned as to whether the Kaiser could restore order at the head of his army, and whether the army could be relied on to fight the Bolshevists. To both questions the majority response was in the negative, and this finally dispelled any hope that the Kaiser might have had of the army's loyalty. Clutching at straws, he announced that he was prepared to renounce the Imperial Crown, but remain as King of Prussia; a hopelessly impractical and unconstitutional notion.

Meanwhile the Chancellor took matters into his own hands by issuing a statement:

The Kaiser and King has resolved to renounce the throne. The Imperial Chancellor will remain at his post until decisions have been made on questions connected with the Kaiser's abdication, the Crown Prince's renunciation of the Imperial and Prussian thrones, and the creation of a regency...[12]

Shortly afterwards he resigned. On 9 November the chancellorship passed to Friedrich Ebert, the Social Democrat leader, and at 2 p.m. Germany was proclaimed a republic. At Spa, Hindenburg told the Kaiser: 'I cannot accept the responsibility of seeing the Emperor hauled to Berlin by insurgent troops and delivered over as a prisoner to the Revolutionary Government. I must advise Your Majesty to abdicate and to proceed to Holland.' At 5 a.m. on the 10th, the Kaiser left by train to Holland and exile, followed shortly afterwards by the Crown Prince.

The German Armistice Commission, waiting anxiously in their train at Compiègne, received two messages, almost simultaneously, on the early evening of the 10th: 'The German Government accepts the conditions of the Armistice communicated to it on November 8th.' The other authorised Erzberger to sign the Armistice and have inserted in the record:

The German Government will undertake to carry out all the conditions laid down. At the same time the undersigned feel obliged to point out that the fulfilment of some points of these conditions will drive into famine the population of those parts of Germany which will not be occupied.

By leaving all provisions which were intended for troops in the areas to be evacuated, by restricting the means of communication and at the same time keeping up the blockade (which is equivalent to the withholding of food) any effort at dealing with the food question and organising the same is impossible...

At 2.15 a.m. on Monday, 11 November, the final armistice session began, and at 5 a.m. or shortly after, the German delegates signed with a declaration on the lines above, and concluded: 'The German nation which for fifty months has defied a world of enemies, will preserve, in spite of every kind of violence, its liberty and unity. A nation of seventy millions suffers but does not die.'

Marshal Foch then declared the meeting closed and the German delegates withdrew.

The following telegram was immediately sent along the whole front by radio and by telephone to the Commanders-in-Chief.

'1. Hostilities will cease on the entire front on November 11 at 11 a.m. French time.

2. Allied troops are not to pass until further orders beyond the line reached on that day at that hour.

3. All communication with the enemy is forbidden until receipt of instructions by Army Commanders.'[13]

This message was repeated by GHQ at 6.50 a.m. to the headquarters of the five British Armies and received, at the latest, by 7.30 a.m. This gave less than four hours for the order to be communicated to front-line troops, and operations continued until the last moment. These consisted of little more than pushing patrols forward against very little opposition, although in some places artillery fire was encountered, but more for the purpose of getting rid of ammunition than from hostile intent. Further orders from GHQ followed later in the morning:

1. Our own troops will not advance east of a line gained by them at hour when hostilities ceased. Our aeroplanes will keep a distance of not less than a mile behind this line, except for the purpose of driving back hostile aeroplanes as indicated in paragraph 3.

2. There is to be no unauthorised intercourse or fraternisation of any description with the enemy. He will not be permitted to approach our lines and any attempt to do so will be immediately stopped, if necessary by fire. Any parties of enemy coming over to our lines under a white flag will be made prisoner and [the] fact reported.

3. No enemy aircraft will be permitted to cross the line. Should any make an attempt to do so they will be attacked by fire from ground and from the air.

4. All commanders are to pay strictest attention to discipline, smartness and well-being of their troops, so as to ensure highest state of efficiency being maintained throughout British forces. Troops will be given every opportunity for rest, training, recreation and leave.

5. Passage of civilians through our lines in either direction will be regulated in accordance with instructions which will be issued separately. In the meantime no civilians will be permitted to pass in either direction.

According to the *Official History*: 'When 11 a.m. came the troops took the occasion in their usual matter of fact way: there was no outburst of cheering, no wild scene of rejoicing. Those who could lay down to sleep. The others went quietly about their duty with the strange feeling that all danger was absent.'

* * *

Very early on the last morning Shadbolt was watching the men dragging the heavy howitzers into a little clearing in the wood. The day was grey and overcast and the raindrops from a previous shower were dripping sadly off the trees. Above them a few pigeons, disturbed by the movements and cries of men, circled and wheeled. A dispatch rider rode up and handed him a message form. 'Hostilities will cease at 11 a.m. today. A.A.A. No firing will take place after this hour.' He sat down on the stump of a tree. In any case the order did not affect them. The enemy was already out of range, and they could move no further. This then was the end. Visions of the early days, their hopes and ambitions, swam before his eyes. He saw again his prehistoric howitzer in the orchard at Festubert, and Alington's long legs moved towards him through the trees. He was back with the Australians in their dug-out below Pozières. He saw the long slope of the hill at Heninel, covered with guns, ammunition dumps, tents and dug-outs. Ypres, the Salient, Trois Tours, St Julien – the names made unforgettable pictures in his mind. Happy days at Beugny and Beaussart, they were gone and the bad ones with them. Hugh was gone, and Tyler and little Rawson; Sergeant Powell, that brave old man: Elliot and James and Johnson – the names of his dead gunners strung themselves before him. This was the very end. What good had it all been? To serve what purpose had they all died? For the moment he could find no answer. His brain was too numb with memories.

'Mr Straker.'

'Sir.'

'You can fall the men out for breakfast. The war is over.'

'Very good, sir.'

Overhead the pigeons wheeled and circled.[14]

Notes

1. Max, Prince of Baden, *Memoirs* (2 vols.) Constable (London, 1928)
2. *Ibid.*
3. *Ibid.*
4. Hammerton, Sir J. (ed.), *World War 1914–1918: A Pictured History*, Amalgamated Press (London)
5. *Ibid.*
6. Max, *op. cit.*
7. Edmonds, Brigadier-General Sir James, and Maxwell-Hyslop, Lieutenant-Colonel R., (comp.), *Official History of the War: Military Operations France and Belgium 1918*, Vol. V, HMSO, 1947
8. *Ibid.*
9. Foch, Marshal F., *The Memoirs of Marshal Foch*, Heinemann (London, 1931)
10. *Ibid.*
11. Baumont, M., *The Fall of the Kaiser*, Knopf (New York, 1931)
12. Max, *op. cit.*
13. Foch, *op. cit.*
14. Severn, Mark, *The Gambardiers*, Ernest Benn (London, 1930)

Epilogue

It is now almost eighty years since the momentous events of 1918 accelerated the end of the Great War. In this remove in time, punctuated as it is by a second world war, it is not easy to comprehend how these events brought an end to the stalemate that had existed on the Western Front for almost four years: nor, indeed, how they had caused the sudden and unexpected collapse of Germany. Between March and early June the Allies had suffered a series of reverses so calamitous that by the end of May, following the German offensive at the Chemin des Dames, it seemed that defeat was a real possibility. The mood at the time is captured in the diary of Sir Maurice Hankey who accompanied the Prime Minister on 31 May to a meeting of the Supreme War Council at Versailles. Prior to the Council meeting he had a conversation with Lieutenant-General Sir John Du Cane (Head of the British Mission at Foch's headquarters):

> He [Du Cane] expressed considerable misgivings about the future and was particularly anxious at the idea of our having two and half million hostages on the Continent in the event of a French defeat. He envisages the possibility of the French Army being smashed and cut off from us, the enemy demanding as a condition of peace the handing over of all the ports from Rouen and Havre to Dunkirk, and, in the event of a refusal, the remorseless hammering of our Army by the whole German Army. He does not think we can get our Army away and considers that, if we wanted to go on with the war, we should have to face the prospect of over a million prisoners in France. He evidently thinks that a situation of this kind might develop quite soon.[1]

On his return to England, Hankey's diary for 5 June records:

> After lunch Milner and Wilson came to 10 Downing Street and we discussed the question of the reserves and the proposed evacuation of Ypres and Dunkirk. Decided that Milner and CIGS [Wilson] should discuss the question with Foch. The latter refuses to budge an inch; Wilson says that, if he does not, there will be a disaster. We also discussed the possibility of withdrawing the whole Army from France if the French crack. It was a very gloomy meeting.[2]

Up until May 1918 there had been two great crises in the Great War when it appeared that all had virtually been lost: in September 1914, when it seemed that nothing could arrest the German advance through Belgium and France, and in March 1918 when there was the imminent danger of the British and French armies being separated and the British driven back to the Channel ports. On the face of it, the German offensive on the Aisne in May appeared to present the third crisis, but the Germans, surprised by the success they had gained, had outrun their transport and were unwilling further to exploit the position. Instead they embarked on two more diversionary offensives – on the Matz in June and the Marne in July. By mid-July Foch, in spite of the continuous arrival of American troops, did not believe that the Allies had sufficient strength to launch a powerful counter-offensive until 1919: '[They] must have an undoubted numerical superiority over the 220 or 240 German divisions; this means the presence of 80 American divisions in the month of April and 100 in July 1919.'[3]

There was a meeting of the British and Dominion Prime Ministers in London on 31 July and Wilson's diary records: '[Lord]Milner is clear that we shall never thrash the Boches, and he suggests holding them on the West with 55 British, 65 French, and 65 American divisions, and sending 10 British divisions to other theatres.'[4] On 21 August, Haig wrote in his diary that Winston Churchill told him that 'the General Staff calculate that the decisive period of the war cannot arise until next July',[5] and this was after Haig had told him 'that we ought to do our utmost to get a decision this autumn...' Thus not only Foch but the War Cabinet in London believed that the war could not be ended in 1918. Haig stood alone in believing that it was possible and, significantly, Rawlinson's diary entry for 18 July records:

> He [Haig] seemed to think the Germans would not, or could not, continue fighting during the winter, and that they would do their utmost to come to terms in the autumn, especially if they failed in Champagne, as now seems possible.

By September, however, Foch too had begun to believe that victory was possible in 1918, but even as late as 19 October, Lloyd George, in his summing up of a meeting of the War Cabinet, saw no prospect of an 'immediate termination of the war'.

There is no single reason that would explain Germany's collapse. It was a cumulative combination of factors, but nearly all of them impacted, either directly or indirectly, on army morale. The decline in morale was evident, somewhat surprisingly, during the German offensive that had begun on 21 March when it might have been presumed to be at a high point. Released from three weary years of defence on the Western Front, the sweeping successes gained at the outset, and on the succeeding days, gave every indication that victory was at last in sight, yet Ludendorff wrote in his *Memoirs*:

Strategically we had not achieved what the events of 23rd, 24th and 25th had encouraged us to hope for. That we also failed to take Amiens, which would have rendered communication between the enemy's forces astride the Somme exceedingly difficult, was specially disappointing. Long-range bombardment of the railway establishments of Amiens was by no means an equivalent. However, our troops had beaten the French and English and proved themselves superior. That they did not achieve all the success that was possible was due not only to their reduced fighting value, but, above all, to their not being always under the firm control of their officers.[6]

Before the March offensive, Ludendorff's problem had been the conversion of his armies on the Western Front from the ingrained tactics of the defence to those of the offensive and, to this end, he had adopted General von Hutier's policy of the employment of storm troops to lead the assault.[7] It had been successfully used on a small scale on the Eastern Front and also in the German counter-attack at Cambrai in November 1917. Under cover of the creeping barrage, the storm troops, armed with light machine guns, flame throwers and light trench mortars would 'press on over weakly held trenches, past centres of resistance and machine-gun nests', leaving these to be dealt with later by succeeding waves. The essence was speed and surprise. It has been shown how successfully this policy had worked in the March offensive, but the difficulty was that the supply of highly motivated and specially trained men for what was, in effect, an élite force was by no means infinite. Ludendorff wrote that OHL 'regretted that the distinction between "attack" and "trench" divisions became established in the Army. We tried to eradicate it without being able to alter the situation which gave rise to it.'[8] Not surprisingly, storm troop casualties were heavy, and difficult to replace after the March and April offensives, with the result that the burden of Allied counter-attacks from July onwards had, in the main, to be borne by the 'trench' divisions, which might predictably be less motivated.

There were other contributory factors. Examples have been given earlier of the slowing down, on occasions, of the German advance through the discovery of the vast stores, particularly of food, left by the retreating Allied armies. The reality proved the lie to the propaganda that unrestricted submarine warfare had brought Britain close to starvation, and pointed to the stark contrast between the quality of German army rations and those of their enemies. A German soldier wrote in his diary:

The daily ration consisted of one-third of a loaf of dark bread, half-filled mess kit of thin soup and a small piece of sausage. Our stomachs shrunk, we were always hungry and grew leaner than ever. A delegation was sent to Major Rhine to complain, but the only answer received was, that he was sorry but couldn't help it; that he too wasn't receiving any more food than we were since the regiment was occupying such a quiet trench it was not entitled to larger rations...[9]

The influenza pandemic that had begun in the spring and early summer of 1918 affected all the combatants on the Western Front, although there were few fatalities. It had a greater effect, however, on German troops because of their poor diet. In June, Ludendorff described the spirit of the troops in the west as 'already weakened by influenza and depressed by a uniform diet', and he complained that it was 'a grievous business having to listen every morning about the weakness of troops if the English attacked again'. In July, Crown Prince Rupprecht noted that Operation 'Hagen', the proposed German offensive in Flanders, might have to be postponed because of influenza. The epidemic returned again in October, but in a much deadlier form. It had a devastating effect, not only on German civilians but worldwide. The effects of the blockade imposed on Germany by the Royal Navy in 1914 have already been described. With food at less than subsistence level, German civilians had an even poorer diet than that provided to the army, and their resistance was correspondingly lower.[10]

Towards the end of July, the decline in German army morale extended to Ludendorff himself. In May, he had decided to close down the Flanders offensive for the time being and apply pressure to the French on the Aisne in the hope that Allied reserves would be diverted from Flanders. Once again he achieved a sweeping success, but he miscalculated by continuing the offensive into July. It was the French counter-offensive on the 18th between Soissons and Reims that was to have such a crucial impact. Two German Armies were driven back over four miles, although the counter-offensive slowed over the following days and was halted four days later. Nevertheless, a German account reads:

> The OHL's failure to understand that the combat strength of the German army was already severely shattered in July 1918 and required systematic rebuilding, which would certainly have succeeded if the troops had received their urgently necessary recuperation in proper camps, finally drove us to the position in which we found ourselves at the war's end.[11]

Ludendorff had not expected the French to launch a counter-offensive, which not only forced the withdrawal from the Marne salient, but ultimately caused the abandonment of the Flanders offensive.

In terms of casualties, the Allies had suffered severely from the German offensives between March and June, the British Army alone incurring over 400,000 in this period, and the French about the same. (German casualties in the period were over 700,000.) The dramatic success of the German offensive on the fronts of the

British Fifth and Third Armies in March, demonstrating that the enemy had found the key to what appeared to be the decisive breakthrough – a key that had so long eluded the British Army – had come as a severe shock. Nevertheless, Ludendorff's decision to switch the offensive to the Aisne, with the consequent abandonment of the Flanders offensive, allowed the British a valuable breathing-space of three months in which to re-equip and train reinforcements. It was now the turn of the British Army to launch a counter-offensive.

The last British set-piece offensive had been in November 1917 when an armada of over 400 tanks, followed by the infantry of the Third Army, blasted their way through the formidable Hindenburg Line defences west of Cambrai and achieved an unprecedented advance of nearly four miles on the first day. The euphoria was such that London's church bells were rung in celebration. Over the following days, however, the rate of progress could not be maintained, and the Germans, recovering from their surprise, launched a counter-attack ten days later and regained most of the ground they had lost. Coming so soon after the ill-fated Passchendaele offensive, it was a dismal end to a dismal year, and yet the military historian Liddell Hart saw Cambrai as the watershed, 'pointing and paving the way to the victorious method of 1918...'

The British counter-offensive at Amiens on 8 August had its genesis in the Battle of Cambrai, but bore little or no resemblance to the offensives that had gone before. It demonstrated how much had been learned from Cambrai and, indeed, how much had been absorbed from the lessons of past failures. To some extent, the circumstances at Cambrai and Amiens were similar. By November 1917 the British Army was exhausted after the Arras and Passchendaele battles, and of the nineteen divisions employed at Cambrai, fourteen had already fought in the latter battle. The British Army was similarly exhausted after the March and April battles of 1918, and the casualties had been replaced by conscripted men of eighteen; it was reckoned that 50 per cent infantry strength comprised men in this age group:

> It is a thousand pities that they should have been sent from England at all. Owing to age and physique some of these immature boys were quite incapable of carrying the weight and doing the work required of an infantry soldier in the line; their presence in the ranks rendered them a danger to their units. To use them at the time was only a waste of those who might later on, with proper training and physical development, have become valuable reinforcements for the army.[12]

The decision was made to use the Australian and Canadian Corps in the main attack south of the Somme because neither corps had been involved in the retreat and were comparatively fresh, albeit the Australians had been engaged in April during the critical days of the German Lys offensive, and also in the recapture of

Villers Bretonneux. On the other hand, the British III Corps entrusted with the attack north of the Somme had suffered severe casualties in the March retreat, and its losses had been replaced by inexperienced conscripts. There were other corps or divisions that had not been involved in the retreat, and the choice of III Corps seems, in retrospect, to have been questionable.

A significant factor in the morale of the Australian and Canadian Corps was that they enjoyed advantages not available to British troops:

> Their men when wounded and sick were sent eventually to their own depot and so back to their own units; the staffs at the British depots did not take the trouble to sort convalescent reinforcements and, not understanding a soldier's love for his unit as a war home, and the craving for the society of old comrades, dispatched these old soldiers to the first unit that required its ranks refilled ... the Australian divisions were kept together as a corps: they had, in addition, a team spirit, which Highlanders thrust into County battalions, or Londoners drafted into Welsh battalions, could not be expected to acquire; it was true esprit de corps enhanced by a very valuable patriotism.[13]

The assembly of the forces to be involved in the Cambrai and Amiens offensives was orchestrated with great secrecy, and the sophistication and ingenuity employed in the assembly for the Amiens offensive demonstrated how far the British Army had progressed not only in the achievement of surprise but in the combination of all arms – artillery, tanks, infantry and aircraft – in a simultaneous assault. The force of fighting tanks (excluding Whippets) engaged in both offensives was approximately similar, but the artillery barrage at Amiens was far heavier. In terms of divisions, the Germans had been outnumbered nineteen to six at Cambrai, but they had believed themselves to be relatively secure behind the Hindenburg Line defences. At Amiens the disparity was less marked, twenty-two divisions (including French) to fourteen, but the German defences were not constructed to repel an attack and were merely those reached at the conclusion of the March offensive. They consisted of little more than a single trench, with no dug-outs, and were inadequately wired. The combination of the simultaneous assault by a vast armada of over 500 tanks and accompanying infantry under cover of a massive artillery barrage, the latter having a devastating effect on the enemy's battery positions, came as a complete surprise to the Germans, and their divisions facing the Australians and Canadians were simply swept away.

There would never be another occasion in 1918, however, when tanks in such overwhelming force could be used again. On the next day after the 8 August offensive only 145 tanks were fit for action, and by the 11th the number had fallen to 38. Indeed, on 31 August there were only nine Mark Vs for service in the Fourth Army area, and none at all in the Third Army area. Thereafter, the employment of tanks was mainly confined to infantry support where they provided a useful service in knocking out enemy machine-gun nests. Their last great battle was on 29 September in the assault on the Hindenburg Line when 140 were employed, although over a half became casualties. The problem was that the supply of crews and machines was never enough to keep pace with losses. In spite of the growing German success in destroying tanks through artillery fire, they continued to have a powerful impact on German morale, even to the extent of regimental histories reporting the presence of tanks when there were none:

> Since the German Higher Command could explain away failure in the event of a tank attack the German regimental officer very naturally came to consider that the presence of tanks was a sufficient reason for the loss of any position entrusted to his care. His men came to consider that in the presence of tanks they could not be expected to hold out... From this time onwards explanations became very simple: 'The tanks had arrived, there was nothing to be done.' The failure of the Higher Command to produce tanks to combat those used by the Allies began to undermine the faith of troops in their generals.[14]

Artillery had now become the dominant weapon on the battlefield. The barrage, coupled with a tank assault and accompanied by ground-attack aircraft had mechanised the tactics of the advance. This combination of fire-power preceded the infantry advance, and was designed to destroy or neutralise enemy resistance, whether from artillery or machine guns, and thus conserve scarce infantry resources. German regimental histories speak of the power of the creeping barrage: 'It was not that it was directed on one line or a narrow zone and then moved forward, but from the very beginning a zone more than a kilometre in depth was overwhelmed with a perfect hail of shell.'[15] Bearing in mind the lack of experience of a significant proportion of the infantry after March 1918, the day-by-day advances attained could not have been accomplished without this immense increase in fire-power. What was seriously lacking, however, was the means to exploit the situation; this was the traditional rôle of cavalry, but despite a number of gallant attempts, it could not find the answer to wire entanglements and the machine gun. After 8 August, the main opposition came from machine gunners and artillery as the Germans steadily withdrew, halting for brief periods behind the natural obstacles of canals or rivers until the Hindenburg Line was reached. It was here that they hoped to make a determined stand, but to no avail.

The decisive successes gained by the British Army in August and September should be viewed alongside Allied successes elsewhere. The French had made good progress between the Oise and the Aisne, and the attack of the Tenth Army on 20 August was described by Ludendorff as 'another black day'; and in September, the Americans, in their first major operation, had been successful in reducing the St

Mihiel salient. Nevertheless, the blows struck by the British Army in August, and against the Hindenburg Line in September, were the two factors that persuaded Ludendorff to seek an armistice. These blows, in spite of their successes, were tactical rather than strategic and, in scale, nothing like that achieved by the Germans in March, yet on 1 October, Ludendorff was telling his senior staff officers that 'OHL and the German army were finished, the war no longer to be won, unavoidable and final defeat was close at hand'.[16] All these operations had been part of Foch's strategy of convergent attacks, and at this point the question might be asked: if unified command had ultimately brought about victory, why had it not been introduced earlier in the war? After the war, Field-Marshal Sir William Robertson wrote:

> While we may acknowledge with gratitude the services rendered by General Foch at a most critical period, and admire the ability and tact with which he eventually restored the situation, it need not be taken for granted that his appointment at some earlier date would have made any material difference to the course of the war. He took up the post of the Generalissimo at a moment when Ministers were at their wits' end to know what to do, and he was accorded a much freer hand than any Commander-in-Chief had previously enjoyed. The plans of operations were his plans, and they were not, as sometimes in the past, a compromise between what the soldiers wanted and what Ministers allowed them to have.[17]

Between August 1914 and the end of 1916, General Joffre had been Commander-in-Chief of the French Armies of the North and North-East and had exercised a *de facto* role as a Generalissimo on the Western Front. He had no power to order the British Army to undertake operations, but as the British Army was the junior partner with the French, the British government had instructed Sir John French and, after him, Haig, to co-operate with his plans. This they did at the Battles of Loos (1915) and the Somme (1916) but the failure of the latter battle brought about Joffre's removal. At the time of the March crisis in 1918, Foch was the only general (created a *Maréchal de France* in August 1918) who would have been acceptable to the French government to command the Allied Armies: Pétain, despite his undoubted capabilities, had become prey to pessimism and had lost his fighting spirit. Although Foch had become the Allied Commander-in-Chief, and nominally in a stronger position than that held by Joffre, he could not order the Allied commanders to undertake operations, only persuade; in the last resort they could have appealed over his head to their governments if they thought their armies were being endangered by his plans. Nevertheless, it was Foch's personality, his determination and his unfailing optimism that successfully harnessed the efforts of the Allied commanders, although, perhaps not surprisingly, he had his differences with

Haig and Pershing. On the whole, Haig co-operated well with Foch, the most serious disagreement being over Foch's insistence that the Amiens offensive should be continued when Haig believed that it had run its course and a diversion should be made elsewhere. Foch, recognising that Haig and the British Army were the best weapons in his armoury, gave way, but in his pique withdrew the French First Army from Haig's command. It can only be conjectured whether the First Army's subsequent lacklustre performance would have improved had it remained under Haig in the renewed advance by the British Fourth Army.

Two final questions can perhaps be posed. The first is when, or what, was the turning point in the war? One German account ascribed it to 18 July when the French launched their counter-offensive on the Marne. On the other hand, the British attack on 8 August at Amiens, described by Ludendorff as 'the black day of the German Army in the history of this war', or the breaching of the Hindenburg Line on 29 September might each have equal claim. It is suggested here, however, that the turning point of the war was not in 1918 but in January 1917 when Germany decided to engage in unrestricted submarine warfare. It was realised that this decision would be likely to bring America into the war, but it was a calculated gamble that Britain would be starved into submission before America could provide a substantial presence on the Western Front. The build-up of American forces was at first slow: by August 1917 only two divisions had arrived in France, increased to four by December, reaching a total of 130,000 men. By March 1918, however, the number had risen to over 300,000, and almost one and a half million by August. Ludendorff had not realised that such a rapid increase was possible, and although at the time he did not have a high opinion of American military capability, he was concerned that their divisions could release Allied divisions from quiet sectors, and wrote that this 'helps to explain the influence exerted by the American Contingent on the issue of the conflict. It was for this reason that America became the deciding factor in the war.'[18]

The second question remains: if Germany, instead of launching the series of offensives beginning in March, had decided to stand on the defensive on the Western Front, would the Allies have been victorious in 1918? The answer, obviously, can only be conjectured. The German Army on the Western Front, although substantially strengthened by divisions from the east, would have been increasingly subject to convergent attacks from the Allied Armies, in particular from the American Army. The developments in fire-power already described would have brought about severe German casualties and further sapped morale which, it would appear, was already on the decline even before the March offensive. If, alternatively, the Germans had decided to relinquish territorial gains in France and Belgium and retire to the Rhine, the knowledge that they would be defending the Homeland might have provided a moral uplift not only to the Army but to the civilian population, even despite the privations it had suffered. The Allies would then have had logistical problems in bringing up their forces to assault the new German positions and, moreover, would have been faced with the depressing prospect of a return to siege warfare. Either alternative would point to the unlikelihood of an Allied victory in 1918; yet if, after retiring to the Rhine, Germany had then decided to seek an armistice, there is a strong possibility that less stringent armistice terms might have been secured from the Allies. In that event, the legend subsequently spread by Nazi propaganda between the two wars that the German Army 'had been stabbed in the back' because of Government weakness and civilian insurrection, would not have arisen.

Notes

1. Hankey, Lord, *The Supreme Command 1914–1918*, Vol. 2, Allen & Unwin (London, 1961)
2. *Ibid.*
3. Foch, Marshal F., *The Memoirs of Marshal Foch*, Heinemann (London, 1931)
4. Callwell, Major-General Sir C. E., *Field-Marshal Sir Henry Wilson*, Vol. 2, Cassell (London, 1931)
5. Blake, Robert, (ed.), *The Private Papers of Douglas Haig 1914–1919*, Eyre & Spottiswoode, (London, 1952)
6. Ludendorff, General, *Concise Ludendorff Memoirs*, Hutchinson (London, 1933)
7. The employment of storm troops was advocated in a pamphlet written by a French captain in 1915, and although issued to French army units, it was not formally adopted as a policy. The pamphlet was found by the Germans in 1916 and issued as an official training manual.
8. Ludendorff, General, *My War Memoirs* (2 vols), Hutchinson (London, 1919)
9. Meisel, F., Papers of, held in the Department of Documents, Imperial War Museum, London
10. The influenza pandemic of 1918 has been described as the most destructive in history. It has been estimated that at least 25 million persons died of the disease – far more than total battle casualties of the war.
11. Quoted in Edmonds, Brigadier-General Sir James, and Maxwell-Hyslop, Lieutenant-Colonel R., (comp.), *Official History of the War: Military Operations France and Belgium 1918*, Vol. V, HMSO, 1947
12. Kincaid-Smith, M., *The 25th Division in France and Flanders*, Harrison (London, 1920)
13. Edmonds, *op. cit.*
14. Fuller, J. F. C., *Tanks in the Great War 1914–1918*, Murray (London, 1920)
15. Quoted in Edmonds, *op. cit.*, Vol. IV
16. Quoted in Asprey, R. B., *The German High Command at War*, Little, Brown & Co. (London, 1993)
17. Robertson, Field Marshal Sir William, *Soldiers and Statesmen*, Vol. 2, Cassell (London, 1926)
18. Ludendorff, *op. cit.*

Appendix: Casualties

S tatistics of casualties incurred in the Great War have always been difficult to assess, particularly German, where the figures of lightly wounded were excluded from the totals. Total British and Dominion casualties on the Western Front between the outbreak of war in August 1914 and the Armistice in November 1918 amounted to 2,700,000, representing 96 per cent of total casualties for all theatres (excluding the Royal Navy and the Mercantile Marine). Of this total, 830,000 casualties were suffered between March and November 1918, making this the most expensive period of the entire war. Only the year 1917 came close (818,000), including as it did the Battles of Arras, 3rd Ypres (Passchendaele) and Cambrai. French casualties on the Western Front for the year 1918 have been estimated at almost one million, and German approaching one-and-a-half million, although there is reason to believe that this figure is understated. When American casualties of roundly 300,000 are included, however, a tentative conclusion could be reached that the Allied total was in excess of that for the Germans. Nevertheless, German losses could be least afforded when it is borne in mind that, although as the year progressed there were no significant reinforcements to fill the ranks of the British and French Armies, there were nearly one-and-a-half million American troops in France in August 1918, increasing to slightly over two million by the end of November.

Select Bibliography

Unpublished Sources
Imperial War Museum, London
Lieutenant-General Sir Richard Butler papers
Lieutenant-General Sir Aylmer Haldane papers
Lieutenant-General Sir Hugh Jeudwine papers
General Sir Ivor Maxse papers
Field Marshal Sir Henry Wilson papers
National Army Museum
General Lord Rawlinson of Trent papers

Published Sources
Asprey, Robert B., *Hindenburg and Ludendorff and the First World War*, Little Brown and Company (1991)
Barnett, Corelli, *The Swordbearers: Studies in Supreme Command in the First World War*, Hodder & Stoughton (1981)
Bidwell, S., and Graham, D., *Firepower*, George Allen & Unwin (1982)
Blake, Robert, (ed.), *The Private Papers of Douglas Haig 1914–1919*, Eyre & Spottiswoode (1952)
Blunden, Edmund, *Undertones of War*, Collins (1965)
Callwell, Major-General, Sir C. E., *Field-Marshal Sir Henry Wilson*, Cassell and Company (1927)
Campbell, P. J., *The Ebb and Flow of Battle*, Oxford University Press (1979)
Chapman, Guy, *A Passionate Prodigality*, Nicholson & Watson (1933)
Churchill, Winston S., *The World Crisis 1911–1918*, Odhams (1938)
Cruttwell, C. R. M. F., *A History of the Great War 1914–1918*, Oxford: Clarendon (1934)
De Groot, G. J., *Douglas Haig 1861–1928*, Unwin Hyman (1938)
Edmonds, Brigadier-General Sir James, *A Short History of World War 1*, Oxford University Press (1951)
— (comp.), *Official History of the War: Military Operations, France and Belgium 1918, Vol I*, Macmillan (1935), *Vol II*, Macmillan (1937), *Vol III*, Macmillan (1939), *Vol IV*, HMSO (1947), *Vol V*, HMSO (1947)

Essame, H., *The Battle for Europe, 1918*, Batsford (1972)

Falls, Captain Cyril, *The First World War*, Longmans (1960)

Farrar-Hockley, A. H., *Goughie: The Life of General Sir Hubert Gough*, Hart-Davis, MacGibbon (1975)

Foch, Marshal F., *The Memoirs of Marshal Foch*, Heinemann (1931)

French, David, *The Strategy of the Lloyd George Coalition 1916–1918*, Oxford: Clarendon Press (1995)

Fussell, P., *The Great War and Modern Memory*, Oxford University Press (1975)

Gough, General Sir Hubert, *TheFifth Army*, Hodder & Stoughton (1931)

Hankey, Lord, *The Supreme Command 1914–1918*, George Allen & Unwin (1961)

Haythornthwaite, P. J., *The World War One Source Book*, Arms and Armour (1992)

Hutchison, Lt. Col. G. S., *Warrior*, Hutchinson (1932)

Liddell Hart, B. H., *A History of the World War 1914–1918*, Faber (1934)

Lloyd George, D., *War Memoirs*, Odhams (1938)

Ludendorff, E., *My War Memoirs*, Hutchinson (1919)

Maurice, Major-General Sir F., *The Life of General Lord Rawlinson of Trent*, Cassell and Company (1928)

Middlebrook, M., *The Kaiser's Battle: 21 March 1918*, Lane (1978)

Pitt, B., *1918: The Last Act*, Cassell and Company (1962)

Powell, G., *Plumer: The Soldier's General*, Leo Cooper (1990)

Prior, P., and Wilson, T., *Command on the Western Front*, Blackwell (1992)

Robertson, Field Marshal Sir W., *Soldiers and Statesmen*, Cassell and Company (1928)

Severn, Mark, *The Gambardiers*, Ernest Benn (1930)

Sixsmith, E. K.G., *Douglas Haig*, Weidenfeld & Nicholson (1976)

Terraine, J., *Impacts of War, 1914 & 1918*, Hutchinson (1970)

— *The Great War 1914–1918*, Arrow Books (1977)

— *To Win a War, 1918 – The Year of Victory*, Sidgwick & Jackson (1978)

Toland, J., *No Man's Land – The Story of 1918*, Book Club Associates (1980)

Travers, T., *The Killing Ground*, Allen & Unwin (1987)

— *How the War was Won*, Routledge (1992)

Wilson, T., *The Myriad Faces of War*, Polity Press (1988)

Winter, D., *Haig's Command: A Reassessment*, Viking (1991)

Woodward, D., *Lloyd George and the Generals*, University of Delaware (1983)

Index